FUTURE ETHICS

Also available from Continuum:

The Ethics of Climate Change, James Garvey
Climate Change and Philosophy, edited by Ruth Irwin
Heidegger, Politics and Climate Change, Ruth Irwin
The Ethics of Metropolitan Growth, Robert Kirkman

Forthcoming:

Key Terms in Ethics, Oskari Kuusela

FUTURE ETHICS

CLIMATE CHANGE AND
APOCALYPTIC IMAGINATION

EDITED BY STEFAN SKRIMSHIRE

continuum

Continuum International Publishing Group

The Tower Building   80 Maiden Lane
11 York Road   Suite 704
London SE1 7NX   New York, NY 10038

www.continuumbooks.com

British Library Cataloguing-in-Publication Data
A catalogue record for this book is available from the British Library.

ISBN: HB: 978-1-4411-7655-4
        PB: 978-1-4411-3958-0

Library of Congress Cataloging-in-Publication Data
A catalog record for this book is available from the Library of Congress.

Typeset by Newgen Imaging Systems Pvt Ltd, Chennai, India
Printed and bound in Great Britain by CPI Antony Rowe Ltd,
Chippenham, Wiltshire

CONTENTS

CONTENTS

Part III: Action/Inaction

Part IV: Religion

FOREWORD

ALASTAIR MCINTOSH

By placing a notion like 'apocalypse' back on the table, anthropogenic global warming exposes a very old fault line in scholarship. Ever since Aristotle, academe has evolved mostly in a departmentalized, disciplinary direction. But the earliest philosophers had a penchant not just for the rational, but also for the mythopoetic. They were able to be more at ease employing meta-constructs to make sense of their observations.

For example, both Plato's *Critias* and *The Laws* interweave accounts of prehistoric Greek climate change or natural disasters with a mythology that sets them in a socially instructive context. Put briefly, Plato's message was that hubris in human affairs eventually meets its nemesis in ecocide. But modern academia runs more in the footsteps of Aristotle than as footnotes to Plato. We are more hamstrung, because our disciplinary specialization furnishes fruitful attention to detail, but often at the expense of the wider grounding necessary to develop a generalist overview. Our strengths are many, but their downside is to be tripped up by a limited capacity to discern 'meaning' and to translate this into policy that shapes how we collectively live.

Because climate change is such a multi-faceted and far-reaching phenomenon this shortcoming is becoming more and more apparent. The science both derives from and has implications for the human condition. Potentially these are very severe. The otherwise quaintly melodramatic term, 'apocalypse', has therefore pushed its way back into informed discourse. For example, a researcher whose normal comfort zone is, say, atmospheric modelling, or the latitude of an electorate to countenance social change, may suddenly find their work casts them into the perceived or actual role of a latter-day apocalyptic prophet. Having been trained to pursue tightly defined constructs, they now have to field balls of a meta-constructual nature with implications that may overstep their reach – especially when spun by the media.

The position that climate change places scholars in can therefore be likened to a group of specialized doctors investigating a sickness that permeates the patient's body. One tests the liver. Another wires up the heart. A third probes this or that structure in the brain and, on finding nothing obvious, wonders if the whole hoo-hah might just be a delusion. But the actual cause of the problem is bigger than any of these parts. It runs in the blood. It underpins the functioning of everything else because it is the very 'oil' that lubricates and energizes the engine of our society.

But nobody really wants to look at that. Everybody knows that the haematologist, notwithstanding his sweet-talk of a painless green new deal transition, is an old-fashioned blood-letter. The body of the rich world has got used to running on a full eight pints of blood. The blood-letter's remedy would have that reduced to just one pint; or perhaps two if the patient is well blessed with fossil fuel alternatives.

Quite apart from the question of electoral will, we also have to ask whether cuts in greenhouse gas emissions of 80 percent or 90 percent for the rich world are even do-able. We have only become a planet of nearly seven billion people, half of us urban, because oil or other fossil fuels lubricate a globalized trading system that interlocks rich and poor alike. Oil helps to produce, transport and process increasingly vast quantities of 'stuff' from distant hinterlands. The system only stacks up thanks to the competitive economics of comparative advantage that degrades biodiversity and mines natural capital. But to cut away radically at this would entail questioning the very basis by which social cohesion at such a high population level is sustained. Many of us have, of course, been advocating precisely such questioning for years, and exploring alternative patterns and examples in our own lives. But now that the carbon crunch is hitting mainstream consciousness, those politicians who seek re-election know that they must be very careful about how to act upon the urgency with which scientific advice indicates cold turkey.

The global financial crisis of 2008 has raised awareness that only so much sudden braking of the economic system can be sustained without apocalyptically compounding injury. Had bankers' lines of credit frozen up, as they very nearly did, our globally interlinked just-in-time food supply system would have gridlocked. Panic buying would have completed the chaos. Social unrest and resultant national emergency are only days away because we've lost the resilience that local sourcing of much of our food and energy gave us until the post-World War II years.

The political fear of throwing our growth-predicated world economy into reverse must partly account for the failure of the United Nations Climate Change Conference of December 2009 in Copenhagen. The question is how to accept a modicum of pain today . . . not even for jam tomorrow . . . but so that future generations might simply live in decency. As this book's introductory chapter surmises: 'How do we create the means to empathise with people we may never meet, in a future we may never inhabit?' The rich have never before done this for the poor. So why should they act for the far away and the mostly as-yet unborn, unless the water's already lapping at their own castle walls? In which case tipping point scenarios suggest it would be too late. What the 'rich' have to understand is that, this time, we're all in it together. Addictive consumerism is the cutting edge driver of climate change and we can run from such reality, but never run away – because we've only got one planet. As The Eagles put it in 'Hotel California', that iconic rock ballad from 1976 in which west coast America becomes a metaphor for the wider world, "'Relax' said the night man, 'We are programmed to receive' / 'You can check out any time you like, but you can never leave.'"

And so, assuming that the consensus science is broadly right, the slow apocalypse of the world rolls on. This is what today draws 'apocalypse' from out of its Biblical backwater and gives this volume such pertinence. But as several of the contributors here point out, apocalypse is more than just the doom and gloom of millenarian end times. Etymologically the Greek *apokalyptein* has its roots in *apo-* 'from', and *kalyptein*, 'to cover or conceal'. Apocalypse is therefore an uncovering, a *revelation*. The word has a technical usage that implies a transformation, perhaps in consciousness, by which an existing corrupt socio-ecological order is turned upside down by the astonishing irruption of new hope.

The classical articulation of this and one that has historically shaped imagination in the West is the Biblical Apocalypse, or Revelation, of St John of Patmos. Here 'Babylon' stands metaphorically for the violent imperial order of Rome, which is overthrown by the transformative meekness (which is not the same as weakness) of the 'lamb' of God. Another example is with Mary near the start of Luke's gospel. This celebrates the divine upheaval of worldly powers in her 'magnificat' or song: 'He has brought down the mighty from their thrones / And lifted up the lowly. / He has filled the hungry with good things, / And sent the rich away with empty hands.'

Irrespective of whether we see such cultural resonances as an enhancement or an encumbrance to modern understanding, apocalyptic scenarios of climate change present us with a choice. We can either do nothing; and risk sliding into barbarism from our lack of preparedness and resilience. For example, the rich world might act as if it can simply pull up the drawbridge as the suffering kicks in. Alternatively, we can look for revelation in the signs of the times. We might do all we can to mitigate the causes of global warming, but also view what is happening as an incredible opportunity to evolve culturally in what it means to be human beings, growing in decency and dignity to help one another and other species to adapt better to come-what-may in the come-to-pass.

One way chooses death; the other, life. And that is the challenge of our times, because the political, economic and technological responses to climate change will not be enough on their own. We also need a change of heart: a shift from seeking fulfilment primarily from the things of outer quantitative consumption, and a move to the more qualitative realms of empathy in relationships, elemental connections to nature, depth of community, sensitivity to beauty and a deepening of the inner life.

Like a persistent wind, climate change tugs at how we think about the world, how we relate to it and how we can envisage the future. That is why the 'apocalyptic imagination' of this book's subtitle has become so powerfully activated in popular consciousness. At such a juncture we are taken beyond the realm of cognition. The unconscious also wells up . . . filling out our movie screens and the nightmares of our children who are locked in a destiny not of their own election . . . calling us to nothing less than the further reaches of human nature.

This is a book that, at last, begins to face the ecological crisis at the scholarly depth that intimations of apocalypse command. Yes, for some it may upset the epistemic innards. But for too long the mainstream Academy has wallowed in philosophical torpor. Now is the time for scholarship to realign itself; to bridge the epistemological divide between detail and context, the sciences and the humanities, Aristotle and Plato, so as to recover a richness we have neglected.

Perhaps, too, we might ask ourselves a touchstone question: does our work ultimately serve the poor or the broken in nature?; because this is about values, and how to act on them. Climate change is our wake-up call to get real.

ACKNOWLEDGMENTS

This book was conceived and produced as part of a three-year research project of the Lincoln Theological Institute (LTI) at The University of Manchester. I am deeply grateful for the encouragement and financial support of the LTI trustees that made this possible.

Particular thanks are due to the LTI's director, Peter Scott, with whom lengthy conversations about climate change, religion and activism kick-started the whole project in 2007. He has been, variously, an advisor, sounding board, proof-reader, contributor and good friend from start to finish.

As well as to the contributors to this volume, I would like to express thanks to all who participated in and shaped the workshop series in Manchester, Future Ethics, from which many of the ideas in the book arose. The advice and friendship of Mark Levene and Barbara Adam were instrumental in getting the project off the ground. The tireless efforts of our camera man, Damien Mahoney, and group facilitators Ben Gilchrist and Topsy Page, made each workshop much more than a workshop. Jemma and the rest of the team at Bridge-5 Mill, and Manchester Environmental Resource Centre initiative (MERCi) were inspiring and enthusiastic hosts.

I am also indebted to the advice and inspiration of many friends and colleagues, in particular: Ralph Skrimshire, Lucy Williams, Katja Stuerzenhofecker, Alastair McIntosh, Simon Dale, Benjamin Morris, Bradon Smith, Mike Hulme, Christopher Rowland, Philip Goodchild, Jonathon Atkinson and the EcoDharma community.

Reprint permission was kindly granted by Wiley-Blackwell for Stephen Gardiner's chapter, which first appeared in *Journal of Social Philosophy*, Vol. 40, Number 2 (Summer 2009), edited by Carol C. Gould.

Many thanks to all at Continuum who made this book happen, and to Andrew Brooks for the cover image.

CONTRIBUTORS

Sarah S. Amsler is Lecturer in Sociology at Aston University. She is the author of *The Politics of Knowledge in Central Asia: Science between Marx and the Market* (Routledge, 2007) and various articles on the dynamics of cultural power, knowledge and social action in education and everyday life. She is currently working on projects in critical pedagogy and the cultural politics of hope.

Andrew Bowman is a PhD candidate in the Centre for the History of Science, Technology and Medicine at the University of Manchester, researching the history of science and expertise in African agricultural development, with additional research interests in the science and politics of climate change. He has been involved with a variety of different environmental and social justice campaign organizations, and is currently an editor for *The Mule* (www.themule.info) and *Red Pepper* magazine (www.redpepper.org.uk).

Frederick Buell is professor of English at Queens College and also a member of the World Studies, American Studies and Environmental Studies programmes. Poet and essayist as well as cultural critic, he has authored numerous essays and five books, most recently *National Culture and the New Global System* (John Hopkins University Press, 2004) and *From Apocalypse to Way of Life: Environmental Crisis in the American Century* (Routledge, 2004). A scholar committed to interdisciplinary studies, he has written extensively on culture and contemporary globalization, migration, environment and technology.

Celia Deane-Drummond holds a chair in theology and the biological sciences at the University of Chester, is Director of the Centre for Religion and the Biosciences that she founded in 2002 and in 2009 was elected Vice Chair of the European Forum for the Study of Religion and Environment. She holds degrees and doctorates in natural science (Cambridge and Reading) and theology (CNAA and Manchester). She has lectured widely nationally and internationally. Her more recent books include *Brave New World* (ed.) (T&T Clark, 2003), *Reordering Nature* (joint ed.) (Continuum, 2003), *The Ethics of Nature* (Blackwell, 2004), *Future Perfect?*, (joint ed.) (Continuum, 2006), *Ecotheology* (Dartman, Longman and Tood, 2008), *Christ and Evolution* (Augsberg Fortress, 2009) and *Creaturely Theology*, (joint ed.) (SCM, 2009).

Richard McNeill Douglas has published essays on the philosophy and politics of climate change denial in the *Political Quarterly; International Journal of Green Economics and Social Epistemology*. He is currently writing a book on the philosophical, political and economic implications of the central message of environmentalism, that there are limits to growth. In his spare time he writes songs, drama and short stories.

Stephen M. Gardiner is an Associate Professor in the Department of Philosophy and the Program on Values in Society at the University of Washington. He specializes in ethics, political philosophy and environmental ethics. His recent publications include articles on climate justice, precaution, the ethics of geoengineering and intergenerational political theory. He is also the editor of *Virtue Ethics, Old and New* (Cornell, 2005) and a coeditor (with Simon Caney, Dale Jamieson and Henry Shue) of the upcoming *Climate Ethics: Essential Readings* (Oxford, 2010).

Christopher Groves' work draws on a background of scholarship in German Idealism, contemporary French philosophy and sociology in tracing three interlinked themes: how the future is socially constructed within diverse social practices, how attachment, expectation and stability play a role in promoting human flourishing, and how the widespread use of advanced technology foregrounds risk and uncertainty as ethically and politically significant concerns. These themes are brought together in the monograph Future Matters: Action, Knowledge, Ethics (Brill, 2007), co-authored with the eminent sociologist and time theorist Professor Barbara Adam. Drawing on the work of figures like Hans Jonas, F. W. J. Schelling and Deleuze and Guattari, his ongoing research aims to develop an original social theory and ethics of (and for) the future.

Mike Hulme is professor of climate change in the School of Environmental Sciences at the University of East Anglia (UEA) and was the Founding Director of the Tyndall Centre for Climate Change Research from 2000 to 2007. His most recent books are *Making Climate Change Work For Us*, an edited synthesis of the findings of the EU FP6 Integrated Project 'ADAM: Adaptation and Mitigation Strategies', and *Why We Disagree about Climate Change* (CUP, 2009), an exploration of the different beliefs, values and ideologies at work in climate change framing and discourse. He is editor-in-chief of the newly launched *Wiley's Interdisciplinary Reviews: Climate Change*.

Roman Krznaric is a founding faculty member of The School of Life in London, where he teaches courses on Work and Politics, and is the resident expert on Empathy. He also acts as an advisor to organizations such as Oxfam and the United Nations on empathy development and social change. He studied at the universities of Oxford, London and Essex, where he obtained his PhD in political sociology. He is editor, with Theodore Zeldin, of *Guide to an Unknown University* (The Oxford Muse, 2006), and author of a forthcoming book, *Empathy* (Acumen).

Mark Levene is Reader in Comparative History at Southampton University and a member of the Parkes Institute for Jewish/non-Jewish relations. He writes extensively on genocide and related themes. He is also a long-term peace and environmental activist, co-founder of Crisis Forum (the Forum for the Study of the Crisis in the twenty-first century) and founder of its sister organization Rescue! History dedicated to galvanizing students of the past to be active around issues of anthropogenic climate change.

Alastair McIntosh is a Fellow of the Centre for Human Ecology and Visiting Professor of Human Ecology at the University of Strathclyde's Department of Geography and Sociology. His seminal *Soil and Soul* explores activism in rekindling people and place. His recent *Hell and High Water: Climate Change, Hope and the Human Condition* argues that politics, economics and technology are insufficient: we must also explore the spiritual roots of addictive consumerism; even a 'cultural psychotherapy'. His writing is described as 'very scientifically rigorous' by Radio 4's Open Book, 'life-changing' by the Bishop of Liverpool, and 'truly mental' by Radiohead's Thom Yorke.

Peter Manley Scott is Senior Lecturer in Christian Social Thought & Director of the Lincoln Theological Institute at the University of Manchester, UK. He is author of *Theology, Ideology and Liberation* (CUP, 1994; paperback edition 2009), *A Political Theology of Nature* (CUP, 2003) and *Anti-human Theology: Nature, Technology and the Postnatural* (SCM, 2010). His research is to be found at the intersection between theology and studies of nature, technology and society, and he is widely published on these topics. His current research is towards a monograph, *A Theology of Postnatural Right*.

Stefan Skrimshire is a postdoctoral research associate in philosophy of religion at the University of Manchester and has been active in various social and environmental movements. He researches and teaches the roots of apocalyptic thought in political life and continental philosophy. He is broadly interested in the function of three core ideas in contemporary political cultures: apocalypse, eschatology and utopia. He is the author of *Politics of Fear, Practices of Hope* (Continuum, 2008), and director of *Beyond the Tipping Point? Conversations on climate, action and the future* (2010). He is a member of Single Cell, a Manchester based music collective.

INTRODUCTION

HOW SHOULD WE THINK ABOUT THE FUTURE?

STEFAN SKRIMSHIRE

Three decades after the publication of *The Limits to Growth*, Donella Meadows, one of its authors, recalled the controversy that had followed them back in 1972: 'I remember finding one of my co-authors, Jørgen Randers, pacing the office in frustration. In his lilting Norwegian-English, he lamented, "People just don't know how to think about the future!"' (Meadows, 1999: 106). Meadows claimed that their attempt at *predicting* the future of the planet (as one of the first earth system modelling exercises) had been interpreted as an attempt at its *predetermination*. People, it had seemed, wanted to engage imaginatively with the future; they didn't want to see it written in advance, as if set in stone but as data sets on computer screens.

But Meadows also believed that as scientists, the authors of *The Limits to Growth* had ignored the centrality that mythic, dramatic and narrative ways of communicating possible futures have played, and continue to play, even in the imagination of 'secular' human cultures: 'we had not thought much about the culture in which we were speaking, though we ourselves were part of that culture. But we were at MIT; we had been trained in science. The way we thought about the future was utterly logical: if you tell people there's a disaster ahead, they will change course. If you give them a choice between a good future and a bad one, they will pick the good. They might even be grateful. Naive, weren't we' (ibid.).

Perhaps, taking this admission of 'naiveté' to a fuller conclusion today should force us to turn around Randers' comment about people not knowing 'how to think about the future'.

Perhaps the problem facing activists and campaigners attempting to galvanize action on climate change is the very fact that *we* don't know how *most people* actually think about the future, and upon which philosophical, political or religious ideas or any such thinking is based.

A need to take this problem seriously is the premise of this book. The authors all examine how different ways of thinking, imagining, knowing and believing in the future impact upon political action and inaction. To make connections between the representations of the future, and the behaviour and action of people in the present, has practical and ethical ramifications. And if it addresses an every day, almost banal question about the reception of bad news, it is yet one that repeatedly dogs environmental activists and policymakers alike: why doesn't the imagination of a catastrophic future galvanize people to act to avert it? Is it simply a question of denial, on a par with asking why people choose to smoke, over-eat or work too hard? No doubt psychologists have their own, useful responses. But, looking a little deeper, the question, posed implicitly through the contributions in this book, also reveals a dilemma in the perceived reality of a far future: how can one know and grasp meaningfully such a thing, let alone relate ethically and politically to it? Can one imagine, believe in, empathize with the future of the human at all?

CLIMATE CHANGE

The consensus, of sorts, that emerged over anthropogenic climate change from the Intergovernmental Panel on Climate Change (IPCC) in 2007 made this task – of understanding how we think about the future – more, not less, relevant than ever. The same exasperation as Randers' expression is palpable in voices today that are coming to terms with the failure of scientific authority in radically altering human behaviour. It is the implicit exasperation of the archivist from the future in the film *The Age of Stupid*: 'what state of mind were we in, to face extinction, and simply shrug it off?'

Understanding climate change as a political and social construction *as well as* a physical reality (Pettenger, 2007; Hulme, 2009) means sensitivity not just to the objective changes in the earth system but also to those psychological and cultural spheres through which the changes are made meaningful. This need is nowhere stronger than in relation to the cluster of concepts in climate change rhetoric that convey the *decisive moment* or ultimate temporal point: tipping points, points of no return, and levels of warming that will trigger / have already triggered, irreversible or 'runaway' climate change. Contemporary political rhetoric reflects intimately such concepts of temporal urgency. The 15th UN Climate Change convention in Copenhagen, 2009, was dubbed the 'last chance saloon' and the 'world's last chance'; UK Prime Minister Gordon Brown declared unequivocally that the meeting represented the world's last chance: 'If we do not reach a deal at this time, let us be in no doubt: once the damage from unchecked emissions growth is done, no retrospective global agreement in some future period can undo that choice. By then it will be irretrievably too late' (Wintour and Sparrow, 2009). Looking back on the failures of that very meeting, are we now bound to say that it is 'irretrievably too late'? The political ramifications of tipping points depend upon much more than their scientific verifiability, and provoke deeper questions. Too late for what? What *are* we actually trying to save? Our own lives? The life of our species; biota; habitat, our current population level and *way* of life?

Answering such seemingly fundamental ethical questions requires understanding how the apprehension of future crises generates specific ways of viewing ourselves and acting in the world, in relation to other humans and non-humans, and ultimately upon which values such actions are based. With the continual loss of animal and plant species, habitats and cultures, aren't points of no return being reached all the time? In what sense then, does one invoke the threat of irreversibility? As NASA scientist Gavin Schmidt has put it, waiting for one allegedly definitive and final point 'can lead to two seemingly opposite, and erroneous, conclusions – that nothing will happen until we reach the "point" and conversely, that once we've reached it, there will be nothing that can be done about it, i.e. it promotes both a cavalier and fatalistic outlook' (2006).

APOCALYPTIC IMAGINATION
In its temporal representation, climate change constitutes a form of global crisis for which we have no precedent. Unlike fear of

'the bomb' in previous decades, climate crisis is represented as a reality both to be avoided and, in other senses, unavoidable (as well as a crisis that we're mostly all complicit in bringing on ourselves). It invites the discourse of tipping points that have already been passed, and those approaching that must be resisted at all costs. But it also puts a new spin on the perennial fascination with 'apocalyptic' language and belief. Thus many of the chapters in this volume either explicitly or implicitly explore how, and why, climate change generates such engagement with this terminology.

While the term apocalypse itself refers to a specific genre of text linked predominantly to Jewish and Christian traditions, the book acknowledges the diffuse manner in which the concept has come to be associated with contemporary cultural and political ideas. Most people will have some idea of how apocalyptic relates to the broad discourse of catastrophe (whether they relate it to film, art, biblical text or other references in English literature). But the implications of that association can be incredibly diverse, true, perhaps, to the different elements that originally defined the Greek word from which 'apocalypse' is derived: a *revelation* or *disclosure* of the spatial and temporal transformation of the world, not simply a prediction of the 'end times'. Thus, to some authors 'apocalyptic' will refer to the anticipation of sudden calamity and possibly the end of the human or the known 'world'; others will draw insight from the vision of an entirely other world order: the imaginative ability to see the world turned upside down and dominant powers crushed.

While an appreciation of the historical origins of 'apocalypse' is not irrelevant here, the approach has been not to invite biblical or linguistic experts to define its meaning before engaging with its significance to contemporary culture. Our task, rather, is to understand apocalyptic as one diffuse facet of the ways in which our society as a whole talks about, and understands, the future. It is in this sense that the book's purpose is to address apocalyptic *imagination* as opposed to merely the 'rhetoric' or 'discourse' of catastrophe. It draws together, that is, the many different modes of discourse, practice, and vision that colour the various and often contradictory elements of a contemporary understanding of apocalyptic: our sense of such concepts as crisis, endings, transformations, destructions and renewals of the future.

4

POLITICAL ACTION

Interesting though such representations are in their own right, the contextual focus throughout the book is the way in which apocalyptic imagination shapes political action. Some authors welcome the notion of 'apocalyptic rhetoric' as a deepening of the imaginative engagement – a true *revelation* of sorts – with reality, or the gravity of a situation; others see in it a mode of disengagement, fantasy or imaginative closing down.

The forms of action and social engagement that we would call 'political' here are, of course, diverse, ranging from civil disobedience to shifts in consumer behaviour. While some authors do outline the strengths or weaknesses of certain types of action, however, a survey of the contemporary political environment is not our purpose. A common starting point of many of the chapters would actually seem to be an acknowledgement of the problem of *inaction*. That is, a presumption that a disparity between the gravity of climate change and the extent of global and individual responses – between its moral demands and our moral responses – presents a philosophical as much as a political problem. What *are* the bases for taking action, and do we understand adequately their relationship to ways of 'thinking the future'? Upon which physical, logical, cultural, psychological, ideological or theological reasons is *inaction* premised, and how might we reverse them, if we can?

STRUCTURE OF THE BOOK

The volume is divided into four parts. In the first part, under the theme of 'History', a number of issues are explored that reflect the very diverse ways in which the future scenarios sketched by climate change have altered (or, in some cases, *failed* to alter) social behaviour, cultural norms and political allegiances. In 'A Short History of Environmental Apocalypse', Frederick Buell gives us an overview of how the perception of environmental catastrophe has been shaped by different cultural forces, from Hollywood to advertisements and then to government policy, over the past four decades (in the United States principally, but with resonances around the world). A crucial insight from history turns out to be a theme resonating throughout the whole book: contemporary attitudes reflect the *normalization* of crisis, or apocalypse as 'way of life' – a theme that casts an altogether different hue on the idea of living with risk. In 'Four Meanings of Climate Change', Mike Hulme explores the more fundamental narrative roots of how climate change as scientific reality became the capitalized 'Climate Change', a cultural and political phenomenon used to justify any number of ideological and technocratic agendas. He asks whether climate change, far from uniting causes, has now become 'a malleable envoy enlisted in support of too many princes and principalities'. A slightly different approach, however, is suggested by Mark Levene, who, in 'The Apocalyptic as Contemporary Dialectic: From Thanatos (violence) to Eros (transformation)', argues that the experience of future crisis, and the possibility of responding to it, is defined by the radical inequalities and power relationships that shape our political landscape. Thus environmental catastrophe has historically played by default into the hands of technocrats whose desire to 'manage' climate risks resembles most closely a Freudian death-drive. The alternative, he argues, is to use the spiritual trope of apocalyptic prophecy to argue the necessity of seeing climate change as humanity's 'kairos' moment, a call for social transformation from below rather than its management from above.

The second part of the book, 'Ethics', consists of two chapters that explain some of the fundamental philosophical questions that frame 'acting upon' uncertain futures in the context of climate change. Both argue that our received ethical frameworks are inadequate for dealing with the parameters of uncertainty generated by climate change, and particularly with reference to possible future catastrophic scenarios. In 'Saved By Disaster? Abrupt Climate Change, Political Inertia and the Possibility of an Intergenerational Arms Race', Stephen Gardiner challenges some basic assumptions about the ethical choices people make when faced with a catastrophic future. An unsettling possibility emerges: not only do people find it difficult *psychologically* to take actions to avoid future disaster, they may even base their decisions *not* to act on traditionally *rational* moral bases. And Christopher Groves proposes, in 'Living in Uncertainty: Anthropogenic Global Warming and the Limits of "Risk Thinking"' that confronting anthropogenic global warming requires a radically new 'ethical imagination' based on the notion of care. This would afford 'different ways to live in and with uncertainty' as opposed to the technical 'management' of risks associated with climate change.

Taking forward the practical implications of these challenges, Part III reflects on the parameters of both action and inaction within recent political responses to climate change. In doing so, each chapter presents, in very different ways, its own suggestion as to why there exists such a gap between awareness of a climate crisis, and willingness to act upon it. What new barriers, whether intellectual or physical, lie in the way of responding effectively to future crisis, and how might these be overcome? Sarah Amsler, in 'Bringing Hope "to crisis": Crisis Thinking, Ethical Action and Social Change', seeks responses from more sociological sources to the same problem outlined by Gardiner: what does it mean when awareness of deep crisis does *not* correspond proportionally to an increase in activism (however that might be conceived)? Amsler's suggestions bear similarities to Groves': While 'apocalyptic narrative' as discourse of fear – and fear of an end to the human in particular – shuts down political participation, an ethics that brings crisis to the 'centre of consciousness', 'decentring' everyday experience, is capable of acting decisively and creatively in the world. Roman Krznaric might well agree, emphasizing as he does, in 'Empathy and Climate Change: Proposals for a Revolution of Human Relationships', the need to move beyond the singular experience of what environmental crisis means for *oneself*. The claim is that climate change can only generate social change when its effects are made tangible to people across vast differences of space and time. This generates a fascinating and practical task to activists and campaigners: how do we create the means to empathize with people we may never meet, in a future we may never inhabit? Though certainly not mutually exclusive, such a proposal can be distinguished from a contemporary trend in direct activism that focuses on the *now* of action. It is, moreover, a trend that has seen significant increases in participation, with a new generation of activists taking part in 'climate camps' in the United Kingdom and around the world; direct action groups such as Plane Stupid; and international networks like Climate Justice Action.

In the following chapter, 'Are We Armed Only with Peer-Reviewed Science? The Scientization of Politics in the Radical Environmental Movement', Andrew Bowman looks at what he sees as a problematic dynamic in *some* forms of climate protest in the United Kingdom. Namely, the 'depoliticisation' of climate change to a task that involves rapid carbon cutting at all cost, without a robust political critique of the sort of future society and form of governance that such a principle might be forced to usher in. The discourse and imagination of a catastrophic future (in this case its use of 'the science'), Bowman argues, must come under close scrutiny. Alongside visions of an apocalyptic threat, what visions of the type of world we'd like to create in its place, are implied by direct action? Which paradigms of power are legitimized in the process? An even profounder conceptual shift is called for in the following chapter. Richard McNeill Douglas also critiques the attempt to confront climate crisis without also rejecting a dominant economic paradigm of unlimited growth that underpins it. In 'The Ultimate Paradigm Shift: Environmentalism as Antithesis to the Modern Paradigm of Progress', Douglas also argues that environmentalism (and, by consequence, environmental action) has been unwilling to acknowledge the most radical of its conclusions, namely, the fundamental reality of our individual and collective mortality.

Perhaps the questions that must attend all activism, then, are these: what sort of future is worth fighting for? Would we defend it at *any* cost? If Douglas' chapter asserts the ethical importance of engaging with questions of finitude and the limits to life, then the chapters in Part IV extend this discussion further. They consider in more detail what aspects of thought originating in our religious heritage either condition, or propose solutions to, our engagement with the notion of 'the end'. Rather than attempting an overview of the diversity of religious perspectives on the end of the world and the future of humanity (for which one volume alone would hardly be exhaustive!), the chapters focus on some nuances of the Western, broadly Christian idea of apocalypse from which so much of the preceding discussion on 'apocalyptic imagination' takes its cue. In 'Eternal Return of Apocalypse', my chapter argues that viewing contemporary attitudes to climate change as apocalyptic *is* appropriate but not, perhaps, for the reasons commonly assumed. Rather than confirming our obsessions and fantasies of a final conflagration or catastrophic storm, apocalypse as the revelation of *world progress* actually presents the much more frightening prospect of *no end*: a narrative of a world in crisis unfolding constantly. Celia Deane-Drummond, on the other hand, takes issue with this 'narrative' format of apocalypse. In 'Beyond Humanity's End: An Exploration of a Dramatic versus Narrative Rhetoric and its Ethical Implications', she argues that it is the potential to portray humanity's destiny in *dramatic* terms that opens up the radical potential of apocalypse. In distinction to the epic narrative format in which humanity stands as passive spectator to an unfolding cosmic story, a dramatic reading of apocalypse empowers people to identify the significance not only of their own actions, but those of the entire non-human ecological community – a truly cosmic drama of possible transformation. In the final chapter, Peter Manley Scott also sees a theological / philosophical exploration of apocalypse as useful to the debate on climate change, but for very different reasons to the previous two chapters. In 'Are We There Yet? Coming to the End of the Line – a Postnatural Enquiry', an ambiguity over whether Western thinkers have historically inferred a sense of ending as 'terminus' or as 'goal' also reflects the dilemma facing an ethics of climate action. The question can thus be raised: is action premised on the value of preserving human life at all costs? And, if it isn't, in what sense is human action responsible for some other destiny for the world?

Each of the contributors to this book come with very different perceptions and ideas of what 'apocalyptic imagination' might mean with regard to climate change: where it comes from; how it constitutes our thinking, and whether or not it fosters political responses. This very diversity may simply confirm the complex nature of the relationship between *knowing about* and *acting upon* perceived dangers. But by attending to the related, fundamental questions of how the future is imagined and communicated, this book may help us to connect to the issues from a profoundly human perspective, and not simply a scientific or technocratic one. Only by so doing might we begin to understand what will be required of individuals and communities that rise to the challenge of our present and future crises.

REFERENCES

Hulme, M. (2009), *Why We Disagree About Climate Change: Understanding Controversy, Inaction and Opportunity.* Cambridge: CUP.

Meadows, D. H. (1999), 'Chicken little, Cassandra and the real wolf: so many ways to think about the future', *Whole Earth Spring,* vol. 96, Spring, pp. 106–111.

Pettenger, M. E. (2007), *The Social Construction of Climate Change: Power, Knowledge, Norms, Discourses.* London: Ashgate.

Schmidt, G. (2006), 'Runaway tipping points of no return', *Real Climate,* 5 July. Available at: www.realclimate.org/index.php/archives/2006/07/runaway-tipping-points-of-no-return/. Accessed 29 June 2009.

Wintour, P. and Sparrow, A. (2009), 'Copenhagen climate change talks are last chance, says Gordon Brown', *The Guardian* 19 October 2009.

PART I

HISTORY

CHAPTER ONE

A SHORT HISTORY OF ENVIRONMENTAL APOCALYPSE

FREDERICK BUELL

ORIGINS AND FIRST USES

Perry Miller, in an essay entitled 'End of the World', wrote that with the dropping of the atomic bomb on Hiroshima on 6 August 1945, the 'narrative [of *The Book of Revelation*] for the first time becomes historical' (Miller, 1956: 238). Miller envisioned nuclear destruction in biblical terms, as a horrific singularity, a complete end to a completely unique creation; he differentiated it, however, as one brought about by human action, not divine intervention. Invoking still further features of biblical tradition, Winston Churchill fused them together with nuclear devastation to make a powerfully novel image. He called the atomic bomb 'the Second Coming in Wrath', adding that 'the atomic bomb is the good news of damnation' (Noble, 1999: 108).

The horror of the bomb's use against Japan did not prevent Christian preachers from going further to erase all differences between nuclear and biblical apocalypse. As David Noble notes, 'the fundamentalist preacher Jerry Falwell pointedly identified Armageddon with nuclear war and encouraged his followers to embrace the prospect as a promise of deliverance. 'I believe there will be some nuclear holocaust on this earth', said Falwell. 'There will be one last skirmish and then God will dispose of this Cosmos' (Noble, 1999: 109).

But it was reinvention that made the most difference in the following years. By the 1960s, Miller's subtler perception – that the narrative of the apocalypse had suddenly become one of human, not divine history – had acquired a different referent. What military technology did in an instant, human society was doing in a somewhat slower way thanks to its environmental impacts. What had previously been unimaginable was now happening. People were altering and destroying all of nature, despite its vastness; they now needed to realize that they were poised on the very brink of finishing the job. This perception quickly became fundamental to the phenomenal success of the post-war environmental movement. Indeed, two contrary, but mutually reinforcing strains of feeling animated that movement: a sudden and passionate upsurge in the idealization of wilderness, of unspoiled nature – one that associated nature with beauty, purity, pristinity, equilibrium and health – was paired with an equally irruptive awareness of the fact that an ecological doomsday was imminently at hand.

Behind the sudden appearance of nuclear and then environmental apocalypse thus lay an equally sudden world-historical change in humanity's understanding of its position in the world. Against a wide variety of contrary scientific, cultural and religious traditions, the notion that human beings had acquired the power to change everything on the earth everywhere – and to do so suddenly – became a mainstream concern. The environmental component of this immense power emerged first with Rachel Carson's *Silent Spring* in 1962. She translated – with a prophetic urgency and ardour still powerful today – nuclear holocaust into an apocalypse brought about by the 'mysterious blight' of 'white granular powder' (in reality, chemicals like DDT) falling on fields, silencing life there and a 'sea of carcinogens' (in fact household chemicals) that had flooded human indoor environments (Carson, 1962: 14, 213). Her depiction of a completely silent spring (brought out by the chemical poisoning of all the birds) drew explicitly on a number of strains of nuclear imagery – silence being one of them, familiar to the audiences of Nevil Shute's *On the Beach* (1957) and the film starring Gregory Peck made from it (1959).

By 1968, Paul Ehrlich had deepened and diversified analysis of environmental apocalypse. He envisioned a grotesquely overpopulated world about to be visited by plagues, famines and diseases. Reality cooperated, as choking pollution events fouled air and threatened lives in cities like New York (Merril Eisenbud, Mayor Lindsay's environmental director, warned that pollution could destroy the city); the Cuyahoga river in Ohio caught fire; Lake Erie eutrophied; and birds died in a catastrophic oil spill off Santa Barbara. In 1972, Donella Meadows, Dennis

Meadows, Jorgen Randers and William Behrens, in *The Limits to Growth*, published their global-systemic analysis of the imminent collision between human populations, economies and technology, one they embodied in a computer model that ran projections based on varying inputs – projections that, when they followed current trends, pointed consistently to global ecological melt-down. Imaginative literature did not lag behind, as vivid versions of environmental apocalypse inspired Harry Harrison's novel, *Make Room, Make Room!* (1966) and the movie made from it, *Soylent Green* (1973); Philip Wylie's *The End of the Dream* (1972); John Brunner's *The Sheep Look Up* (1972); Philip Disch's anthology *The Ruins of Earth* (1973); and a series of memorable short stories by J. G. Ballard (*The Best Stories of J. G. Ballard*, 1978).

One thing that all of this literature and some of the non-fiction make clear is that the environmental apocalyptic mode continued and complicated what nuclear apocalypse began. It incorporated and revised what I see as four main features of the Judeo-Christian apocalyptic tradition, simultaneously invoking and modifying them. These four features – sudden rupture with the past, presentation of a revelation, narration of a world-end and dramatization of a last judgment – were what seemed to Churchill to be all fused together in the flash of an atomic explosion. The world-end environmental apocalypse depicted was, by contrast, the result of much more slowly unfolding processes; as society neared the brink it finally stood at in the 1960s, humanity's plunge to destruction had accelerated fearfully. Realizing this, people faced both sudden rupture with their planetary past and an imminent end to all life on earth. If rupture and world-end were inflected in novel ways by environmental writers, so also was revelation. Here, environmental apocalypse was closer to biblical tradition than nuclear events in that its coming world-end needed to be discerned from within human history by people embedded in it and announced by people (often unwillingly) made to be prophets. A feeling that forces far larger than any individual (albeit ones people acting collectively had created) compelled them to bring to their readers a last-minute, intensely-urgent, hitherto unsuspected and terrible truth, one that could just possibly be redemptive. It was a truth that could change the lives of all who had ears and hearts open enough to receive it.

Environmental apocalypse was thus closer than nuclear to the biblical tradition of salvific truth. But once again differences quickly become apparent: environmentalists' revelation was not like that of St. John – absolute in its decree of the shape of the imminent end times and absolute in its promise of redemption for the faithful. Environmental prophets' truth was far more difficult. It was a revelation of an apocalypse human beings created for themselves; that revelation, moreover, might very well not be a saving one. To 'save' it had to instigate change not just by the enlightened few, but by the collective, and if that happened the revelation would cease to be. True, if it didn't yield such change, it would indeed come true – releasing forces that would come, if not in wrath, then in withering or tragic irony to deny salvation to all.

Environmental apocalypse thus differentiates itself from yet a fourth feature of Judeo-Christian apocalypse: the drama of judgment, the separation of sheep from the goats, the faithful to Christ and the minions of the Devil. The wrath that Churchill invoked as a key part of a nuclear holocaust is, in biblical tradition, heaped on an evil outgroup. Despite Churchill's imagery, Miller felt that nuclear apocalypse diverged from this tradition. The Hiroshima bomb brought a catastrophe, but no real judgment. Its slaughter finally had nothing to do with separating good and evil. With environmental apocalypse, the situation was even muddier. Some environmental prophets, like Paul Ehrlich (1968) and Garrett Hardin (1968), have been justly criticized for targeting an outgroup: for being neo-Malthusians who stigmatized the too-fecund (particularly third world) poor as the cause of environmental crisis. Worse, they advocated policies against them that were positively cruel. On the other hand, the other regular enemies of environmental crisis screeds were Carson's chemical industry, the Meadows' corporate capitalism, and Wylie's demagogic politicians; stigmatizing these, however, hardly seems cruel. More important still than this lack of clear judgment was that all judgment was called into question by the dominant rhetoric of environmental apocalypticism. As the comic strip *Pogo* famously put it, this message was 'we have met the enemy and they is us' (Kelly, 1970). Humankind is judged; at the same time, to judge all is really to outgroup none.

Once again, the religious right made literal what nuclear and environmental apocalypse reinvented. Falwell, having celebrated nuclear holocaust as world-end, continued, gloating that when that end came, he would not be around to see it. He would be saved; the damned would be punished. Right-wing Christians thus showed little reticence when it came to stigmatizing and punishing wrong outgroups – An attitude that helped give particular edge to their political rhetoric, as they became more active in and essential to the Republican Party. As we shall see, this edge was turned very effectively against environmentalists in the 1980s and 1990s.

The first generation of environmental apocalyptics thus proceeded to construct an extremely complex discourse: one which fused nature traditions with apocalypticism, reworking both, even as it united scientific analysis with political urgency. That urgency, moreover, expressed itself through powerfully and artfully crafted prophetic-apocalyptic rhetoric. Most familiar to us is the achievement of writers like Carson and Ehrlich in fashioning prophetic-apocalyptic imagery and voices (Carson, 1962; Ehrlich, 1968). Less noted is the way they and numerous others also displayed and invented a remarkable variety of more scientifically and ecologically based rhetoric, rhetoric that presented patently terrible logics of accretion and proliferation. First came invocations of the logic of doublings; this was encapsulated in a familiar environmental parable. Ecological damage did not just accumulate, but doubled and redoubled: the process was like algae that took over a pond by periodically doubling. The day before the last doubling, the pond would still be half clear; thus the final blow would come 'like a thief in the night' – that is, suddenly, without warning – and be as shocking and final as the events of the Biblical apocalypse (of John), such as the opening of the seals, the tribulation or the Last Judgment. At the same time, perception of the algae's last doubling would be revelation. A second strain of rhetoric invoked the startling, out-of-control consequences of interactions that followed a non-linear logic of irruptive magnification, of the sudden state-changes catastrophe theory describes; in Wylie's fiction, for example, a chemical film devised to seal off the flammable pollution in the Cuyahoga river in fact, as a result of its success in containing the pollution, created a nuclear-scale explosion that levelled Cleveland. As this example also makes clear, yet another – a third – logic was at work: that of unintended side effects and of Barry Commoner's principle that, in world of ecological systems, you cannot just do one thing.

A fourth rhetoric spelled out a process that lay behind these sudden leaps – a process of tipping points and positive feedback loops, moments of discontinuity that kicked momentum towards apocalypse up onto a terrible new level. For example, as the earth warms, huge reserves of Arctic methane await their release, something that will in turn catastrophically accelerate global warming. A fifth was simply (yet powerfully) a rhetoric of hysterically accumulating hyper abundance, of the dynamic proliferation of problems that came not in ones and twos, but as whole congeries so intertwined they exceeded our capacity to ever neatly separate them or arrest their multiplication in a static description. In these complex meltdowns, environmental crises interact (worse, non-linearly interact) as air becomes unbreathable, water turns undrinkable, forests disappear, crops fail, temperatures warm, diseases are unleashed, population spikes make for starvation, and all together creates global conflict. Even Carson, who concentrated on just one issue, used this logic of proliferation forcefully; she multiplied chemicals and their multiple impacts. Finally, crisis-discourse deployed a sixth rhetoric, one it used in extremely various ways: irony. This included not just the overarching irony of human-created doom, but subtler tracings of the ways unnoticed feedback signals preceded tipping points and catastrophes. Thus another familiar environmental parable recounts the story of the frog in the pot; if the heat beneath the pot is turned up fast, the frog escapes; if the temperature rises slowly (say at the speed of much pre-tipping point ecological change), the frog stays in and is cooked.

For writers in the 1960s and 1970s, these rhetorics were all equally logics and revelations. Deployed against the era's fundamental attitudes, they overturned them: they revealed. Depicting humans as having trapped themselves in a terrible rush towards world-end, they expressed a terrible logic. Together, they distinctively and creatively gave force to the feeling that the environmental problems of the day amounted to apocalypse – to rupture, world-end and a last judgment on humanity.

The imaginative writing inspired by environmental apocalypse was equally richly inventive, artful and varied. It also cannot be reduced to monotonal doomsaying. The film *Soylent Green* (1973) depicts a future New York City as situated in a world already far advanced in ecological and social decay, one created through a fearful logic of doublings (the film's introductory slideshow) and marked by a terrible efflorescence of problems (the end of almost all non-human life, claustrophobic over-population, rapacious capitalism, air pollution, social and techno-logical decay, even an early depiction of hothouse weather thanks to global warming). It climaxes in a final, terrible revela-tion: the oceans, earth's last ecosystem, are finally dead, and people are now eating not plankton, as they are told they are, but each other. But along with this maximally gloomy, ironic revelation, the film presents a second, more genuinely powerful one. In the famous scene in the euthanasia centre, the film reaches beyond itself to create enormous pathos. It dramatizes the last minutes and death of Sol (Edward G. Robinson), the beloved elderly friend of the young hero, Detective Thorn (Charlton Heston). Catching up with Sol too late, Thorn views, with him, the one real attraction the future world offers: the opportunity to watch lush nature films from the 1960s. Accom-panied by a soundtrack drawn from Beethoven's *Pastorale*, they lavishly evoke all the beauties of the nature this claustropho-bically dying world has irretrievably lost. All-encompassing claustrophobia, irony and doom open into gorgeous passion and pathos, and a new, later very important subgenre of environ-mental mourning is born.

Another strain of literary work represents environmental apocalypse startlingly differently – not with prophetic irony and pathos, but with (of all things) comedy, even high comedy. These fictions – Wylie's *The End of the Dream* (1972), Brunner's *The Sheep Look Up* (1972), and, for example, Ballard's 'Billennium' (1978) – amuse and surprise (in Ballard's restrained version) or erupt into wildly inventive, outrageously entertaining farce (Wylie and Brunner). Richly connected with an avant-garde tradition of provocation, one committed irresponsibly to discov-ering ever more inventive ways to *épater la bourgeoisie*, writing like this presses the rhetorics of out-of-control superabundance into a crafting of wry parables or into headlong, hysterical

overdrive. Either way, it decisively refutes charges that environmental crisis writers of the 1970s did nothing but purvey doom.

SUDDENLY ON THE DEFENSIVE

In just a few short years, however, proponents of environmental
apocalypse were made to seem just that – a bunch of monotonal, gloomy, anti-human, neo-Malthusian purveyors of doom,
nothing but doom. In what I see as a second, major phase in the
tradition of environmental apocalyptics, the assertion was so
often repeated in so many places its truth seemed self-evident.
Starting in the 1980s, environmental commitments of all sorts
came under sustained attack in the United States by activists
and ideologues of the neoconservative/new right coalition.
Assuming power, it began its domination of public discourse.
Policy Review, the organ of the Heritage Foundation, one of the
leading conservative think tanks, described the environmental
movement as 'the greatest single threat to the American economy', and numerous observers remarked that the environmental
movement was taking the place of communism as the US Right's
chief bugbear and enemy (Helvarg, 1994: 20). And particular
fire was turned on the notion that human society was on an
apocalyptic collision course with the planet.

Sheer abuse was probably the most overt strategy of the
neoconservative Right in this area (as it was, to be sure, in
numerous others).[1] Because it had been one of the great motiva-
tors of the environmental movement, the issue of environmental
apocalypse drew some of the Right's most outrageous and
inventive fire. Environmental rhetoric was widely and famously
stigmatized as coming from anti-human misanthropes; from
gloomy, moralistic, people-hating Calvinists; from plain old
doomsters or doomsayers; from wooly-headed, hysterical Chicken
Littles (Bailey, 1993); and/or from (to pick a few of my favour-
ites) as toxic terrorists (Whelan, 1985) or apocalypse-abusers or
chic-apocalyptic neoprimitives (Efron, 1984) or people suffering
from an Armageddon complex (Wildavsky, 1982). These terms
were used not just in low-end, Rush-Limbaugh style conservative talk shows, but also across the entire spectrum of US public
discourse. They were disseminated in conservative talk-shows

like Limbaugh's; in right-wing grassroots activism (so much of which was top-down organized and corporately funded it has been called 'Astroturf' activism); in created anti-environmental media outlets and via 'experts' placed in mainstream media; in an enormously well-funded corporate PR industry; in varieties of politically committed professional organizations created for the purpose; in a rapidly growing number of new-style 'think tanks' pre-committed to conservative ideology and the creation of new anti-environmental 'counter-science' meant to drown serious research in a sea of disinformation. What Jeremy Leggett wrote about the treatment of global warming in the United States applies, in fact, to the achievement of the anti-environmental across all its issues: 'every country', he wrote, 'had its companies lost in skepticism about climate change. But in the United States the scale of the collective denial was unique. There was something primitive, even frightening about it' (Leggett, 2001: 264).

Julian Simon was at the forefront of the counter-science movement. He was, paradoxically, the most important denier of environmental apocalypse and the most important renewer/ reshaper of the tradition it started. Simon was the coiner and/or disseminator-in-chief of some of the above terms (e.g. 'doomsayers') and the most encyclopaedic in his footnote-studded presentation of anti-environmental counter-science. He was also the Right's most witty, gifted and provocative stylist. His most significant contribution was his pseudo-dialectical reworking of the most environmentally sacred formulation of crisis-rhetoric: the I=PAT formula (Environmental Impact = Population growth × Affluence × Technology).

Simon argued first that population growth was not bad, but good for us, because it increased the quantity of human geniuses alive (Simon, 1996: 67). Second, he maintained that all the other supposedly civilization-ending environmental crises were also good, not bad, for us, because the increasing proliferation of human genius, tasked urgently with coming up with solutions for these critical problems, would find transformative technological answers (Simon, 1996: 59). These answers would not just solve the crises, but kick human civilization up to a whole new level, fuelling the creative–destructive energies of capitalism and producing economic growth that would yield the capital necessary for still further innovation.

Simon thus did not just try to pooh-pooh crisis; he also welcomed it. He changed environmental apocalypse from an end into a beginning, from a cause of accelerating decay into a dynamical principle of (literally, he maintained) unlimited growth and unimaginable possibility (Simon, 1996: 81). The logic of doublings became the acceleration of progress; limits to growth became no limits to growth. Doublings of environmental stresses and problems, which meant apocalypse to environmental writers of the 1970s, became today's new motors of progress; the end of the world they formerly led to became a secular technological millennium. For the most part, Simon's critics (as he planned) got lost in his forest of disinformation. Few have seen how deeply dependent his ingenious central idea was on the environmental thought it repudiated.

Though startlingly threadbare as a theory of actual social dynamics, Simon's mechanism worked beautifully as ideology. But no ideology, however artfully constructed and relentlessly disseminated, could have had such an effect were it not for the participation of other, more material and less resistible forces. Neoconservative/right-wing anti-environmental ideology in fact was allied with and buttressed on a number of deeper, though near-term, structural changes in society, ones which gave Simon's arguments a powerful lift. If the well-known woes of the Carter era made an opening, four of these changes made the crucial subsequent difference. All contributed to what seemed like a decisive and exuberant takeoff in economic, social and technological development. Most important and most surprisingly, all helped extend, not repeal, the post-war apocalyptic tradition.

Most notable was the way a set of emerging industries, namely computers and telecommunications, genetic engineering, robotics and nanotechnology, were packaged as parts of a whole new era in human history. Suddenly appearing, the era was styled as a new industrial revolution, a post-industrial age, a second Renaissance, an information age, the post-scarcity economy, late capitalism, the third wave, postmodernity, and posthumanity. Crucial was the fact that all of these celebrations did not simply ignore environmental apocalypse; as was clear from Alvin Toffler's formulation of the 'third wave', they all sprang dialectically from it. In essence, the dialectic went as follows. Humanity's heroic era of mastery of nature (thesis) was opposed by the belated, but powerful appearance of environmental apocalypse (antithesis); the new, boundless possibilities of society, just now being revealed as incorporating both the ideology of mastery and the logic of environmental crisis were the triumphant synthesis. Gloomy second-wave pessimism – which Toffler linked explicitly to *The Limits to Growth* – was transformed into an era in which pessimism was a 'sin' (Toffler, 1981: 20).

Specific claims by the proponents of the new industries reinforced this point. Computers promised, among other things, dematerialization of the economy (providing answers to environmental problems in this biosphere) and the opening up of a boundless, unlimited cyberspace (providing an alternative to that biosphere). More pointedly, Moore's law of the rapid doublings of computer processor power slyly evoked and then reversed environmental apocalypticism's fear of doublings, turning it from crisis to celebration – a blow which became far worse when the law was extended to describe not just a specific technological advance, but the new acceleration of economic growth as a whole. Genetic engineers, meanwhile, publicized the promise of their field by seeing it as providing antidotes to specific environmental woes, from the biodiversity crisis to potential food crisis to toxic waste problems (the first patented organism was one manufactured to eat toxic waste). Conceptually, they maintained that their new industry simply undid what for environmentalists were the foundational limits of nature – limits on human ingenuity and to human interventions imposed by biology, ecology and evolution. Now, those limits seemed to be removed – something which many then generalized to the whole era. Even the Meadowses, updating *The Limits to Growth* (1972), renamed their book *Beyond the Limits* (1992).

The pseudo-dialectic that used environmental crisis thought as its now wholly surpassed antithesis also left a mark, surprisingly, on a wide swath of critical cultural and social theory. In the work of Fredric Jameson (1991), Donna Haraway (1997), David Harvey (1996), and Noel Castree and Bruce Braun (2001), founders of the 'social nature' movement, this dialectic did not lead to a millennium or end-of-time transcendence, but yielded a new phase of an old inequitable system. Still, they repeatedly styled this new phase as the result of the dialectic, described above – a dialectic that comprehensively dismissed the environmental thought and advocacy of the previous era. The most provocative and sweeping formulation came from Fredric Jameson, who pronounced nature 'over' thanks to its at last complete penetration by industrial agriculture on the one hand and by culture on the other and who saw this as signalling the emergence of 'late capitalism' (Jameson, 1991: 36, ix).

A second structural change also greatly enabled the dismissal of environmental crisis in the 1980s and 1990s, but did not represent a new phase in the tradition it started. By the end of the 1980s, globalization hit mainstream discourse. It promised millennial possibilities for economic, social and cultural transformations, for example, global modernization and integration, an end to destructive nationalism, and a new, cosmopolitan cultural hybridism. The exploration of these possibilities simply left out emergent global environmental discourse, which for the most part elaborated global environmental crisis on a separate track. Only by the end of the 1990s were students of globalization working to try to create grand unified theories of all four forces.[2]

Essential to these developments, ensuring the success of their claims, was a third, very well-publicized event. The predictions that Paul Ehrlich and the Meadowses seemed to have made about dates for the appearance of system-ending consequences were wrong. The end did not come. Population growth did not produce the famine, war and ecological devastation Ehrlich foresaw for the world by the 1990s. The interaction of systemic factors didn't result in the damage the Meadowses saw for the same time period. Indeed, as we have seen, just the opposite seemed to happen. Uh-oh.

A final short-term structural factor behind the rout of apocalyptic environmental crisis discourse was quite different. The 1970s saw vast disruptions caused by OPEC quotas meant to punish the United States for supporting Israel in the Yom Kippur war and the loss of Iranian oil thanks to the ouster of the Shah. By the end of the decade, however, oil supplies had been building up, eventually reaching glut-level. If the era of Reagan and Thatcher celebrated itself as transformative in the ways described above, it did not inquire about the extent to which its was indebted for its celebrations to the plunge in prices of oil – a plunge that began shortly after Reagan took office and accelerated dramatically into the mid-1980s, as expanded trading on oil spot markets continued to undercut the OPEC cartel, and oil from Alaska and the North Sea flooded in. Claims of the sin of pessimism, and the widespread respinning of environmental crisis into post-environmental possibility, apocalypse into millennium, floated to victory, in part, on a sea of oil. Thus the end of environmental crisis was fuelled by an oil economy that, in a few short years, would emerge as environmental crisis *redux*.

REGROUPING; REINVENTION

It is impossible to overemphasize the importance of these political and structural factors in turning the force of apocalyptic rhetoric unhappily back on environmentalists. But it is also profoundly wrong to portray environmental apocalypticism, let alone environmental thought and activism, as 'over'. Just the opposite is the case. For, as it lost ground, the predominantly nature-based environmental movement of the 1970s (including large mainstream environmental organizations like the Sierra Club and the World Wildlife Fund [the 'majors'], philosophical movements like Deep Ecology, and smaller radical groups like Earth First!) began going through considerable change. One important strand of this process involved a transformation of the discourse of environmental apocalypse.

First and foremost came a conundrum. Though neither obvious rupture with the past, nor times of great tribulation, nor final judgment and world-end arrived as predicted, it was painfully clear to those who still consulted environmental science that index after index showed biospheric conditions not getting better, but becoming much, much worse. Indeed, in the last decade, a whole bookshelf of new volumes about urgent global environmental crisis has appeared.[3] Claims of dematerialization of the economy were not credible. Statistics showed growth without dematerialization; conservative appeal to Kuznet's curve analysis (supposedly revealing that, as societies became wealthier environmental problems lessened) dissolved under scholarly microscopes. The computer industry created more problems than answers. It generated huge new amounts of pollution, prodigally used huge amounts of freshwater and energy. Genetic engineering did less than it claimed and opened up new areas of risk.

Old environmental problems became worse, not better. Measurements of ecological damage showed deterioration on far vaster scales. If the economy had globalized dramatically, so had damage to oceans, fisheries, soils, tropical forests, mangrove swamps, wetlands and coral reefs; depletion of freshwater and erosion of the atmosphere had dramatically worsened. The ozone hole(s) had indeed surprised scientists and society with a further demonstration of humanity's ability to erode the entire biosphere in a short period of time; despite the Reagan administration's attempts to neutralize this concern by sneering, an urgent global initiative was created to arrest the damage. Climate change science presented steadily more certain and alarming pictures of major crisis ahead; concern was kicked up to a significant new level with the formation of the IPCC in 1990. Population growth had indeed been accommodated by the Green Revolution and rates of population increase were even declining, but Green Revolution agricultural techniques and fossil-fuel dependencies were becoming increasingly seen not as solutions, but as having created near-future human and ecological risks. Species extinctions appeared now truly major. They showed contemporary society to be creating an era of biological collapse comparable to the great extinction events in biological history. Whereas Rachel Carson saw Americans swimming in a sea of carcinogens, Theo Colborn and colleagues saw global populations swimming equally in a sea of endocrine disrupters, with every human everywhere having a burden of toxic chemicals in his or her body (Colborn et al., 1997: 91–2).

This worsening of old issues was accompanied by the appearance of new ones. If ozone depletion had indeed brought rapid action to avert increased future harm, present human health problems related to environmental stress had substantially risen. Though few have called HIV-AIDS an environmental disease, it indeed emerged and spread, thanks to traditional environmental problems like habitat destruction and ecologically harmful development, as well as from developments traditionally seen as social, such as increased poverty, inequality, and the new global mobility of people. But even apart from AIDS, new disease prospects today are severe. Today, worries include zoonotic flu pandemics resulting from a complex of environmental and social changes and the spread of non-exotic tropical diseases thanks to globalization and global warming. These specifics indicate a more fundamental change. Human health concerns are fusing today with environmental ones.

Even more fundamentally, environmental and social problems formed hybrids across a wider variety of fronts. The study of environmental security and conflict appeared as a new crisis discourse. The environmental consequences and concomitants of poverty and inequality – on both local and global levels – became clear. The environmental justice movement succeeded in changing a movement that initially resisted it. As important, inequality was targeted as an important structural cause of ecological as well as social harm. Off-shored pollution and off-shoring of dirty industries clearly allowed, for example, rich-world economies to ignore their environmental impacts. Increasingly, the only credible remedies to environmental problems are environmental-social ones. The effect on environmental thought and activism has been marked; examples are numerous. Robert Gottlieb (1993) and Mark Dowie (1997) have written about the reshaping of activism, thanks to a fusion of environmental and public health advocacy and the emergence of the eco-justice movement and localist anti-toxic crusades; James Gustave Speth (2008), acknowledging the failure of the nature-based advocacy of the 1970s to reach its goals, now argues for the necessary inseparability of environmental and social activism and calls for systemic change in the form of developing non-socialist alternatives to capitalism. Similarly embracing systemic change, Paul Hawken and Amory and L. Hunter Lovins (1999) have called for an environmental revolution within capitalism.

APOCALYPSE REDUX

As environmental analyses and activism changed, so have the concepts behind the rhetoric of environmental apocalypse. This tradition has not been cast aside; its reinvention has been part of the reinvention of environmentalism today. Today, nature is no longer either practically or theoretically separable from culture. Where for social theory, this conclusion was drawn in dialectical opposition to environmental thought and practice, environmentalists' similar revision has come for the most part from heightened awareness of the still rising erosion of, and stress on, the environment. Damage is everywhere; no outside-the-system seems left; we exist in Herman Daly's 'full world' (Daly, 2004). Previous (i.e. modern) assumptions of the foundational separation of humans and nature now appear not as true, but as constructions of a particular cultural period – one in which cultural denial of embeddedness in nature helped create all the environmental woes that now so clearly mar both our world and us. The increasing transparency today of the actual intertwining of nature and society, and nature and culture, is thus an artefact of a time that cries out for more environmental concern, rather than less.

Second, as human's capacity to alter the environment every-where fast has become everywhere unhappily apparent, the fact of it is no longer startlingly new to us, but familiarly old. It has become a given today, a norm. For we are heirs to the era of environmental apocalypse; we are in a second generation of intense public concern about the environment; our problems have distinct histories; we have already once tried to control, manage and adapt to them without real success. If Carson showed us something new – that we were swimming in seas of carcinogens – Theo Coburn enriched that sea further with endocrine disruptors; Sandra Steingraber then grimly pointed out just how familiarly aware of the situation we have become: we have been swimming in these waters for so long that we have already learned how to swim better by jettisoning our breasts and prostates (Steingraber, 1998: 263). Both privately and pub-licly, we live with complex awareness and experience of environ-mental deterioration and constraint. We are no longer sheep who need a prophet to make them look up. We've lost the innocence of sheep, and need more and more to lose their docility.

With our present awareness of this new, tight coupling with the environment, we are in the process, I believe, of further revising apocalyptic tradition, itself revised by the writers of the 1960s and 1970s. Rupture, revelation, world-end and judg-ment are no longer what they were then. We do not encounter revelations of sudden ruptures with the past; environmental problems and constraints *are* that past. Even more, we don't any longer see nature as so categorically separate from human impact. The nature many sought to defend in the 1970s – the nature they feared society was destroying – appears today to have been more certain as an ideal than a truth. The Right succeeded in caricaturing nature-based philosophies and movements like Deep Ecology and Earth First! as people-hating and extremist. Old environmental standards began to appear to their friends, not just their foes, unworkable and incorrect. Pristinity and purity could not in fact be primeval; the biosphere and everything in it has always been evolving and changing, and human-affected changes of landscapes and biota date back certainly to agriculture, and arguably to our early hunter-gatherer existence (Ponting, 1991). Equilibrium also never really existed (Catton, 1982); and continuous biospheric evolution has been driven in fact by disequilibrium, setting it and us firmly on a one-way path through time (Botkin, 1990). Moreover, in the contemporary science of complex systems, disequilibrium has been shown to be a creative force, not just an index of damage and agent of collapse (Prigogine and Stengers, 1984).

Even the notion of external limits came to seem an idealization – an idealized brake on our potential impacts. Instead of being haunted by a sudden world-end brought on by the violation of limits, we more realistically worry about a world that doesn't end, but which descends and further descends (Beck, 1986). Visions of the future today have less of the terrible novelty or even closure they once had; a large-scale change has taken place. In many ways, the third world today, once seen from the first-world as an image of its past and idealized as the site of nature at its purest, has been thoroughly re-worked. Today it appears to the first world as an exemplar of advanced environmental-social deterioration and misery – a vision of its possible future, not past. The primeval has disappeared, and the future will bring no novel apocalypse, but an immensely heightened version of old woes getting worse and still worse.

Challenges to pristinity, equilibrium and limits have undermined both standard-setting in environmental policy discourse and strains of feeling in nature art and practice. I don't mean to say that they have simply gone away. Their value continues for many, especially those who are or wish themselves to be outside metropolitan-based contemporary culture; their value also survives as idea and as sentiment underpinning still important cultures of nature. At the same time, new aesthetics, ethics and even policy invention based on embeddedness in a changing, wounded world is also emerging. As this happens, I see apocalypse being reinvented again in two ways. One is in more intimately realistic portrayals of damage done and in discourses of human-environmental mourning. The second is in depicting humans' one-way trip through time as not a rush to doom, but a conscious immersion in uncertainty and rising risk. Risk awareness is definitely on the rise today; indeed, the discipline of risk-management is an attempt to contain it. But, as Ulrich Beck, risk's preeminent theoretician, makes clear, risk today is actually not finally manageable or limitable. Increased consciousness of it, today, haunts us far more than any sense of ends to come (Beck, 1996: 28).

To fully understand these changes, I argue, we need not to discard but reinvent apocalypse. To this end, I have proposed seeing apocalypse as turning paradoxically into way of life (Buell, 2003). Its magnitudes are all about us as we experience and in fact dwell in present risk. This metaphor is in fact a multifaceted one. It does not just underwrite a program for progressive action today; it also provides a tough description of the challenges we face. More complexly still, it indicates a crucial direction that contemporary anti-environmental discourse is already taking. Both description and source of prescriptions, the metaphor is crucial to understanding and also shaping our environmental circumstances today. It indicates vividly just how the discourse of environmental apocalypse is being, once again, successfully reinvented, and how influential it still is to our environmental-social analysis and activism today.

To say that apocalypse has become today a way of life is, of course, to suggest an attitude that undergirds much environmental passivity and quiet desperation today. The metaphor is, in short, a central expression of our current environmental dilemmas. It also is something that, strange as it may seem, can and already is being used to help escort us further and further into catastrophe. The most recent addition to anti-environmental discourse on global warming, for example, is a claim that global warming has already happened; that we cannot stop it; and that we must face facts and adapt to it. Already this wisdom has resulted in (shockingly ironic) attempts by nations to claim likely places for future oil development, in preparation for the time they will emerge from under melting ice-sheets. Geo-engineering – a source of hitherto scary fringe-solutions to climate change is gaining respectability (Tierney, 2009).

A pathway for developments like these has already been cleared by this popular culture's fascination with environmental apocalypse, something that began as early as the 1980s. Today, speculative visions of the future in film almost obligatorily present a dystopian vision of environmental-social apocalypse, one as extreme and multifactoral as that of the early environmental prophets. But this vision is not meant to shock us into our senses and make us seek alternatives. Instead it is something audiences are meant to and indeed do *consume*: sci-fi's obsession with wrecked, militarized, post-natural environments of social meltdown and perpetual high-tech combat (and its invention of special effects to present these scenes and wow audiences) is directed at transforming apocalypse into exciting entertainment for the multitudes. The original *Terminator* (1984) movie excited many viewers to fantasize their bodies as robotically invulnerable and to go around repeating the famous phrase 'Hasta la vista, Baby' on all sorts of inappropriate occasions. The original *Matrix* (1999) movie, while making recovery of the human also its official theme, stylized cyberworld violence so vividly as to make that what moviegoers dreamed most of taking part in, not seeking alternatives to. Homologous with this phenomenon in popular culture is thus, I believe, an expansion of what Naomi Klein (2007) has described as 'disaster capitalism' – capitalism that welcomes environmental and social disaster as a source of profit.

But the metaphor of apocalypse as way of life can also authorize action more informed, open-eyed and responsive to recent change than before. The creeping spread of crisis into more physical, social and psychological places, and the intimacy with which we feel it, opens up new sites for action and coalitions for change. Risk represents a much more sustainable sense of urgency, and uncertainty fosters experiment, small and large. Perception that the global environment is as sensitively dependent on us as we are on it extends sensitivities and interests in ways difficult to anticipate in advance. Nowhere is the dissemination of such sentiment so important today as in the emergence of concern about global warming, something that has become today's foremost environmental concern and thus site for reinventing apocalypse.

GLOBAL WARMING TODAY

The cornucopian exuberance of the 1990s disappeared quickly – so quickly as to reveal it was indeed based on the most short term of trends and shaky of cultural-intellectual dialectics. Terrorism brought down the towers; Americans discovered whole new areas of risk. The new millennium put an end to a tech bubble that had thrived on visions of a new millennium. Two wars commenced and stretched themselves out, troubling not just their participants but the world. A disastrous two-term presidency in the United States made it clear that history hadn't ended yet – that it continued both in a host of large vehemences and a still larger host of mundane, small-scale struggles. An oil crisis indicating the possible arrival of peak oil promised massive, disruptive global change. A far more comprehensive systemic economic crisis proved to be that presidency's crown jewel.

Global warming right now is our model environmental crisis. It embodies and features all the changes noted above. It is a crisis inseparably entwining people and nature. It is not revealed to us by prophets; it is more potently a part of us; it has worked its way deeper and deeper into our daily consciousness. It is a crisis about which, as James Hansen remarks, we cannot later claim we did not know. It represents no sudden rupture with a totally different past. It promises intimate damage to our lives and the continued existence of people and places we love. It is happening even now; and it points clearly to present risk – to small daily paths mined, gravely, with the large, unpredictable tipping points. It is a crisis decisively in-process, one that, thanks to the diffusion of fossil fuel dependency, woven into society at seemingly every imaginable point (its transportation, its manufacturing, its food production, its consumerism, its entertainment, its healthcare). And more than ever before, the enemy is, as the saying goes, us; stigmatizing others doesn't work.

Michael Shellenberger and Ted Nordhaus (2004) could not be more incorrect when they try to rule out crisis-talk for environmentalism today by saying that Martin Luther King Jr. did not proclaim, 'I have a nightmare'. Gore's PowerPoint and film, *An Inconvenient Truth* – which they specifically criticized as flawed in this way – has done the most of any single intervention to push global warming towards the front of social concern. Constructing new rhetoric, it explores global warming as a well-known, well-studied crisis. It keeps audiences' focus on climate change as a key part of their present allotment of rising risk and uncertainty, even as the damage (represented in often stunningly aesthetic film clips) it is now doing accompanies them personally and collectively on their one-way journey into the future. Personalizing his narrative and self-presentation, Gore speaks not as a prophet but as a member of a community that includes everyone listening to him. He uses many of the forms of ecological rhetoric pioneered by the first generation of post-war environmental apocalyptics, and he makes the stakes of climate change seem almost as large as the crises of his predecessors; yet he makes them part of a shared awareness of our risky, vulnerable way of presently dwelling in the world today, not a cataclysmic end to come in the future.

But it is perhaps James Gustave Speth who gives us the most decisive answer to Schellenberger and Nordhaus. 'My reply to them', Speth writes, 'was that he [King] did not need to say it – his people were living a nightmare. They needed a dream. But we, I fear, are living a dream. We need to be reminded of the nightmare ahead' (Speth, 2008: 233–4).

Conceptual neatness makes me prefer reminders of present risk and deep, near-term uncertainties. But my conviction is that reminders like these (reminders, not prophecies) will and should keep on coming.

NOTES

1 For fuller discussions of the strategies and institutionalization of the politics of anti-environmentalism, see books by Sharon Beder titled *Global Spin*, Paul and Anne Ehrlich's *Betrayal of Science and*

Reason, Daniel Helvarg's *War Against the Greens* and my *From Apocalypse to Way of Life.*
2 Immanuel Wallerstein, the great pioneer of contemporary globalization study, is paradigmatic here. His *Modern World System* (1974) laid groundwork for the analysis of economic, social and cultural globalization without noticing Donella Meadows' *Limits to Growth*, which came out two years before. Wallerstein wrote about the ongoing process of globalization; Meadows about what would end it. In 1999, he integrated the environment into the picture; the new book was called *The End of the World as We Know It.*
3 James Gustave Speth gives a list of seven of these in his book *The Bridge at the End of the World*, itself one of the best guides to crisis-deepening today and what to do about it (Speth, 2008: 5.)

REFERENCES

Bailey, R. (1993), *Ecoscam: The False Prophets of Ecological Apocalypse*. New York: St. Martin's Press.
Ballard, J. G. (1978), 'Billennium', *The Best Stories of J. G. Ballard*. New York: Henry Holt.
Beck, U. (1986), *Risk Society: Towards a New Modernity*. London: Sage.
—(1996), 'Risk Society and the Provident State', in *Risk, Environment & Modernity: Towards a New Ecology* (Lash, S., Szerszynski, B., and Wynne, B., eds). London: Sage Publications.
Botkin, D. (1990), *Discordant Harmonies: A New Ecology for the Twenty-First Century*. New York: Oxford University Press.
Brunner, J. (1972), *The Sheep Look Up*. New York: Ballantine Books.
Buell, F. (2003), *From Apocalypse to Way of Life: Environmental Crisis in the American Century*. New York: Routledge.
Cameron, J. (Director) (1984), *The Terminator* [Film]. United States: Orion Pictures.
Carson, R. (1962), *Silent Spring*. Greenwich, CT: Fawcett Crest.
Castree, N. and Braun, B. (2001), *Social Nature: Theory, Practice and Politics*. Malden, MA: Wiley-Blackwell.
Catton, W. (1982), *Overshoot: The Ecological Basis of Revolutionary Change*. Urbana and Chicago: University of Illinois Press.
Colborn, T., Dumanoski, D., and Myers, J. P. (1997), *Our Stolen Future: Are We Threatening Our Fertility, Intelligence, and Survival? A Scientific Detective Story*. New York: Plume.
Daly, H. (1997), *Beyond Growth: The Economics of Sustainable Development*. Boston, MA: Beacon Press.
Daly, H. and Farley, J. (2004), *Ecological Economics: Principles and Applications*. Washington, D. C.: Island Press.
Disch, P. (ed.) (1973), *The Ruins of Earth*. New York: Berkeley Publishing.
Dowie, M. (1997), *Losing Ground: American Environmentalism at the Close of the Twentieth Century*. Cambridge, MA: MIT Press.

Efron, E. (1984), *The Apocalyptics: Cancer and the Big Lie – How Environmental Politics Controls What We Know About Cancer.* New York: Simon & Schuster.

Ehrlich, P. (1968), *The Population Bomb.* New York: Ballantine Books.

Ehrlich, P. and Ehrlich, A. (1996), *Betrayal of Science and Reason: How Anti-Environmental Rhetoric Threatens Our Future.* Washington, D.C.: Island Press.

Fleischer, R. (Director) (1973), *Soylent Green* [Film]. United States: Metro-Goldwin-Mayer.

Gottlieb, R. (1993), *Forcing the Spring.* Washington, D. C.: Island Press.

Guggenheim, D. (Director), *An Inconvenient Truth* [Film]. United States: Paramount Home Entertainment.

Haraway, D. (1997), *Modest Witness @Second_Millennium. Female-Man©_Meets_OncoMouse™.* New York: Routledge.

Hardin, Garrett (1968), 'The Tragedy of the Commons', *Science* 162, 1243–8.

Harrison, H. (1966), *Make Room, Make Room!* New York: Doubleday.

Harvey, D. (1996), *Justice, Nature, and the Geography of Difference.* Cambridge, MA: Blackwell.

Hawken, P., Lovins, A. and Lovins, H. (1999), *Natural Capitalism: Creating the Next Industrial Revolution.* Boston, MA: Little, Brown and Company.

Helvarg, D. (1994), *The War Against the Greens.* San Francisco, CA: Sierra Club Books.

Jameson, F. (1991), *Postmodernism: or, the Cultural Logic of Late Capitalism.* Durham, NC: Duke University Press.

Kelly, W. (1970), *We have met the enemy . . . and he is us.* Retrieved 13 August 2009, from www.igopogo.com/we_have_met.htm.

Klein, N. (2007), *The Shock Doctrine: The Rise of Disaster Capitalism.* New York: Henry Holt and Co.

Kramer, S. (Director) (1959), *On the Beach* [Film]. United States: Stanley Kramer Productions.

Leggett, J. (2001), *The Carbon War: Global Warming and the End of the Oil Era.* New York: Routledge.

Meadows, D., Meadows, D. and Randers, J. (1972), *Limits to Growth.* New York: New American Library.

—(1992), *Beyond the Limits: Confronting Global Collapse, Envisioning a Sustainable Future.* White River Junction, VT: Chelsea Green Publishing.

Miller, P. (1956), *Errand into the Wilderness.* New York: Harper Torchbooks.

Noble, D. F. (1999), *The Religion of Technology.* New York: Penguin.

Ponting, C. (1991), *A Green History of the World: The Environment and the Collapse of Great Civilizations.* New York: Penguin.

Prigogine, I. and Stengers, I. (1984), *Order out of Chaos: Man's New Dialogue with Nature.* New York: Bantam Books.

Shellenberger, M. and Nordhaus, T. (2004), *The Death of Environmentalism: Global Warming Politics in a Post-Environmental World*. New York: Nathan Cummings Foundation.

Shute, N. (1957, 1983), *On the Beach*. New York: Ballantine.

Simon, J. (1996), *The Ultimate Resource 2*. Princeton, NJ: Princeton University Press.

Speth, J. G. (2008), *The Bridge at the End of the World: Capitalism, the Environment, and Crossing from Crisis to Sustainability*. New Haven, CT: Yale University Press.

Steingraber, S. (1998), *Living Downstream: A Scientist's Personal Investigation of Cancer and the Environment*. New York: Vintage.

Tierney, J. (2009, 11 August.) The Earth Is Warming? Adjust the Thermostat. *New York Times*. Retrieved 13 August 2009, from www.nytimes.com/2009/08/11/science/11tier.html

Toffler, A. (1981), *The Third Wave*. New York: Bantam Books.

Wachowski, A. and Wachowski, L. (Directors) (1999), *The Matrix* [Film]. United States: Warner Brothers.

Wallerstein, I. (1999), *The End of the World as We Know It*. Minneapolis, MN: University of Minnesota Press.

Whelan, E. (1985), *Toxic Terror*. Ottawa, IL: Jameson Books.

Wildavsky, A. (1982), 'Pollution as Moral Concern: Culture, Perception, and Libertarian Values', *Cato Journal* 2, 305–7.

Wylie, P. (1972), *The End of the Dream*. New York: DAW Books.

CHAPTER TWO

FOUR MEANINGS OF CLIMATE CHANGE

MIKE HULME

What is not always so clear – what the history of environmental rhetoric amply illustrates – is just how hard it is to predict the effect of a particular discourse on an audience at any given time.

Killingsworth and Palmer (1996: 41)

The climate change 'activist' world, and indeed the environmental world, has all too often sought refuge in random use of apocalyptic imagery without seeking to harness the power of narrative. Without narrative, few people are ever moved to change or adapt. [But] the faiths have been masters of [such narratives] for centuries.

Alliance of Religions and Conservation (2007)
ARC/UNDP Programme Statement on Climate Change

RE-EXAMINING CLIMATE CHANGE

Throughout human history and pre-history the relationships between societies and their climates have been dynamic (Boia, 2005). They have been simultaneously material and imaginative and variously elemental, creative and fearful. These changing relationships have now taken a more intimate turn. The cumulative impact of the aggregation of an almost infinite number of individual human actions across the world taken over the last 200 years is changing the gaseous composition of the global atmosphere. And as scientists Joseph Fourier, John Tyndall and Svante Arrhenius knew in the nineteenth century (Fleming, 2005), changing the composition of the atmosphere alters the performance of weather – or what scientists today would call 'the functioning of the climate system'. We thus have good grounds for believing that future climates will not be like past climates.

Our ancestors have often worried about this possibility and now the knowledge claims of science have offered new reasons for this current generation to be concerned. Humanity is firmly embedded *within* the physical climate system, straining further the artificially constructed boundaries between the natural and the human. But at the same time as physical climates are changing, the imaginative *idea* of anthropogenic climate change[1] is penetrating and changing political discourse and social organization in novel ways. The past (through historic emissions of greenhouse gases) and the future (through lurid descriptions of the effects of predicted climates to come[2]) are interacting in new ways to provide a novel motor for cultural change. And this is all happening under the symbolism of global warming.

Yet the proliferating narratives around climate change remain strongly rooted in the knowledge claims of the natural sciences and aligned to a policy framing in which climate change is a 'problem' to be 'solved' (Hulme, 2009). The universalizing authority of science, and its expectations of progressive 'improvements' in its predictions of the future, is invoked in this dominant framing of climate change. It is a framing which both demands and claims global assent. So for example, the goal of restricting global warming to no more than 2°C above the mid-nineteenth century global temperature – a policy position originating with the European Union in 1996 and recently adopted by the G20 in 2009 as an aspirational target – is seemingly powerful, yet fundamentally fragile. This goal appears powerful because it traces its lineage to the positivist and predictive sciences. It remains fragile, however, because it is largely a construction of elite scientists and of neo-liberal Western politics. This constructed policy goal is unlikely to be one around which the world will easily be re-engineered. In the turbulent geo-politics and social transformations of the twenty-first century, neither positivist science nor Western neo-liberalism seems likely to retain global hegemony.

For these reasons the emergent global phenomenon of climate change needs a new examination. And this re-examination should have a different starting point from that adopted in the late decades of the twentieth century. Those origins – notably in the 1980s – were to be found in the disciplines of the physical sciences and in the institutional processes which led in 1988 to the creation of the Intergovernmental Panel on Climate Change (IPCC) (see Agrawala, 1998). This is an institution whose pronouncements rapidly came to dominate climate change framing and discourse. They still do, as evidenced by the kudos conferred on the Panel by the 2007 award of the Nobel Peace Prize. Instead, the re-examination of climate change I propose here starts with contributions from the interpretative humanities and social sciences, married to a critical reading of the natural sciences, and informed by a spatially and historically contingent view of knowledge. In this chapter I offer one way in which we may begin to embed culture and myth in our understanding of climate change.[3]

Why is such a re-examination necessary? It is necessary I believe because the dominating construction of climate change as an overly physical phenomenon (what we might designate as lower case 'climate change') readily allows the idea of climate change to be appropriated uncritically in support of an expand-ing range of ideologies . . . the ideologies, for example, of green colonialism, of the commodification of Nature, of national security, of celebrity culture, of localism and many others (let us designate these latter interpretations as upper case 'Climate Change'). I am not arguing here whether or not any of these creeds are desirable. My central point is that the existing framing of climate change – with its dominating material, global and universal properties and its consequential exclusion of situated and heterogeneous cultural anchors – endows the idea of climate change with a convenient plasticity. 'Climate Change' is there-fore used to justify, *inter alia*, emissions trading, large-scale solar radiation engineering, vegetarianism, nuclear power, national identity cards, flight rationing, carbon offsetting and so on. Rather than leading to a convergence in thinking, the idea of climate change acts as a proxy for, and a revealer of, conflict in the human world. 'Climate Change' thus becomes a malleable envoy enlisted in support of too many princes and principalities. We need to understand the roles played by the idea of climate change in the contemporary world.

This chapter makes a small contribution to the re-examination I call for by suggesting four ways in which climate change gets loaded with deeper sets of assumptions about the natural world and our relationship with it – in other words how 'climate change' becomes 'Climate Change'. I am not suggesting that these are the only myths or ideologies,[4] nor even claiming that they are the four most important ones. But they are four that have struck me repeatedly over recent years as I have observed the language and rhetoric of climate change discourse. Because of the religious tradition with which I am most familiar, I have given Biblical metaphors to these four myths: lamenting Eden, presaging Apocalypse, constructing Babel and celebrating Jubilee.

By approaching climate change in this way, by seeking to reveal the underlying myths and cultural narratives which shape and inflect the idea of climate change, I am hoping to make easier the task of thinking ethically about the future. Narrating climate change as an idea situated in cultural spaces rather than as one correlating solely with a physical reality, makes it easier to understand the diverse and diverging calls for action we hear circulating through the networks of advocates and echoing in the corridors of power.[5]

LAMENTING EDEN

The lament for Eden views climate as a symbol of what is natural, something that is pure and pristine and (should be) beyond the reach of humans. In this mythical position, climate therefore becomes something that is fragile and needs to be protected or 'saved', just as much as do 'wild' landscapes or animal species. These are goals which have fuelled the Romantic, wilderness and environmental movements of the Western Enlightenment over two centuries and more.

To characterize this myth I adopt the image of a lost Eden, the idea of loss, lament and a yearning for restoration:

> So the Lord God banished him from the Garden of Eden to work the ground from which he had been taken. After he drove the man out, he placed on the east side of the Garden of Eden cherubim and a flaming sword flashing back and forth to guard the way to the tree of life. (Genesis 3/23–4)

This idea in relation to climate change has been developed in part by the sociologist Steve Yearley. He proposes that rather than being concerned about climate change for its substantive diminution of human welfare, there is a strong element of symbolism involved (Yearley, 2006). We are so concerned about anthropogenic climate change because our climate has come to symbolize the last stronghold of Nature, untainted by Man.

Bill McKibben in *The End of Nature* (1989) adopted this position with respect to reasoning why we are concerned about climate change. His powerful lament for the end of Nature finds its highest expression in the transition from a natural climate to a climate which is being modified through human interference with the global atmosphere. That 'a child will now never know a natural summer' is for McKibben a cause of deep sadness and of loss. That global climate is no longer safe from the contaminating influences of the human species speaks symbolically of just how deeply humans have penetrated and changed the natural world.

Now, of course, when and why Nature first became a separate category in the human imagination can be endlessly disputed, as indeed can whether an independent category of 'wildness' exists in any substantive sense. Many anthropologists and environmental historians (such as Julie Cruikshank, Michael Thompson, Bill Cronon) have argued that the idea of Nature *as* a separate category, distinct from our interior worlds and therefore something that can be objectively studied and hence physically 'damaged' by us, is an idea – an ideology – originating only in the Western Enlightenment. It is an interpretation of the world that finds rarer expression in traditional or non-Western societies where Nature and Culture are consistently viewed as mutually embedded categories: there is no Nature unless interpreted by Culture and no Culture disembodied from Nature. There is no denying, however, that the idea of wildness – Nature *as* separate – has been a persistent mode of discourse in Western rationalist cultures over recent centuries ever since that proto-Romantic Jean-Jacques Rousseau proposed a project to reclaim a pure Nature freed from human oppression (see Grove, 1998).

This mythical position – what I call the lament for Eden – contends that by changing the climate, by losing wildness in one of the last 'untouched' places, humans are diminishing not just themselves, but also something beyond themselves. And that we are the poorer for it . . . as too maybe are the gods. This mythic position emphasizes the symbolic over the substantive. It is a lament which underpins the deep ecology movement and which surfaces in some forms of eco-theology. Variants of this thinking in relation to climate change permeate, subliminally perhaps, mainstream environmentalism. And they lie hidden in even broader climate change discourses across neo-liberal Western societies. Thus we find ecological economist Paul Baer challenging the World Bank economists by rhetorically asking what an ice-sheet is worth (Baer, 2007), and the polar bear – that hackneyed icon of climate change – ends up not just worrying about its own survival, but has also to carry a huge additional weight on its shoulders, the weight of human nostalgia. Camille Seaman's recent haunting photographic exhibition *The Last Iceberg*[6] also plays to this lament. The Last Iceberg *chronicles just a handful of the many thousands of icebergs that are currently headed to their end. I approach the images of icebergs as portraits of individuals, much like family photos of my ancestors. I seek a moment in their life in which they convey their unique personality, some connection to our own experience and a glimpse of their soul which endures.*

But if we approach climate change through *this* myth we have to ask exactly what is it that is being lost as climates change? Climate is not like biodiversity – an absolute decline in species numbers or a loss of ecosystem function – or even like ozone, a direct physiological health hazard. As climates change the various categories of weather are re-arranged to occur in different places and in different sequences. We are not losing clouds, abandoning rainfall, denying the sun. We are changing climate, not depleting it. Certain climates may become extinct in one place, but only for new climates to emerge somewhere else. There is no such thing as a 'good' climate or a 'bad' climate, only 'good' or 'bad' ways of imagining and living with climate. There is a parallel here with the emerging deliberations among ecologists about 'novel ecosystems': how to define, categorize and manage them (see Hobbs et al., 2006).

And if this position is merely lamenting the loss of 'the natural' as McKibben suggests, then climate change is simply one more staging post on the long human journey starting half a million years ago with the domestication of fire as an agent of manipulation and control. Climate change then is no new category; and lamenting Eden really is romantic idealism.

PRESAGING APOCALYPSE

Environmental discourses have long been clothed in the language of apocalypse.[7] Over ten years ago, Jimmie Killingsworth and Jacquie Palmer (1996) traced part of this genealogy from the appearance of Rachel Carson's seminal book *Silent Spring* in 1962 to what they identified then as the new apocalypse of global warming, passing along the way through Paul Ehrlich's 1968 *The Population Bomb* and the Club of Rome's 1972 *The Limits to Growth*. Since Killingsworth and Palmer wrote this in 1996, and especially over the last few years in Western Europe and North America, I suggest that this apocalyptic narrative of climate change has become even more dominant.

The linguistic repertoire of this apocalyptic myth deploys categories such as 'irreversible tipping points', 'billions of humans at risk of devastation, if not death', 'climate genocide'. There is an endless supply of headlines in print and on screen that are so phrased. 'Global warming: be worried; be very worried' said *Time Magazine* in April 2006; 'Ten years to avoid catastrophic tipping points' wrote Tony Blair to European leaders in 2006. A separate category of climate change is invented – 'catastrophic climate change' as distinct from climate change. It's as though there are now two distinct sub-species of the phenomenon. A Green Party politician from the United Kingdom puts it clearly:

> 'Climate change' is a criminally-vague and anodyne term that is dangerous for us to use. Let's not fool ourselves by using warm words such as 'climate change'. Talking instead about averting 'climate catastrophe' is not alarmism. It is simply calling things by their true names.[8]

We see evidence of this linguistic trope not just in the places we would expect it – in the media, from environmental campaigners – but also in the words of civil servants such as the former chief scientific advisor in the United Kingdom Sir David King (2004), 'I believe that climate change is a bigger threat than global terrorism', and from some scientists such as Jim Lovelock (2006): '. . . we [humans] are now so abusing the Earth that it may rise and move back to the hot state it was in fifty-five million years ago and if it does, most of us and our descendants will die.'

These tones contrast, for example, with the less passionate and loaded language used by the IPCC (2007: 123): 'Abrupt climate changes, such as the collapse of the West Antarctic Ice Sheet, the rapid loss of the Greenland Ice Sheet or large-scale changes in ocean circulation systems, are not considered likely to occur in the twenty-first century.' In the Synthesis Report of the Fourth Assessment Report of the IPCC in 2007, the word catastrophe does not appear. Visual imagery too becomes deployed in support of this myth of Apocalypse, the calving of ice from the Greenland Ice Sheet, cities drowned under imaginary floods of water, doomsday movies such as *The Day After Tomorrow* being some of the more evocative.

What does this framing of climate change do to audiences around the world? It undoubtedly lends a sense of danger, fear and urgency to discourses around climate change. Thus *The Independent* newspaper in the United Kingdom asked the startling question in two-inch bold print on its front page on 28 April 2007: 'Will this be the summer when Britain reaches 40 degrees?' In fact it wasn't, as maximum temperatures during the subsequent, rather uneventful, summer barely made 30°C. Such stark language and urgent tones certainly deny audiences the choice to ignore the phenomenon of climate change. We hear the claim that we only have ten (or maybe it is eight or fifteen) years to 'save the planet' (e.g. *The Times* newspaper, January 2007) and the New Economics Foundation and others have established an internet clock, ticking second-by-second to climate meltdown predicted for 1 December 2016 if 'emissions are not reduced'.[9] Campaigning movements in the United Kingdom such as *Rising Tide* and *Stop Climate Chaos* have become expert in deploying such urgency in their lobbying of Parliament and in their public protestations (e.g. against expansion of Heathrow Airport or the building of a coal power station at Kingsnorth).

Yet heightening saliency and awareness of climate change is rather too easy a goal. The counter-intuitive outcome of such language is that it leads to disempowerment, apathy and scepticism among its intended audience. Several studies – not only in relation to climate change – have shown that promoting fear is an ineffective, even counterproductive, way of inducing attitudinal and behavioural change (Moser, 2007; O'Neill and Nicholson-Cole, 2009). In recent years, although the proportion of the British public being concerned about climate change has remained steady, there are now (2009) twice as many as before (2004) who believe that media representations of climate change are too alarmist (Whitmarsh, 2009). If pro-environmental behaviour change is what the myth of apocalypse really is seeking, then it may in the end be self-defeating.

So why should climate change be framed this way? How does it so easily lend itself to the trope of apocalypse? Anthropogenic climate change has not always been talked about in this way. I suggest here three dimensions to the consolidation of climatic apocalypse that we have seen in recent years. First, drawing from the myth of a fragile Earth and a disappearing climate – as in the Lament for Eden above – the enduring human fear of the future has fuelled these descriptions of a climate system on the point of collapse. It resonates with a particular view of Nature as fragile or ephemeral, as originally proposed by Buzz Holling (1986).

Second, the rhetoric has also been fuelled by the new paradigm now driving Earth system science: the ideas of complexity, thresholds and non-linearity. Working within this paradigm, Earth system models are able to find an increasing number of 'tipping elements' in their model worlds where non-linear changes in climate function can occur (Lenton et al., 2008). And third, I suggest that the myth of apocalypse has been partly a response of frustration to the apparent failures of international negotiations to establish agreements and policies which are effective in slowing the growth of global carbon emissions. Global greenhouse gas emissions continue to grow at the rate of about 2.5 per cent per year, and indeed have accelerated in recent years.[10] The instinctive reaction to such perceived failure in international climate diplomacy is to turn the dial on the rhetorical amplifier a notch higher and proclaim that the risks of climate change are even greater than first thought.

Of course the primary purpose of environmental rhetoric has always been to change the future rather than merely to predict it. Paul Ehrlich, for example, now claims that by painting in the late 1960s a scenario of a dysfunctional and Malthusian world owing to unfettered population growth he in fact contributed to a slowing down of population growth thereby averting the very scenario he foresaw. A similar normative goal may now be being served by portrayals of climatic Apocalypse. But I sense there is a new literalism pervading this mythic position on climate change. This normative role for myth-making enlists powerful scientific predictions in its cause. Spokes-persons such as Jim Lovelock and Jim Hansen claim to be basing *their* claims of impending disaster on the science of the IPCC, a body not acting in an advocacy role. I think these spokes-persons believe they are being literal rather than rhetorical.

Climate change as Apocalypse is essentially a call to action but now, rather than a call based on ideological conviction and rhetoric, it is a call that invokes 'sound science' as its legitimizer. In the summer of 2007 the protestors against the third runway at London Heathrow Airport proudly marched chanting 'armed only with the weapons of peer-reviewed science', holding aloft their scientific reports (see Bowman's chapter in this volume). In at least this sense then the myth of climate Apocalypse is different from 1960s environmental radicalism which was deeply suspicious of establishment science. This is demonstrated by the fact that this apocalyptic tone can easily bifurcate into a number of quite different policy discourses: radical ecology, ecological modernization, social activism, neo-liberal conservatism are all projects which can claim ascendency from the promotion of climate change as fear. The one thing these discourses all share, however, is the need for some form of control: whether controlling the impulse to consume, the levers of state power, the networks of communication or the operation of the market.

CONSTRUCTING BABEL

This brings us to a third mythical position on climate change, the one I call 'constructing Babel'. This is an ideology not necessarily orthogonal to either of the previous two and indeed gains some of its legitimacy from narrating climate change as catastrophe. As the Genesis myth of Babel relates, a confident and independent humanity, re-populated after the traumas of the Flood, claimed: 'Come, let us build ourselves a city, with a tower that reaches to the heavens, so that we might make a name for ourselves and not be scattered over the face of the Earth' (Genesis, 11/4). This aspiration towards god-like status, acclaim and personal glory exemplifies the idea of hubris.

I want to suggest that this confident belief in the human ability to control and to plan is a dominant characteristic of the modern state. It is a view developed at length in James Scott's book *Seeing Like a State* (1999). This ideological position sees the challenges of climate change in essentially modernist terms. As with acidified air, tobacco-stained lungs and depleted ozone, once a risk is identified then the apparatus of the State – or in the case of climate change the apparatus of many states – needs to be mobilized to mitigate the risk. Sociologist John Lie captures this mindset: 'Even if God-like control is unattainable – and the very idea of conquest of nature is unattainable – a deeply optimistic strain in the scientific mindset envisions nature as increasingly colonised and controlled by human conceptual inventions and technological interventions' (Lie, 2007: 234). Perhaps drawing emotional power from the overwhelming language of climate change as Apocalypse, the management of climate change becomes the latest project over which human governance, control and mastery is demanded. Thus Jim Hansen's recent appeal to the 'loss' of control as a reason for concern: 'An important point is that the nonlinear response could easily run out of control, because of positive feedbacks and system inertias' (Hansen, 2007: 4).

This instinct for control can explain the optimism which greeted the Kyoto Protocol on its signing in 1997 and again on its ratification in 2005. It was an agreement which mimicked the Montreal Protocol for the Control of Ozone Depleting Substances and bolstered claims that we were on the way to full climate control. This instinct can also explain the urgent tones to the Stern Review (2006) which laid out, using the tools of economics, a rational argument as to why stabilization of carbon dioxide concentrations at between 450 ppm and 550 ppm should and could be achieved. It explains, too, a range of advocacy positions, from biofuels, to emissions trading, to green taxes.

This myth claims, 'The climate needs saving and we can do it', prompting for example the green gold rush for carbon offsetting:

> The growing political salience of environmental politics has sparked a 'green gold rush', which has seen a dramatic expansion in the number of businesses offering both companies and individuals the chance to go 'carbon neutral', offsetting their own energy use by buying carbon credits that cancel out their contribution to global warming. (*Financial Times*, 25 April 2007)

This myth of political control and climatic mastery also has an interesting variant, the sub-myth of climate-engineering. This narrative – drawing power from the new modelling claims of the Earth system scientists – argues that exactly because we are *unlikely* to realize our Tower of Babel using the conventional instruments of diplomacy, trade and fiscal regulation, we need a new form of intervention to bring a runaway climate under human management. Jim Lovelock and Chris Rapley capture this mood perfectly: ' . . . [amplifying] feedbacks, the inertia of the Earth System – and that of our response – make it doubtful that any of the well-intentioned technical or social schemes for carbon dieting will restore the status quo' (Lovelock and Rapley, 2007: 403). They then propose a large-scale scheme for sucking up cold, nutrient rich waters from the deep ocean to the surface where they can fertilize algae who will feed on carbon dioxide in the atmosphere: 'If we can't heal the planet directly, we may be able to help the planet heal itself' (Lovelock and Rapley, 2007: 403). More recently, the Royal Society has reviewed the feasibility of a number of such technologies, divided between large-scale solar radiation management and large-scale carbon dioxide removal from the atmosphere (Royal Society, 2009).

There is a deep irony displayed in this sub-myth. The inadvertent side-effects of carbon-fuelled economic growth – the 'great geophysical experiment' with the planet first described by Roger Revelle in 1957 – are charged with de-stabilizing our naturally controlled climate. All efforts to reign in the damage using conventional human control systems of politics, diplomacy and economics are deemed to be failing (witness the outcome of

COP15 at Copenhagen in December 2009). What is therefore proposed is a new and now deliberate great geophysical experiment with the planet. The only difference between this new purposeful experiment and our ongoing inadvertent one is that we now have the 'wisdom' of Earth system models to guide us.

Whether one believes in the finance offices of the World Bank, the efficacy of the traditional nation state, or the scientific high priests of Gaia, believing that we can 'make a name for ourselves' by stabilizing global climate requires an inordinate degree of faith.

CELEBRATING JUBILEE

The fourth mythic position on climate change I suggest here relates to the ways in which we think and talk about climate change using the language of morality and ethics. I have examined elsewhere (chapter 5 of Hulme, 2009) the inescapability of adopting ethical positions when we diagnose responsibility for climate change and propose responses; also the ways in which the language of popular discourse about climate change and responsibility echoes the theological language of sin, repentance and atonement. The human instinct for justice fuels this fourth powerful myth about climate change. For some, the desire for justice is synonymous with the entire meaning of climate change. I attach to this myth the metaphor of Jubilee – the idea of justice, freedom and celebration, an idea embedded in the Jewish Torah that every 50 years soil, slaves and debtors should be liberated from their oppression. 'In this way you shall set the fiftieth year apart and proclaim freedom to all the inhabitants of the land' (Leviticus 25/10). The occasion was to be marked by a year-long celebration.

For those in social and/or environmental justice movements, climate change is not primarily a substantive, material problem, nor simply – as in the lament for Eden – a symbolic one. Rather, climate change is an idea around which concerns for social and environmental justice can be mobilized. Indeed, a new category of justice – climate justice – is demanded. It is one that attaches itself easily to other long-standing global justice concerns: 'By and large, the framing of "climate justice" reflects the same social and economic rights perspectives voiced by global movements on debt, trade and globalisation' (Pettit, 2004: 102). A former environment minister in Canada's Liberal Government of the late 1990s clearly revealed the underlying commitment to this mythic position: 'No matter if the science of global warming is all phony . . . climate change provides the greatest opportunity to bring about justice and equality in the world' (Stewart, 1998).

This instinct for justice, and the recognition that climate change demands an engagement with this instinct, is not just to be found within radical social movements. Ideas of justice and equity are threaded through political debates and international negotiations about climate change policies, whether in the context of procedural decision-making, of emissions reduction burden-sharing or of vulnerability, adaptation and compensation. For example, the principle that justice demands that those responsible for altering climate and causing any subsequent damage should be held liable for that damage underpins part of the framing of the UN Framework Convention on Climate Change. Other avenues along which justice might be pursued are those which emphasize procedural or distributive justice – the former making sure decisions made about climate change are fair and the latter making sure that actions taken compensate and benefit those who are most disadvantaged by climate change.

One widely discussed and advocated framework for tackling climate change which claims a strong foundation in this mythic position of climate change as social justice is that of 'contraction-and-convergence' (Meyer, 2001). Contraction-and-convergence has been widely endorsed by organizations ranging from the international negotiating bloc of the Africa Group to the Church of England, and from individuals such as Germany's Chancellor, Angela Merkel. The Indian Prime Minister has repeatedly stressed this principle when articulating the negotiating position of his country in international negotiations: 'Long-term convergence of per capita emissions is . . . the only equitable basis for a global compact on climate change' (Singh, 2008).

Some would argue that with respect to ordinary citizens, this mythic position of climate change as social justice has instinctive, mobilizing power. It appeals to certain intrinsic values held by many – values of fairness and justice around which popular

(Western) campaigns such as Make Poverty History have been able to mobilize. Climate justice may seem to have much going for it, but whether it is a sufficiently crisp and unambiguous concept around which agreed courses of action will emerge is more doubtful. 'It is not surprising that climate justice is contested and means different things for different actors, from parties to the [UN Framework] Convention to national policy constituents and other stakeholders' (Adger et al., 2006: 9). It leaves much room for debates about the precise apportionment of that liability between present and past generations, and whether it should be individuals, corporations or nation states which are held liable. And despite its alluring logic and appeal to foundational principles of equity and justice, the principle of contraction-and-convergence has thus far failed to gain sufficient purchase on the proposed architectures for an international climate change protocol.

By framing climate change as a celebration of Jubilee – at least as an opportunity to create a new potency behind movements for social and environmental justice – this myth offers hope as an antidote to the fear of an impending Apocalypse. Thus campaigner Alastair McIntosh – in his 2008 book *Hell and High Water: Climate Change, Hope and the Human Condition* – elaborates the presence of hope within this mythic position on climate change, while ethicist James Garvey concludes *The Ethics of Climate Change: Right and Wrong in a Warming World* with the observation: 'Many . . . say something remarkable, something uplifting and hopeful. They say that climate change offers humanity the chance to do the right thing' (Garvey, 2008: 155).

CONCLUSION

I have suggested four underlying ideologies – or myths – that shape and inflect contemporary narratives about climate change. They are ways of talking about upper-case 'Climate Change' – climate change as lament, fear, hubris and justice – rather than about lower-case 'climate change', climate change purified by science and stripped of cultural tone and meaning. These four myths do not offer exclusive narratives. Indeed, one very likely finds threads of all four myths entangling themselves in the beliefs about climate change held by many of us and in our expressed claims of what must be done. And they are of course not the only ideological lenses through which climate change can be viewed.

But I do think it is very important that we analyse the phenomenon of climate change at this deeper level, at the level at which science and culture interact. It is simplistic and trite to suggest that there are those who believe in the science of climate change and those who are sceptical of it. Science requires scepticism and thrives on it. This really tells us nothing, certainly nothing about the upper-case phenomenon of 'Climate Change'. Equally, it gets us nowhere to castigate American neo-conservative Republicans and the 'religious right', or the Governments of China and India, as being the *real* obstacles to progress on tackling climate change.

What science can tell us about climate change – whether through IPCC reports, National Science Foundation reviews, academic papers in the journals *Nature* or *Science* – does not present us with a script from which any of the four myths of 'Climate Change' can be read. As an idealized form of inquiry, science endorses no ideology other than itself. We are allowing ourselves to get into a muddle by confusing the lower-case and upper-case variants of the phenomenon, as if we were talking about 'Climate change' or 'climate Change'.

I believe it is only through this deeper level of analysis – revealing the beliefs, values and ethical commitments that drive our various myths about climate change – that we can begin to understand what really is at stake in the politics of climate change.

Should our real focus of concern with climate change lie with the diminution of the invented category called Nature? If we believe the myth of Eden, climate change really *is* about symbolic loss, a loss to our imaginative capacities rather than a loss of something material and substantive. If this is so, it would certainly help explain why the reaction to climate change around the world is so heterogeneous and disputed; the imaginative symbolism of climate has a wide diversity of meanings and interpretations across different cultures and traditions.

Or maybe anthropogenic climate change really has introduced a new and non-negotiable absolute planetary limit to human reproductive fecundity and profligate resource consumption (cf. Rockström et al., 2009). If we believe the myth of Apocalypse, the melting of the Greenland Ice Sheet really might signal the end of civilization as we know it. Perhaps we do only have until 1 December 2016 to save the world. And maybe science, once and for all, has replaced the prophets of religion and astrology by revealing the chronology of 'the end times'.

Or does climate change demand the enlargement and enforcement of global governance – Earth system governance in Biermann's (2007) terminology – offering new institutions for a new millennium delivering the means for new social, economic and environmental control? If we believe the myth of Babel, climate change demands that we deliver on the hubristic goal of re-stabilizing world climate at some new safe level, first by inventing new institutions of global governance and then by allowing our behaviour to be engineered globally towards achieving this long-term goal. In the history of humanity we certainly have never before got close to designing, let alone delivering, such a global project. Stalin's Five Year Plans and Mao's Great Leap Forward in China are not perhaps the best models to emulate.

Or is the power of climate change to be found in its demands that we attend to the enduring questions of injustice and inequity in the world? If we believe the myth of Jubilee, then climate change will not be 'solved' by an abandonment of modernization, not by the roll-out of clean green technology nor by the colonization of space with heat-reflecting mirrors. Instead, climate change is the latest reason why the project we must put above all others is the global redistribution of wealth and the reparation for environmental and social damage caused by an unequal appropriation of ecological space.

Now these are of course rhetorical questions I am asking. So let me end with an alternative proposition.

Notwithstanding the myth of Jubilee, I suggest that we are using climate change to distract ourselves from the really rather uncomfortable perversions that exist in our world – so many of them a result of our infatuation with consumer-driven economic growth at the expense of human health and social justice. We have become blinded by the prospect of a dysfunctional future climate, at worst a dysfunctionality of apocalyptic proportions, and lost sight of our contemporary crisis. Why, for example, do we not see the same political energy and diplomatic capital

being invested in the achievement of the Millennium Development Goals (MDGs) as we see daily being invested in the drive
to establish an international climate regime with its sights half a
century hence? Delivering the MDGs – the eradication of
extreme poverty and hunger, the reduction of child mortality,
the achievement of universal primary education – is now only
five years away. Has climate change allowed a convenient trans-
ference of ethical concern away from the immediate and tract-
able to the distant and unachievable? Is climate change, rather
than being an 'inconvenient truth', in fact being used as a very
'convenient truth' because it offers us a psychological focus for
our loss of the past, our fear of the future, our desire for mastery
and our instinct for justice? We are using climate change to act
as a conduit for serving our deeper psychological needs.

The function of climate change I suggest then is *not* as a
lower-case physical phenomenon to be 'solved'. It really is
not about stopping climate chaos. Our reach as humans is too
limited, our ability to manage ourselves too feeble, our voices
on what to do too plural. Instead, we need to see how we can
use the idea of climate change – the asymmetric matrix of power
relationships, social discourses and symbolic meanings that
climate change reveals – to re-think how we take forward our
various political, social and economic projects over the decades
to come, whatever they may be. We should *use* the idea of climate
change as a magnifying glass in more forensic and honest
examinations than we have been used to of each of these
projects – whether they be projects of human development, free
trade, poverty reduction, community-building, demographic
management, social health and so on. As Rowan Williams, the
Archbishop of Canterbury, claimed recently:

> Instead of a desperate search to find the one great idea that
> will save us from ecological disaster, we are being invited
> [by climate change] to a transformation of individual and
> social goals that will bring us closer to the reality of an inter-
> dependent life in a variegated world – whether or not we
> find we can 'save the planet'. (Williams, 2009)

Climate change has great magnifying power, the things that
'Climate Change' in its socio-cultural manifestation reveals to

us: its focus on the long-term implications of short-term choices, its global reach, its narrative of crisis, its revelation of new centres of power, its attention to both material and cultural values. We can therefore use this magnifying power, this mobilizing idea of climate change, to attend more closely to what we really want to achieve for humanity: whether this be social justice and human well-being or even whether, as it seems for some, to be material affluence and survival at any cost.

NOTES

1 Strictly speaking, the term 'climate change' refers to a change in climate brought about for *any* reason, whether natural or human. The great ice ages are therefore a result of (natural) climate change. However, in popular usage 'climate change' has come to imply a change in climate brought about by human actions (anthropogenic climate change), most notably the changing composition of the global atmosphere. The erasure of this distinction between natural and anthropogenic climate change is of some significance for communications between the worlds of science, society and politics. The term 'global warming' also has the connotation of human causation.

2 The film *Age of Stupid* released in March 2009 in the United Kingdom is one example of such vivid imagination at work, with the world of 2055 inundated under a flood of biblical proportions.

3 I first outlined this approach in chapter 10 of *Why We Disagree About Climate Change* (Hulme, 2009), an approach that is here somewhat elaborated.

4 By ideology I mean the body of doctrine, myth, belief, etc., that guides an individual, social movement, institution, class or large group. And I mean 'myth' in the anthropological sense of 'embodying fundamental truths underlying our assumptions about everyday life and scientific realities' (Thompson and Rayner, 1998). Myths transcend scientific categories of 'truth' and 'falsehood'.

5 These voices and their ideological correlates have been explored in Elizabeth Malone's new book *Debating Climate Change: Pathways Through Argument to Agreement*.

6 [www.camilleseaman.com]

7 I use the word apocalypse in its popular sense, meaning impending large-scale disaster or destruction, rather than in its original Greek – and Biblical – usage, meaning simply disclosure or revelation. See Skrimshire's chapter in this volume for elaboration of the significance of this difference.

8 Rupert Read, private correspondence, 2008.

9 www.onehundredmonths.org/ [accessed 20 October 2009].

10 The *reduction* of about 2.5 per cent in global emissions during 2008 was caused by the global economic recession and most commentators expect the decadal growth trend to resume after 2010.

REFERENCES

Adger, W. N., Paavola, J., Huq, S. and Mace, R. J. (2006), *Equity and Justice in Adaptation to Climate Change.* Cambridge, MA: MIT Press, 319pp.

Agrawala, S. (1998), 'Context and Early Origins of the IPCC', *Climatic Change* 39, 605–20.

Alliance of Religions and Conservation (2007), ARC/UNDP Programme Statement on Climate Change ARC, Bath. Available at: www.arcworld.org/about_ARC.htm

Baer, P. (2007), 'The Worth of an Ice-Sheet. A Critique of the Treatment of Catastrophic Impacts in the Stern Review'. An EcoEquity discussion paper, 10pp. Available at: www.ecoequity.org

Biermann, F. (2007), '"Earth system governance" as a Crosscutting Theme of Global Change Research', *Global Environmental Change* 17(3/4), 326–37.

Boia, L. (2005), *The Weather in the Imagination.* London: Reaktion Books, 200pp.

Camille Seaman quoted at http://www.soulcatcherstudio.com/exhibitions/seaman/index.htm [accessed 24 March 2010].

Carson, R. (1962/2000), *Silent Spring.* London: Penguin Classics, 323pp.

Ehrlich, P. R. (1968), *The Population Bomb.* New York: Ballantyne Books.

Fleming, J. R. (2005), *Historical Perspectives on Climate Change.* 2nd edn. Oxford: Oxford University Press.

Garvey, J. (2008), *The Ethics of Climate Change: Right and Wrong in a Warming World.* London/New York: Continuum International Publishing, 179pp.

Grove, R. H. (1998), *Ecology, Climate and Empire: The Indian Legacy in Global Environmental History, 1400–1940.* Delhi, India: Oxford University Press, 237pp.

Hansen, J. E. (2007), 'Scientific Reticence and Sea Level Rise', *Environmental Research Letters* 2, doi:10.1088/1748–9326/2/2/024002, 6pp.

Hobbs, R. J., Arico, S., Aronson, J. et al. (2006), 'Novel Ecosystems: Theoretical and Management Aspects of the New Ecological World Order', *Global Ecology and Biogeography* 15, 1–7.

Holling, C. S. (1986), 'The Resilience of Terrestrial Ecosystems: Local Surprise and Global Change', in *Sustainable Development of the Biosphere* (Clark, W. C. and Mann, R. E., eds), pp. 217–32. Cambridge, UK: Cambridge University Press, 500pp.

Hulme, M. (2009) *Why We Disagree about Climate Change: Understanding Controversy, Inaction and Opportunity.* Cambridge, UK: Cambridge University Press, 393pp.

IPCC (2007), *Climate Change 2007 – the Physical Science Basis.* Working Group I contribution to the Fourth Assessment Report of the IPCC. Cambridge, UK: Cambridge University Press, 996pp.

Killingsworth, M. J. and Palmer, J. S. (1996), 'Millennial Ecology: The Apocalyptic Narrative from *Silent Spring* to Global Warming', in *Green Culture: Environmental Rhetoric in Contemporary America* (Herndl, C. G. and Brown, S. C., eds), pp. 21–45. Madison, WI: University of Wisconsin Press, 315pp.

King, D. A. (2004), 'Climate Change Science: Adapt, Mitigate or Ignore?' *Science* 303, 176–7.

Lenton, T. M., Held, H., Krieglar, E. et al. (2008), 'Tipping Elements in the Earth's Climate System'. *Proceedings of the National Academy of Sciences* 105(6), 1786–93.

Lie, J. (2007), 'Global Climate Change and the Politics of Disaster', *Sustainability Science* 2, 233–6.

Lovelock, J. (2006), *The Revenge of Gaia: Why The Earth is Fighting Back – and How We Can Still Save Humanity*. London: Penguin, 222pp.

Lovelock, J. and Rapley, C. (2007), 'Ocean Pipes Could Help the Ocean to Cure Itself'. *Nature* 449, 403.

Malone, E. L. (2009), *Debating Climate Change: Pathways Through Argument to Agreement*. London: Earthscan, 176pp.

McIntosh, A. (2008), *Hell and High Water: Climate Change, Hope and the Human Condition*. Edinburgh: Birlinn, 289pp.

McKibben, B. (1989), *The End of Nature*. London: Random House, 230pp.

Meadows, D. H. (1972), *The Limits to Growth: A Report to the Club of Rome*. New York: Universe Books, 208pp.

Meyer, A. (2001), *Contraction and Convergence*. Totnes, UK: Green Books, 96pp.

Moser, S. (2007), 'More Bad News: The Risk of Neglecting Emotional Responses to Climate Change Information', in *Creating a Climate for Change: Communicating Climate Change and Facilitating Social Change*, pp. 64–81. Cambridge, UK: Cambridge University Press, 549pp.

O'Neill, S. J. and Nicholson-Cole, S. (2009), ' "Fear won't do it": Promoting Positive Engagement with Climate Change Through Imagery and Icons', *Science Communication* 30 (3), 355–79.

Pettit, J. (2004), 'Climate Justice: A New Social Movement for Atmospheric Rights', *IDS Bulletin* 35 (3), 102–6.

Rockström, J. et al. (2009), 'A Safe Operating Space for Humanity', *Nature* 461, 472–4.

Royal Society (2009), *Geoengineering the Climate: Science, Governance and Uncertainty*. London: Royal Society Report, 82pp.

Scott, J. C. (1998), *Seeing Like a State: How Certain Schemes to Improve the Human Condition Have Failed*. New Haven, CT: Yale University Press, 445pp.

Singh, M. (2008), PM's speech on release of climate change action plan New Delhi, 30 June. Available at: www.pmindia.nic.in/speech/

Stern Review (2006), *The Economics of Climate Change.* Cambridge, UK: Cambridge University Press, 557pp.

Stewart, C. (1998), Speaking in 1998. Quoted in *Canada Free Press*, 5 February 2007.

Thompson, M. and Rayner, S. (1998), 'Cultural Discourses', in *Human Choice and Climate Change*, vol. 1 *The Societal Framework* (Rayner, S. and Malone, E. L., eds), pp. 265–344. Columbus, OH: Battelle Press, 490pp.

Whitmarsh, L. (2009), UK climate scepticism more common. *BBC News On-line* http://news.bbc.co.uk/1/hi/sci/tech/8249668.stm, 10 September 2009.

Williams, R. (2009), The climate crisis: fashioning a Christian response Speech delivered at Southwark Cathedral, London, 13 October. Available at: www.archbishopofcanterbury.org

Yearley, S. (2006), 'How many "ends" of nature: making sociological and phenomenological sense of the end of nature'. *Nature and Culture* 1(1), 10–21.

CHAPTER THREE

THE APOCALYPTIC AS CONTEMPORARY DIALECTIC

FROM THANATOS (VIOLENCE) TO EROS (TRANSFORMATION)

MARK LEVENE

The Last Days were announced to St. John by a voice like a sound of many waters. But the voice that comes in our day summoning us to play out the dark myth of the reckoning is our meagre own, making casual conversation about the varieties of annihilation. . . . the thermonuclear Armageddon, the death of the seas, the vanishing atmosphere, the massacre of the innocents, the universal famine to come . . .

Roszak (1972: 1)

INTRODUCTION

One might have hoped that with the overwhelming nature of global warming upon us, Theodore Roszak's implicit plea from 1972 that we should now be alert to the apocalyptic quality of our situation would finally have registered with public consciousness. Yet where is that alertness? In the modern Western imagination, 'apocalyptic' has primarily come to be associated with a catastrophic end, or near-end, of either human society or human life, through the intervention of natural or divine beings or events. One thinks of the wave of apocalyptic and post-apocalyptic genre of cinema, for example, that has resurfaced in the past decade. A persistent theme is the collective, violent death of millions of unprepared and *unaware* innocent individuals, in the face of invincible – sometimes invisible – forces. It is not, then, that a sense of the apocalyptic is alien to our culture. On the contrary, it is in some ways very familiar, background noise.

And to that extent, whereas it may remain for the time being something to switch off at the film's 'end', it does offer a premonition of the possibility of a terminal condition, and – perhaps more unsettlingly – of some kind of willingness to embrace it.

Yet we surely cannot but be troubled by this *version* of apocalyptic anticipation, not least when set against the tradition inherent in the original Judeo-Christian or Gnostic texts of apocalypse. The earlier narratives were dependent on hidden truths about humankind's purpose in the world being finally and irrevocably revealed – in so doing, unlocking the path to humankind's *redemption*. In the Hollywood-informed formula, however, the role available to the majority of humanity is nothing more than as passive onlookers. To be sure, there *is* a salvation of sorts for a remnant of survivors, which we might read as a continuation of the bleaker side of the ancient apocalyptic trope. But what is most striking about the Hollywood version – even as it is offered as fantasy – is in the way it provides an uncanny reflection of the workings of our 'normative' Western state and societal organization. The 'saviours', in humanity's hour of need, are invariably an extremely select, indeed, highly *specialized* scientific elite whose esoteric skills (plus grit and daring) determine that only they are able to vanquish the death-dealing danger or enemy. This mirrors a truism about modern Western society as one in which the vast majority of us are entirely dependent for our safety and well-being on the technical know-how of the few. But in the face of the escalating crisis of climate change this also has much more sinister implications.

I will argue in this chapter that the dominant heroic-technological mode of contemporary secular apocalyptic is itself indicative of a pervading, mostly, unwritten premise of today's Western hegemonic system: namely, that there are heavy-duty technical fixes to *all* problems, and that in the event of some overwhelming global, environmental or other catastrophe, the appropriate response is to scale them up accordingly – *regardless* of the ultimate consequences. If this, on the one hand, is simply a statement about Western society as a 'technological society' (Ellul, 1965; Shaw, 2010) it also carries political and military implications which reinforce the widening gap between elite power as largely exercised by state security, scientific and corporate elites, and the rest of us. In short, in the face of an accelerating pace of human-induced global warming, not only will 'we' – the populace – be required to acquiesce to what the Nazi jurist, Carl Schmitt, from a more overtly totalitarian historic moment, would have called 'the state of exception' (Slomp, 2009), but to 'solutions' which are likely to exacerbate the drive, on the one hand, to mass exterminatory violence, on the other, to all-encompassing environmental disaster.

Viewed through the lens of the Hollywood genre, this is clearly paradoxical. Rather than our technocratic heroes being the oppositional bulwark against the certainty of catastrophe, I am proposing that they are actually its harbingers. I call this apocalyptic form, here, the apocalypse of Thanatos, referring to the Greek god of death, which Freud interpreted psychologically as linked to a universal human death-wish.

In the face of this bleak prognosis, is there an alternative version of apocalyptic imagination which might act as an antithetical antidote? The answer may lie, at least in part, in a recovery of the ancient *purposefulness* of the idea of apocalypse – *not* as a prospect simply of obliteration, and with it world-end, but rather as a prophetic warning whose wake-up call to all humanity beckons them to participate in a general act of redeeming planetary reconciliation. It is this implication of apocalypse as an idea geared towards enabling people – in the face of total wipe-out – to utterly change their lives for the *good* which, in our age of total crisis, I submit, remains redolent with potentiality. Using again the Freudian short-hand I call this updated version of the ancient form, the apocalypse of Eros, to denote life, love and affirmation of the will to live in, and with the natural world.[1]

The juxtaposition should, I hope, be clear. As human time runs into its hour-glass, we will be increasingly confronted with a stark dialectic as represented by these two antithetical forecasts of the future – and with rapidly diminishing space for any middle ground between them. We can submit (as indeed we are already being required to do) to the false prophets of the top-down, technical fix, increasingly in alignment with the military-security apparatus of the hegemonic powers, or, as human beings, of our own volition, attempt, against the odds, to resolve the current crisis from the grass-roots in favour of a transformation geared towards social justice and environmental sustainability.

But there is in this proposition clearly a problem and it does not simply reside in the fact that the two competing ideas of apocalypse, in terms of the material forces they can physically bring to bear, are ill-matched. The very fact that the Western-state system has long been at a point where the gap between its technological powers and that of its wider populations are so vast as to induce feelings of utter powerlessness and dependency might actually provide exactly the crisis conditions now, in which an alternative prescription, not of fear but of hope, might appear. Indeed, as the crisis deepens, the need for *ethical* sustenance will surely become an urgent one. Or will it? As Roszak implies at the outset of this piece, re-igniting the ethical fire of the authentic apocalyptic tradition may simply not be possible in a secular society where practically all traces of its relevance and meaning have been lost or submerged. Its voice, where it exists today, is liminal, enigmatic and uncertain. We are again, as with Thanatos, confronted with a paradox. How can modern Western society reconnect with a vision of hope derived from ancient texts of apocalypse in a way that can enable us to repudiate the dominant path of violence, death and obliteration? If in what follows we can more concretely develop the trajectory towards Thanatos, that towards Eros is necessarily more exploratory. My method is to elect three individuals who from their own recent time have personally inspired me as guides. Modernists each undoubtedly were, but through their own personal engagement with global crisis, they also drew, in different ways, on the apocalyptic tradition, to develop visions of the future which might give us food for thought in our own fraught, contemporary quest for redemption.

THANATOS: THE MILITARY-INDUSTRIAL 'MANAGEMENT' OF CLIMATE CRISIS

Most people in the West have yet to reach a moment of either true climate change recognition, let alone of desperation in its face. Behind the scenes, however, the story is quite different. A nexus of government agencies, military planners and technologically driven corporate partners – more specifically those in a burgeoning post-9/11 security sector – *are* thinking through and working towards their own strategic responses. Despite the public veneer of UN-sponsored, multilateral talks geared towards a strengthened Kyoto 2, little of this military-industrial complex analysis is about greenhouse gas (ghg) *mitigation*. Trawl through the increasing plethora of think-tank, defence industry or government-sponsored conferences and it is increasingly evident that the preservation of the political and economic status quo, even in the face of disaster, is their actual sine qua non.[2]

Discreetly at one remove from media attention and thus public purview, we need to understand this effective abandonment of ghg mitigation in its very contemporary setting. What is taking its place is, a reassertion of the nation-state interest, and more exactly, from the politically most powerful and technologically advanced nations, a heightened appetite for a scaled-up technical fix to climate change. It is not our concern here to enumerate all the many and varied geo-engineering schemes presently under discussion. What does matter for our argument is an understanding of what geo-engineering *represents*. First of all, its rationale is dependent on there being no socially achievable route to carbon deceleration. Its proponents can correctly point to the fact that, to date, *all* efforts at 'traditional, regulation-based climate change strategy' (Michaelson, 1998: 4) have failed. Moreover, with scientific evidence mounting that anthropogenic pollution already emitted into the atmosphere may be moving us towards some runaway process of Earth system feedbacks, to do nothing now to stop this would be tantamount to a global case of fiddling while Rome burns. The geo-engineers, in short, legitimate their case as one of absolute necessity. As no other guaranteed solution from politicians, economists or environmentalists has been forthcoming, the scientists and technologists hence take it upon themselves to step into the breach to save the day. Through proposals of giant space mirrors, iron fertilization of the oceans or spraying sulphur aerosols into the stratosphere to reflect solar radiation, the geo-engineers are self-consciously Promethean in their determination to act before it is too late (Webb, 2008b). Yet we must be wary either of dismissing their proposals as science fiction, or as some sudden belated whim on the part of one element of the scientific community. On the contrary, the idea that the climate can be 'controlled' was publicly articulated in a US science advisory report as far back as 1965, though such ideas were already being promulgated a decade earlier by the clearly brilliant mind of John von Neumann (Hulme, 2009: 24, 348).

The name of von Neumann provides a clue as to geo-engineering's antecedents. In the 1950s he was using his mathematical skills to help develop the hydrogen bomb at the US Lawrence Livermore laboratory, alongside both Edward Teller, father of the bomb, and his key protégé, Lowell Wood. Both of the latter two went on to become leading exponents of President Reagan's 1980s Strategic Defence Initiative (Star Wars), and, most recently, of the geo-engineering proposition to pump vast quantities of sulphur particulates into the atmosphere (Broad, 2006; Lifton and Markusen, 1990: 119–20, 140–1). If we trace back these various connections to their starting point we arrive at none other than the Manhattan Project (MP): the wartime, top-secret plan devised by the Anglo-American allies to create the first atomic bomb.

The parallels between what was formulated and acted upon then, and the geo-engineering projects of today, demand a little further exploration. MP was itself a race against time, the fear being that the Nazis (or perhaps, even supposedly allied Soviets) would develop their own bomb *first*. While, moreover, the political impetus for the project came from Roosevelt and Churchill, scientifically they had no choice but to defer to the leading theoretical physicists and technologists of the era to design and operationalize the weapon. MP was the most ambitious scientific project of its kind to that date. It is also significant that it operated beyond the realms of politics, law or for that matter, ethics. It is difficult to imagine, in conditions of contemporary emergency, that large-scale geo-engineering would, or could, be developed under more consensual, for instance, UN sponsored, arrangements. Most keenly, if we return to MP as the progenitor of the current schemes, it is significant in the degree to which state and science were prepared to enter into entirely unknown terrain. During the hours preceding the Trinity explosion on 16 July 1945, one of the team, Enrico Fermi was taking bets among fellow scientists on whether the bomb would take out New Mexico or ignite the atmosphere and so potentially destroy the world. Previous calculations had suggested *only* a 1 in 3 million chance that this might happen (quoted in Webb, 2010). The world, of course, was irrevocably changed by the Trinity moment, humanity henceforth presented with the realization of its potentially terminal status. The awestruck scientists and military men at the test site responded with unequivocally apocalyptic language. Robert Oppenheimer famously intoned from the Bhagavad Gita: 'Now I am become death, the destroyer of worlds', while General Farrell described the roar of the explosion as warning 'of doomsday and made us feel that we puny things were blasphemous to dare tamper with the forces heretofore reserved for the Almighty' (quoted in Jungk, 1960: 183).

Yet, for all this after-shock horror, what is equally striking is how enough of those who had made the bomb possible were able to wrest from its use over Hiroshima and Nagasaki the notion that the bomb was morally justified. Its creation would heal humankind's afflictions, and its further development signalled 'the embodiment of a transcendent rationality which alone can discipline the dark impulses leading humans to make war' (Gusterson, 1993: 69). Scientists, such as Teller, on one level, may also have sought to promote their case for bigger and better bombs as pure 'security' logic. But they hardly seem to have been averse to quasi-religious imagery being employed to describe the post-war US nuclear laboratories at Los Alamos and Livermore as 'sacred centres or even oracles like Delphi' (Thompson, 1982: 13), or their own place within this schema as that of visionary seers of a heroic new age (Lifton and Markusen, 1990: 83–4).

It is surely significant how closely the urge for geo-engineering follows these same ultra-rational, yet, paradoxically, salvationist contours. The latter's proponents have already for some time been speaking openly of geo-engineering as a second MP, justified on the grounds that it would cut out 'the institutional inefficiency inherent in international policymaking bodies . . . reducing the number of decisions, and focusing costs on a small number of parties' (Michaelson, 1998: 23). Urgency, once again, is the driver. If we want 'victory', the time is *now*, which in turn means either affirming or acquiescing to the state or states with the technological advantage to invent and implement the strategy. By dint of the fact that only the United States has the overriding material resource plus military and technologically integrated capacity as well as technical expertise to undertake it, a geo-engineering MP will also primarily be a US MP. But the fact that the future environmental consequences of any such programme are completely in the realms of the unknown (nobody has any real idea what locally or globally, immediately or cumulatively, dumping iron oxide will do to the oceans or what masses of sulphur particles sprayed into the atmosphere will do to the ozone layer) (Webb, 2008b) means that as with the nuclear experiment, what we are being offered is a very peculiar form of salvation. Geo-engineering proposals do not seek to engage with the environmental consequences for the longer term. Like the atom bombs in 1945, they operate on combating a perceived threat as it presents itself now. As a consequence, our children, or children's children, will still have to cope with the burden of our ghg emissions (presumably requiring them to develop some even more extraordinary technical fixes for the purpose) just as they will with our radioactive waste.

One might object that this line of cheerless reasoning is not only speculative but also highly rhetorical. Where we find ourselves now is not yet *there*. By the same token, because Cold War political warriors embraced the possibilities proffered by the most extreme scientific apostles of nuclearism, this presumably does not *have to* mean that the same will happen again. Yet if we were to come down a notch from the most far-reaching technological proposals for tackling climate change to the quotidian business of Western 'security' responses in the years of the 'war on terror', the same apocalyptic mindset which we have identified as Thanatos mode, remains evident.

Naomi Klein's recent analysis of 'disaster capitalism', especially, for instance, her treatment of the 2003 'Shock and Awe' bombing campaign of Iraq, offers some disturbing parallels. Klein demonstrates that the campaign was not simply designed to knock out Saddam's military command and control facilities. It was also intended as a conscious spectacle of emotional and psychological hell for the Iraqi people with the aim of rendering them disorientated, paralysed and impotent. The fear they were to feel was to be like that from 'nature in the form of tornadoes, hurricanes, earthquakes, foods uncontrolled fires, famines and disease'. US news media outlets were also 'conscripted by the Pentagon to 'fear up' Iraq' which in media parlance was renamed as 'A-Day'. The violence of the campaign thus was not simply to topple Saddam but to achieve 'rapid dominance' for Paul

Bremner's announcement two months later that the country was 'open for business' (Klein, 2008: 331–4).

The fact that behind all this was an attempted reassertion of US control over not just Iraqi oilfields but world oil markets has remained largely absent from official communiqués ever since. But if Klein's inference that the invasion was geared towards wiping the slate clean of what was deemed evil in order to make way for Iraq's 'restoration' to the world of 'free' international commerce, the faux-redemptive ring of US self-justification is even more explicit in her account of hurricane Katrina, in 2005. Here Klein demonstrates how the Republican administration took advantage of the cataclysm to, as one developer put it, make of New Orleans a 'clean sheet to start again' (ibid.: 4). In other words, having failed the poorest, mostly black population of the city during the hurricane, corporate interests were given free rein by federal government to knock down the gutted homes of that majority, squeeze them out further by privatizing all services, including education and build condos for the rich where public tenements had once stood. As Klein explains, 'a kind of corporate new Jerusalem' (ibid.: 8).

Corporate self-interest, of course, is nothing new. What is significant about Western *statist* responses to calamity in the here and now is in the degree to which the environmental break-down consequent upon climate change has become simply a pretext for a naked grab of what might otherwise have fed, clothed and kept warm the poor and dispossessed. This is all the more true when it comes to a third-world in free-fall. How else, for instance, should we understand this section from a scoping paper entitled 'Strategic Trends, 2030', prepared by defence analysts working under the British Ministry of Defence?

Climate change and HIV/AIDS, scarcity of food and water and regional conflict could lead to Africa becoming a failed con-tinent, where even large, currently self-sustaining states become chaotic. Outside engagement and intervention would effectively be limited to a small number of well-defended entry points and corridors, which would provide access to raw materials essential to the global economy. Nations or corporations wishing to trade with Africa would increasingly be required to provide security for their nationals and the necessary support to sustain critical areas of access and security (Mabey, 2008: 31).

The other side to this coin is what we might call the motif of the 'barbarian at the gate', in other words keeping the poor and dispossessed out of one's own residually well-fed domains. Such has been a constantly recurring theme in Western security thinking on climate change ever since the 2004 Pentagon report (Webb, 2008: 59–81). In a more recent climate-related war game, devised by a US think-tank, the Centre for New American Security (CNAS), game players representing leading industrialized countries placed migration-prevention as their number one priority in any long-term framework agreement on climate change. How they proposed to repatriate refugees by non-coercive means (especially those from islands already on the point of inundation) was left absent from the discussion (CNAS, 2008). Meanwhile, some months earlier, a bevy of retired NATO generals made public their belief that the Alliance should maintain its ongoing commitment to a nuclear first strike option, citing a threat list which included, alongside climate and energy challenges, mass 'environmental' migration (Traynor, 2008). Meanwhile, literally billions of dollars are being pumped into US, and other Western government R&D programmes on high-tech perimeter control systems, geared towards the 'immoblisation' of waves of border trespassers (Wright, 2007: 82–101; Klein, 2008: 303). Though there is yet still an alternative strategy for keeping the hordes at bay: ensuring that they are kept isolated in their third-world mega-city slums, now seen and planned for by the United States and other Western military think-tanks as the major terrain of future warfare (a.k.a. 'urbicide') (Davis, 2006: 302–4; Graham, 2004).

Even where the hegemonic West does not seem to be directly implicated in third-world violence, the underlying truth usually displays on the one hand, the most extraordinary indifference to suffering, on the other, venal complicity. The 5.4 million casualty figure in the Democratic Republic of Congo over the last decade serves as the most obvious example (IRC, 2007). Why has the West, beyond the most token humanitarian intervention, consistently turned a blind eye to the Congo's ongoing calvary? Not simply because it would inconvenience the proxy supply of key minerals from this resource-rich arena (not least coltan, for our precious mobile-phones), but because it would demand us to consider why third-world peoples do not 'count' when set against the smooth-running at all costs of our global economic system. Notions of triage are already built into standard Western economic cost-benefit analysis of a developing climate change crisis. Put more prosaically, third-world lives are worth vastly less than first-world ones.[3]

We might interpret all this 'banally' in terms of what Paul Rogers has called 'liddism': a signal refusal to deal with the systemic causes of the carbon crisis, opting instead for a control paradigm which responds only to its violent symptoms and, in the process, *perpetuates* that state of violence (Abbott et al., 2008: 28). Necessarily, such responses in the long term are futile as radical changes in the biosphere engulf us all, West and rest alike. But we might equally read such responses as forms of an irresistible technological and military drive towards Thanatos, in other words, as consequences of a dominant mindset, which not only can live happily with violence and destruction but can justify it on the grounds of wresting an albeit ephemeral advantage from the climate emergency. We have already seen by way of Klein's critique of Friedmanite neo-liberalism how powerful states and their corporate partners have sought to positively *encourage* disaster as an opportunity to make a quick buck. But ascendant states, such as Russia or China, pushing against the waning power of the West, may equally reason that global warming offers a unique opportunity to steal a vengeful march – even if it is a final one – on their historic competitors. A melting Arctic, for instance, presents the most obvious arena in which a Kremlin-led drive to get at its sea-bed fossil fuel reserves *first* – thereby potentially disrupting traditional 'downstream' Western monopolies of distribution, marketing and spot price – also provides the obvious goad to a new bipolar confrontation (Borgerson, 2008: 63–77). Here, Kremlin authoritarian diktat has been matched by US technological superiority. Weather modification, not least in the Arctic arena in the form of the Alaska-based High Frequency Active Auroral Research Program (HAARP), has been an active element in quasi-secret US military planning for some time (Webb, 2008a: 73–6). With geo-engineering closely aligned to Pentagon funding and supervision, the likelihood that some of these applications will be weaponized and subsequently deployed against real or perceived geo-political threats, could represent the ultimate twist in humankind's relationship with the Earth's climate though not before the strong possibility that it will precipitate a nuclear Armageddon.

EROS: RESOURCES FOR SOCIAL TRANSFORMATION

Set against this utterly bleak, *uber*-statist prognosis, any alternative version of the future must look weak and unconvincing. It also raises many questions about how we arrived at this impasse, and equally what psychological as well as physical resources we might possess to transcend it. Arnold Toynbee, the great historian of the *Oikumene*: 'the habitat of (hu)mankind', confronting this dichotomy at a time before the issue of climate change had become pressing, responded thus:

> In the biosphere Man is a psychosomatic being, active within a world that is material and finite. On this plane of human activity, Man's objective, ever since he became conscious, has been to make himself master of his non-human environment, and in our day has come within sight of success in this endeavour – possibly to his own undoing. But Man's other home, the spiritual world, is also an integral part of total reality: it differs from the biosphere in being both non-material and infinite; and in his life in the spiritual world Man finds that his mission is to seek, not for a material mastery over his non-human environment, but for a spiritual mastery over himself. (Toynbee, 1976: 18)

If Toynbee is correct, then the key question for us now is, how we can fully draw on (or rediscover) this 'spiritual' dimension? George Monbiot, in his recent representation of humanity's relationship with fossil fuels as akin to a Faustian Pact, (Monbiot, 2008: 1–3) inadvertently reminds us why the quest has become so problematic. So long as humankind, or at the least the Western part of it, has been able to maximize the exploitation of this sequestrated yet finite source of solar energy, Man *is* (in the patriarchal sense) God. With no constraints upon his actions, recognition of the inevitable reckoning – in terms of biospheric blow-back – could always be put off to another day, diminishing in turn the need to confront the fundamental ethical deficit in the trajectory. In such circumstances, the idea of social mobilization for a fundamentally different sort of relationship

with ourselves and our natural world, becomes highly unprom-
ising. Which means that as the opportunity to practically
respond to climate change in a positive way recedes, only the
dystopian apocalypse we have described remains to provide.
Again, we are left with the elusive nature of the prophetic in
a desacralized society, which not only does not want to, but
seemingly cannot hear.

Let me, at this point, introduce three near-contemporary
figures who – even from the far side of the grave – might yet help
us rediscover an alternative response to climate change by way
of the *good* apocalypse. They are the English composer Ralph
Vaughan Williams (1872–1958), the English historian Edward
(E. P.) Thompson (1924–1993), and the Austrian-Jewish existen-
tialist philosopher, Martin Buber (1878–1965). What makes this
trio notably purposeful to this discussion is in the way a visionary quality intruded itself into their expression almost in spite
of themselves. All were modernist, rationalist progressives of a
strongly socialist and humanist hue, making them (at least super-
ficially) part of that much broader artistic-cum-activist stream
striving for a secular, terrestrially based commonweal. Certainly,
none were religious believers in the traditional sense of the word.
Yet in each, their devotion to a vision of a transformed *Oikumene*
took them, directly or indirectly, to an engagement with that
rich, *subversively* millenarian vein of Judeo-Christian faith.

Vaughan Williams' repeated claims to being an agnostic thus
sit somewhat oddly alongside the peal of rapturous hallelujahs
at the culmination of *The Pilgrims Progress*, a work, incident-
ally, that he struggled to perfect throughout almost his entire
working life and to which he designated singular import
(Kennedy, 1997: 31–6). Markers on the way include the decidedly
unsettling ballet *Job* by way of inspiration from William Blake's
engravings of that arguably darkest of all biblical texts. Thompson's
mature self-identification – from being a once paid up and
leading theoretician within the British Communist Party – as
one of 'the Muggletonian Marxists', acclaimed by Thompson
as founded by Blake, must seem even more idiosyncratic and
obscure still (Thompson, 1993: xxi). But then, the Muggletonians
were an eighteenth century, stridently antinomian sect who
Thompson was convinced critically influenced Blake's own
uniquely counter-cultural and utopian brand of Christianity.

This in turn would lead us back to the writings, among others, of the German mystic – and like Blake, literal visionary – Jakob Boehme. It was through initial encounters with Boehmenism that Buber beat his own path to *Jewish* messianism. Yet Buber, insofar as he was religious at all, has been described rather as a 'religious anarchist', reminding us that *his* utopian construct had nothing to do with some other future time or heavenly place, but was something which might happen in the here and now through the active participation of humanity in the task of worldly redemption (Löwy, 1992: 48–52).

These few lines may offer something by way of intellectual connecting threads between our trio. As stimulating an exercise as this might be, development through some sort of Venn diagram misses the point. What matters is not the literal connections or even the degree to which, behind the secular garb, we are actually dealing with three prophetic thinkers. At stake, rather, is how each individually was inspired to see beyond the inhumanity and injustice of the world as it is, to a vision of things as they *could* be. In each case, that world is still one fashioned by *ourselves*. But the potency of the vision rests upon a deep, historically rooted Judeo-Christian idea. The world may have fallen, but it also can be recovered. There is the possibility thus of a divine time beyond the givenness of the present. The *knowledge* – one might even say *gnosis* – that this can be so, of itself repudiates the hegemonic wisdom which would have it that there is no other way but that of the state, economic determinism and military might. This repudiation is all the more significant in the case of our trio because each in their separate ways were profoundly marked and disturbed by the potentialities of Thanatos.

Ralph Vaughan Williams

Nearly 42 years old when the Great War began, and already acknowledged as the leading advocate of a specifically English musical voice, the privileged Vaughan Williams volunteered for service as a private with the Royal Army Medical Corps. As a field ambulance orderly on the Western front he encountered the atrocity and futility of trench warfare at first hand. Thereafter, war as dread motif is insistent and recurrent in his composition.

It is there in what amounts to the mournful, if poignant, requiem for the slaughtered in the third symphony and much more violently so in the fourth and sixth. The eerie Epilogue of the latter, while denied by the composer himself, was almost unanimously received by his first 1948 and then subsequent audiences as a musical representation of a post-atomic wasteland. Yet what is equally insistent is Vaughan Williams' counterpoint, not just the clarion calls *against* war such as in 'Donna Nobis Pacem' but the clearly transcendent, even ethereal quality so evident, for instance in the Romanza of the fifth symphony, and itself a foretaste of that final hallelujah-laden benediction in Pilgrims Progress. It is as if through music Vaughan Williams is telling us: peace is possible, a lost innocence can be refound by way of reconnecting with the sheer beauty of the English landscape, and, as he himself in great old age proposed, we look 'through the magic casements to what lies beyond' (Heffer, 2001: 11).

Edward Thompson

Can we imagine a hopeful apocalypse without music? Can we seriously see ourselves putting our finger on the terminal sickness in our current condition without a proper understanding of the historical processes by which we have arrived here? Hardly a million miles from Vaughan Williams in terms of social background, nearly two generations on, Edward Thompson's overtly Marxist quest to interrogate the socio-cultural underpinnings of Britain's avant-garde industrialization were interrupted by his own induction into the horrors of World War II: on the Italian front; the loss of his beloved brother, Frank; in the fight against fascism; and then, repeatedly throughout the rest of his life by his unflinching involvement in the struggle against nuclear Armageddon. Already long associated with the home-grown British Campaign for Nuclear Disarmament (CND) this commitment was extended in 1980 though his founding of European Nuclear Disarmament (END) at a critical moment when, with the proposed NATO siting of cruise missiles in Europe, the arms race appeared to be in danger of going ballistic. Thompson's analysis of these events was to a high degree in keeping with standard leftist assumptions about the nature of the hegemonic capitalist state, its underpinning violence and willingness to use all forms of social control and media disinformation to stifle grass-roots resistance. Yet, significantly, Thompson cut loose from his Marxist moorings when he proposed in 1982 that the Cold War – as practised by both the United States and the Soviet Union – had already long passed into 'a *self-generating* condition' which, because 'the originating drives, reactions and intentions' had themselves become obscured, could propel the people of the globe towards 'a theatre of the apocalypse' (Thompson, 1982: 8, 21).

In this critique of a condition that Thompson labelled 'exterminism', he came very close to pinpointing the same pathology which could equally presage our current destruction, with or without nuclear weapons. But in proposing that this might not only have taken on the aspect of an irreversible, even roller coaster momentum but even might be without rhyme or reason, Thompson injected more than a whiff of Marxist heresy. The idea that material or structural conditions alone were sufficient to understanding how social organisms operate was one aspect of Thompson's growing disenchantment with a Communist party which he had left in 1956. Yet in using a term such as 'apocalypse' as if to predict the end of the world, he was charged by fellow-leftists with behaving not unlike some of the more colourful eighteenth century millenarian prophets whom he had studied (Levene, 2004: 73). The irony is that Thompson *was* drawn to historical actors who, operating beyond 'a limited horizon of moral norms and practical probabilities', were denounced as purveyors of 'blasphemous, seditious, insane or apocalyptic fantasy' (Thompson, 1993: 108–9). Perhaps, then, he was more than a little aware that he stood – with Blake the towering pinnacle – in a long-line of dissenters who, in their own potent demolitions of the 'reigning hegemony', took on a moral authority not only for what they said, but equally the way they imbued it with a poetic vitality flowing from that wellspring of the Western canon: the prophets. If, from his great magnum opus, what we rightly remember Thompson for is how the 'Making' of the English Working Class came through the people *themselves,* (Thompson, 1963), his implicit question as projected into the future remains: from where does the ethical fire come which might yet enable them to encompass their own earthly transcendence?

Martin Buber

If the point is that Thompson – against the pull of Thanatos – firmly planted human agency as central to that quest, we need to turn to our third and final figure, Martin Buber, to suggest how that might be aligned to and firmly articulated as a more thorough-going anticipation of the apocalypse of Eros. Again, in terms of life history, Buber's was marked by extraordinary violence, in his case not just that of living through the two World Wars but as a Jewish witness to the Nazis' own apocalyptic desire to obliterate a whole people. There was also the violence and injustice meted out by the nascent Jewish nation-state, of which Buber was citizen, against its Arab members or neighbours, a new reality in the modern Jewish experience which Buber, sometimes almost as a lone voice, firmly and forcefully repudiated, in favour of dialogue, good-will and co-existence. The role of what he called Hebrew humanism was intended to crystallize a political ethos which would not only heal the division between morality and politics but restore a 'broken' world (Mendes-Flohr, 1983: 17). But this could only happen through the individual and communitarian action of human beings themselves. Where Buber, thus, was akin to Thompson in identifying agency as critical, was given an altogether more provocative edge by an open embrace of the notion of messianism, which Buber insisted was 'Judaism's most profoundly original idea' (Löwy, 1992: 51).

What is important to reiterate, however, is that Buber did not assert this position from a traditional, and certainly not normative, religious perspective. On the contrary, he both refuted the notion that redemption was in any sense 'written' or predetermined just as he equally did that the messianic age would be other-worldly. His eschatology is thus decidedly open in its insistence on the willed collaboration and striving of each individual with the messianic ideal to 'establish (or *re-establish*) an age of harmony between man and God, between man and nature, and among men' (ibid.: 19). More potently still, that vision for Buber represented neither a return to some Edenic paradise, nor some longing for a distant but unattainable future. It was no slip of the pen that his great paean to libertarian socialism was entitled not paths towards but 'Paths *in* Utopia'. That redemption could be at hand in the here and now was, for Buber, all the more possible as well as urgent because of the bankruptcy of what he called the World of 'It', the functional but sterile nature of the modern capitalist state and, with it, its utter atomization of society. Through dialogue and encounter – Buber's famous 'I–Thou' dialectic – human beings might not simply rediscover the possibilities inherent in a lived communal conviviality but cast off their chains and in so doing transform the nature of political organization itself (Buber, 1949).

In Buber, thus, as with our other two guides, a vision of the world transformed is one predicated on a form of human self-discovery, the release of whose energy could be the driving force anticipating that better place. It is certainly no accident that all three were intensely involved in forms of adult education and so to an implicit or explicit recognition that for the human spirit to take wing something more was necessary than the modern bureaucratic state or traditional religion could ever confer. What is perhaps more surprising is how each in their own personal quests for the truth, found themselves increasingly reaching out for inspiration to prophetic, even overtly millenarian textual sources.

The important question for ourselves, of course, is: are the ideas of these thinkers of any value to our task today? If our purpose is to develop political and social action to mobilize and enable Western society writ-large against the forces of Thanatos, are our main, or only, terms of reference that which is 'given' through the clinical data of the climate science, or more prosaically, government exhortations to dim the lights, while spending *more*? Or, rather, is now the time to dig deep – even against the grain of received modern or post-modern wisdoms – towards a re-engagement with an authentically apocalyptic tradition as the necessary catalyst to that spiritual self-realization, which as Toynbee inferred, might hasten a genuine paradigm shift?

CONCLUSION: TOWARD THE UNKNOWN REGION

Mike Hulme's important and critically received recent work *Why we Disagree about Climate Change*, has emphasized how the phenomenon cannot be understood in purely physical terms to which scientific or policy-making answers simply lend themselves, but is closely intermeshed with a multi-layered plethora of cultural, social and spiritual responses to the world. The mythic narratives which inform our lives are as likely as any science to govern how in turn we respond to the climate challenge, and these may help teach and empower us in our actions (Hulme, 2009: 340–65). Hulme undoubtedly offers us a life-line founded on sane and compassionate analysis. At the same time his study is one in avoidance of the fundamental issues which will determine our fate. We are *not* all equally empowered in our agreement or disagreement as to what to do (or not) about climate change. It is those with incumbent power in the richest and most powerful nations who are most likely to dictate the trajectory of response. And, as we have suggested, as the crisis worsens and any ability to hold back the biospheric blow-back disintegrates, it will be political and economic elites who will refer and defer to heavy-duty military-technological techniques. These will be the main contenders, too, ready to fill the apocalyptized space of a more general societal longing for salvation, thereby heralding the final victory of Thanatos. It is important to remind ourselves how close we have come to that dread verdict. At a major event hosted by the Royal Society in January 2007, the Bulletin of Atomic Scientists, who 60 years earlier, in the first full flush of the nuclear arms race had created a symbolic 'Doomsday Clock' – but after the end of the Cold War had pushed their minute hand back – now symbolically moved it forward once again to five minutes to midnight. The new message from the scientists was stark indeed. If the threat to our collective existence began with nuclear weapons, the inexorable countdown to 'the end' was now coming from two directions: nuclear weapons *and* from the impact of carbon emissions on the biosphere (Osborne, 2007).

But suppose we were to read our symbolic clock in eschatological terms? End-time – as in the Hebrew, *et ketz* – then might take on a very different meaning. It would beckon, as in the truly apocalyptic, the potentiality of a refound purpose for our existence on earth. Our arrival there would be utterly dependent on our own prophetic compass. Yet, as with our three anticipatory guides, the vision impelling us towards this other place will be like the arrow from the future pointing back to our own creative moment, and hence to our blessed task. *As never before* our moment has the potentiality to have that special, kairos quality yet ticking away with its constant refrain that now *is* the time 'to believe and change the way you live'. It is thus, also time for people in the West to be inspired, as our three moderns were, by the classical prophets (and more recent intermediaries like Blake), to speak truth to power, where necessary to run the gauntlet of state preparation for Thanatos, and to cohere around communal action which can be our only practical salvation. Indeed it is time for 'some utopian leap, some human rebirth, from Mystery to renewed imaginative life' (Thompson, 1993: 193), while there is still time.

NOTES

1 The original Freudian idea of Eros and Thanatos has had its most potent and provocative outing to date in Marcuse, 1955/1969.
2 See, for instance, Approdex, 2009.
3 See 'Global Commons Institute, Defending the "Value of Life"', [www.gci.org.uk/vol/vol.html] for Aubrey Meyer's searing critique.

REFERENCES

Abbott, C., Rogers, P., Sloboda, J. (2007), *Global Responses to Global Threats, Sustainable Security for the 21st Century.* Oxford: Oxford Research Group.
Approdex (2009), 'CIA Tackles Climate Change and Its Risk to National Security'. Available at: www.aprodex.com/cia-tackles-climate-change-and-its-risk-to-national-security-418-bl.aspx
Borgerson, S. G. (2008), 'Arctic Meltdown: The Economic And Security Implications Of Global Warming'. *Foreign Affairs* 87 (2).
Broad, W. J. (2006), 'How to cool a planet (maybe)'. *New York Times*, 27 June.
Buber, M. (1949), *Paths in Utopia.* Trans. R. F. C. Hull. London: Routledge and Kegan.
CNAS (2008), 'Climate Change Wargame'. 28–30 July. Available at: www/cnas.org/ClimateWarGame/
Davis, M. (2006), *Planet of Slums.* London and New York: Verso.
Ellul, J. (1965), *The Technological Society.* London: Jonathon Cape.
Graham, S. (ed.) (2004), *Cities, War and Terrorism.* Oxford: Blackwell.
Gusterson, H. (1993), 'Exploding Anthropology's Canon in the World of the Bomb: Ethnographic Writing On Militarism'. *Journal of Contemporary Ethnography* 22 (1).
Heffer, S. (2001), *Vaughan Williams.* London: Phoenix.
Hulme, M. (2009), *Why We Disagree about Climate Change, Understanding Controversy, Inaction and Opportunity.* Cambridge: Cambridge University Press.

International Rescue Committee (2007), *Mortality in the Democratic Republic of Congo, An Ongoing Crisis*. New York: IRC.

Jungk, R. (1960), *Brighter than an Thousand Suns*. Trans. James Cleugh. London: Penguin.

Kennedy, M. (1997), 'The long journey to the delectable mountains'. *The Pilgrims Progress*. London: Royal Opera House programme notes.

Klein, N. (2008), *The Shock Doctrine, the Rise of Disaster Capitalism*. London: Penguin.

Levene, M. (2004), 'Battling Demons or Banal Exterminism? Apocalypse and Statecraft in Modern Mass Murder'. *Journal of Human Rights* 3 (1).

Lifton, R. J. and Markusen, E. (1990), *The Genocidal Mentality, Nazi Holocaust and Nuclear Threat*. London: Macmillan.

Löwy, M. (1992), *Redemption and Utopia, Jewish Libertarian Thought in Central Europe, a Study in Elective Affinity*. Trans. Hope Heaney. London: The Athlone Press.

Mabey, N. (2008), *Delivering Climate Security, International Security Responses to a Climate Changed World, Whitehall Papers*, 69. London: Royal United Services Institute.

Marcuse, H. (1955/1969), *Eros and Civilization, a Philosophical Inquiry into Freud*. London: Penguin.

Mendes-Flohr, P. R. (ed.) (1983), *A Land of Two Peoples, Martin Buber on Jews and Arabs*. New York: Oxford University Press.

Michaelson, J. (1998), 'Geo-Engineering, a Climate Change Manhattan Project'. Available at: www.users.globalnet.co.uk/~mfogg/links.htm (accessed 5 October 2009).

Monbiot, G. (2008), *Heat: How to Stop the Planet Burning*. London: Penguin.

Osborne, H. (2007), 'Doomsday Clock Ticks Closer to Armageddon'. *The Guardian*, 17 January.

Roszak, T. (1972), *Where the Wasteland Ends, Politics and Transcendence in Postindustrial Society*. New York: Doubleday and Co.

Shaw, C. (2010), 'Dangerous Limits: Climate Change and Modernity', in *History at the End of the World? History, Climate Change and the Possibility of Closure* (Levene, M., Johnson, R. and Roberts, P. eds). Penrith, Cumbria: Humanities-Ebooks.

Slomp, G. (2009), *Carl Schmitt and the Politics of Hostility, Violence and Terror*. Basingstoke: Palgrave.

Thompson, E. P. (1963), *The Making of the English Working Class*. London: Penguin Books.

—(1982), 'Notes on Exterminism, the Last Stage of Civilisation', in *New Left Review, ed. Exterminism and the Cold War*. London: Verso.

—(1993), *Witness against the Beast, William Blake and the Moral Law*. New York: The New Press.

Toynbee, A. (1976), *Mankind and Mother Earth, A Narrative History of the World*. New York and Oxford: Oxford University Press.

Traynor, I. (2008), 'Pre-Emptive Nuclear Strike a Key Option, Nato Told'. *Guardian*, 22 January.

Webb, D. (2008a), 'Thinking the Worst, the Pentagon Report', in *Surviving Climate Change: The Struggle to Avert Global Catastrophe* (Cromwell, D. and Levene, M. eds). London: Pluto Press.

—(2008b), 'Geo-Engineering and Its Implications'. Available at: www.crisis-forum.org.uk/events/workshop1_resources.php (accessed 5 October 2009).

—(2010), 'On the Edge of History, the Nuclear Dimension', in *History at the End of the World? History, Climate Change and the Possibility of Closure* (Levene, M., Johnson, R. and Roberts, P. eds). Penrith, Cumbria: Humanities-Ebooks.

Wright, S. (2007), 'Preparing for Mass Refugee Flows, the Corporate-Military Sector', in *Surviving Climate Change: The Struggle to Avert Global Catastrophe* (Cromwell, D. and Mark Levene, eds). London: Pluto Press.

PART II

ETHICS

CHAPTER FOUR

SAVED BY DISASTER?

ABRUPT CLIMATE CHANGE, POLITICAL INERTIA AND THE POSSIBILITY OF AN INTERGENERATIONAL ARMS RACE[1]

STEPHEN M. GARDINER

We are all used to talking about these impacts coming in the lifetimes of our children and grandchildren. Now we know that it's us.

Parry (2007)

INTRODUCTION

In recent years, scientific discussion of climate change has taken a turn for the worse. Traditional concern for the gradual, incremental effects of global warming remains; but now greater attention is being paid to the possibility of encountering major threshold phenomena in the climate system, where breaching such thresholds may have catastrophic consequences. As recently as the 2001 report of the *Intergovernmental Panel on Climate Change* (IPCC), such events were treated as unlikely, at least during the current century (IPCC, 2001). But the work of the last six years tends to suggest that these projections are shaky at best. As the United States' National Research Council warns us, climate surprises are 'inevitable' (US National Research Council, 2002).

In this chapter, I want to explore some ways in which this paradigm shift may make a difference to how we understand the moral and political challenges posed by climate change, and in particular the current problem of political inertia. I will examine two suggestions. The first is that abrupt climate change undermines political inertia, in part through undermining three common explanations for it, based in economic, psychological and intergenerational factors. The second suggestion is that this shift is in one respect beneficial: the focus on abrupt, as opposed to gradual, climate change actually helps us to act. On the one hand, it supplies strong motives to the current generation to do what is necessary to tackle the climate problem on behalf of both itself and future generations; on the other hand, failing this, it acts as a kind of fail-safe device, which at least limits how bad the problem can, ultimately, become.

My thesis is that these suggestions are largely mistaken, for two reasons. First, the possibility of abrupt change tends only to reshape, rather than undermine, the usual concerns; hence, the root causes of moral corruption remain. Second, the possibility may make appropriate action more, rather than less, difficult, and exacerbate, rather than limit, the severity of the problem. Worst of all, if the abrupt change is severe, it may provoke the equivalent of an intergenerational arms race.

ABRUPT CLIMATE CHANGE

The debate on global change has largely failed to factor in the inherently chaotic, sensitively balanced, and threshold-laden nature of Earth's climate system and the increased likelihood of abrupt climate change.

(Gagosian, 2003: 12)

Until recently, scientific discussion of climate change has been dominated by what I shall call 'the gradualist paradigm'. Researchers tended to assume that the response of natural phenomena to increases in greenhouse gas concentrations would be mainly linear and incremental; and this assumption tended to result in analogous claims about likely impacts on human and non-human systems. Hence, for example, the original IPCC report projected a rise in global temperature at an average of 0.3C per decade in the twenty-first century (IPCC, 1990; Brown, 2002), and typical estimates of the economic costs of impacts ran at around 1.5–2 per cent of gross world product (Houghton, 2004, p. 184).

Such results are hardly to be taken lightly, and much of the first three IPCC reports was taken up with showing how and why they are matters of serious concern. But recent research suggests that they may underestimate the problem. This is because there is increasing evidence that the climate system is much less regular than the gradualist paradigm suggests. In particular, there may be major threshold phenomena, and crossing the relevant thresholds may have catastrophic consequences. Scientists have been aware of the possibility of such thresholds for some time. But recent work suggests that the mechanisms governing them are much less robust, and the thresholds themselves much closer to where we are now, than previously thought. This suggests that we need an additional way of understanding the threat posed by climate change. Let us call this, 'the abrupt paradigm'.

Where might this paradigm be instantiated? Three possibilities are especially well known. The first is ice sheet disintegration, accompanied by a major rise in sea level. In the past, such change has occurred very abruptly – as much as 'an average of 1m of sea level rise every 20 years' for four hundred years (Hansen, 2005, p. 269). Furthermore, the current potential for change is substantial. Melting the mountain glaciers and Greenland alone would lead to a sea level rise of around seven meters, and adding the West Antarctic ice sheet would boost the total to fifteen meters (Williams and Ferrigno, 1999). Moreover, it is easy to see why such melting could be catastrophic. Even a total rise of over two meters 'would be sufficient to flood large portions of Bangladesh, the Nile Delta, Florida, and many island nations, causing forced migration of tens to hundreds of millions of people' (Hansen, 2005: 274). Indeed, since 'a large portion of the world's people live within a few meters of sea level, with trillions of dollars of infrastructure' (Hansen, 2004: 73), James Hansen believes that such a rise would 'wreak havoc with civilization' (2005: 275), making the issue of sea level 'the dominant issue in global warming' and one which 'sets a low ceiling on the level of global warming that would constitute dangerous anthropogenic interference' (2004: 73). Given this, it is clearly a matter of concern that the Greenland ice sheet is 'currently thought to be shrinking by 50 cubic kilometers per year', and that this might prime the ice sheets for a sudden, 'explosive' and irreversible disintegration (Schiermeier, 2006: 258; Hansen, 2006).

The second possibility is a weakening of the ocean conveyor of the North Atlantic, which, among other things, supports the Gulf Stream to Western Europe. Again, paleoclimatic evidence suggests that the system is vulnerable to abrupt change. Furthermore, substantial effects on ocean circulation are projected by climate models, and there is little reason to doubt that such change could be catastrophic, at least to some countries (Alley, 2004; Stouffer et al. 2006; Vellinga and Wood, 2002). Given this, it is sobering to see some scientists reporting that the Conveyor may already be showing some signs of disruption (Bryden et al., 2005).

A third, less understood, possibility is that 'vast stores of methane hydrate – a super-greenhouse gas – that are currently frozen under the oceans will, when global warming has reached some point, rise to the surface and dissipate themselves into the atmosphere'. Again, there is precedent. Such a release is said to have caused the biggest extinction of all time, the end of the Permian era 251 million years ago, when 90 per cent of species were suddenly lost (Berner, 2002; Barry, 2005). Clearly, a change of this kind would be catastrophic. A *New York Times* columnist aptly referred to it as 'the Big Burp Theory of the Apocalypse' (Kristof, 2006).

Now, the three prominent examples are of serious interest in their own right. However, it may be that the most important thing about them is the support they lend to the abrupt paradigm. This is because perhaps our greatest uncertainty at the moment concerns how good we are at identifying catastrophic risks. In short, it is reasonable to think that our current grasp of the possibilities is seriously incomplete (Alley, 2004: 69); and this may be the most crucial fact from the point of view of policy.

SOME CAUSES OF POLITICAL INERTIA

Still, perhaps the news is not all grim. For it has been suggested that the possibility of abrupt change may help us out of our current problem of political inertia. Let me first sketch this problem and then suggest why it might be thought that the threat of abrupt change might help.

The fact that climate change poses a serious threat has been known for some time. The IPCC's main conclusions have been endorsed by all major scientific bodies, including the National Academy of Sciences, the American Meteorological Society, the American Geophysical Union, and the American Association for the Advancement of Science. This consensus appears to be remarkably robust (Oreskes, 2005: 1686). Despite this, progress on solving the problem has been minimal. First, as a matter of substance, humanity's annual emissions of the main greenhouse gas, carbon dioxide, have grown by more than 12 per cent since the early 1990s (IPCC, 2007: 2–3). Moreover, there is no sign of serious, sustained reductions either globally or in particular nations: indeed, the rate of growth has increased recently to around 2–3 per cent per year (Hansen, 2006; Moore, 2008). Estimates of future trends vary considerably. But under a scenario usually taken to be representative of 'business as usual', annual carbon dioxide emissions will increase over the century from around 8 gigatonnes of carbon (Gt C) in 2000 to around 20 Gt C in 2100, an increase of 250 per cent (to >700 ppm CO_2) (Houghton, 2004: 116). Plainly, there is a mismatch between the apparent seriousness of the problem and our collective institutional response. What accounts for this? No doubt there are many possible explanations, more than one of which may play a contributing role. Here I shall discuss three particularly prominent suggestions, to see how far they might be undermined by the emergence of the Abrupt Paradigm.

Economics

One explanation for political inertia is, of course, that people believe that action is not justified. Such arguments are often couched in economic terms. So, for example, Bjorn Lomborg asserts that 'economic analyses clearly show that it will be far more expensive to cut CO_2 emissions radically than to pay the costs of adaptation to the increased temperatures' (Lomborg, 2001: 318). Now, in my view, such arguments are dubious even under the gradualist paradigm. Nevertheless, it is worth discussing the impact of the Abrupt Paradigm on them, since it appears to undercut these economic arguments even more decisively.

Let us begin with the usual objections. First, interpreted as a general claim about economic analysis, Lomborg's assertion appears to be false. In fact, the results of economic analyses vary widely, and are inconclusive. Hence, for example, the economist Clive Spash asserts:

> . . . [E]conomic assessment fails to provide an answer as to what should be done. The costs of reducing CO_2 emissions may be quite high or there may be net gains depending on the options chosen by the analyst. The benefits of reducing emissions are beyond economists' ability to estimate so the extent to which control options should be adopted, on efficiency grounds alone, is unknown. (Spash, 2002: 178)

However, second, interpreted more narrowly, Lomborg may be correct. If he means to refer only to standard economic approaches – in particular those relying on current market prices and employing substantial discount rates (of the order of 5 per cent or more) – then it may be true that there is wide agreement in the results of such analyses in the direction he suggests. However, unfortunately, this claim does not have the implication that Lomborg intends – that inaction on climate change is justified – since it is precisely these features of standard economic approaches that many people argue makes them inappropriate tools for assessing long-term impacts. The critics contend that there is too much uncertainty about the technology and preferences of the distant future to render current prices an appropriate guide to future prices (Broome, 1992), and they claim that standard discount rates are far too blunt an instrument, and far too theoretically ungrounded, to serve as a covert theory of intergenerational ethics (Stern, 2008; Gardiner, 2004; forthcoming).

But perhaps there is a rejoinder. Enthusiasts for the standard approach may want to argue that we need not be too concerned about future uncertainty so long as climate change itself has only a minor impact on factor prices; and perhaps they will claim that the worry about discount rates can be overcome if we make sure that we reinvest productive gains and save for the future. Even as it stands, this rejoinder has limited appeal. Still, the abrupt paradigm may undermine even this. For one thing, a severe abrupt change, such as a substantial temperature drop in Europe caused by a major change in ocean circulation in the North Atlantic, would presumably have a large impact on global society, and so on relative prices. Indeed, a report commissioned by the Pentagon speculated that the regional impacts of a shutdown in the thermohaline circulation would be 'a world where Europe will be struggling internally, large numbers of refugees washing up on its shores, and Asia in serious crisis over food and water', such that 'disruption and conflict' would be 'endemic features of life' (Schwartz and Randall, 2003: 14). For another, such a change would probably affect both the productivity of investment, and the possibility of intergenerational saving. If there is a severe abrupt change, we might predict that the current generation would dissave whatever had been set aside for the future in order to address more immediate hardships. (More on this later.) Again, consider the Pentagon report:

> In the event of abrupt climate change, it's likely that food, water, and energy resource constraints will first be managed through economic, political, and diplomatic means such as treaties and trade embargoes. Over time though, conflicts over land and water use are likely to become more severe – and more violent. As states become increasingly desperate, the pressure for action will grow. (Schwartz and Randall, 2003: 22)

In conclusion, a severe abrupt change would surely undermine the reliability of existing cost-benefit analyses of climate change. Hence, there is at least one respect in which the possibility of a catastrophic abrupt climate change does seem to help with the problem of political inertia: it appears to undermine (what was left of) the appeal of the economic arguments.

Psychology

A second prominent explanation for political inertia is psychological. For example, Elke Weber claims that political inertia is not surprising, since neither peoples nor their governments have (yet) become alarmed about climate change, and this has meant that they have not (yet) become motivated enough to act (Weber, 2006: 103).

Why aren't people alarmed? A full explanation would no doubt be very complex. But Weber's account suggests that the outline is accessible enough. In short, human beings have two processing systems – the affective and the analytical (104) – and these two systems are influenced in different ways, and by different kinds of inputs. Moreover, in cases involving risk and uncertainty – such as climate change – the affective system is dominant (104). This gives rise to a number of general problems. First, the two systems can, and often do, offer different judgments for the same cases (104). Second, the reasons for these differences seem shallow. In particular, the two systems acquire information in different ways – the affective tends to rely on personal experience, whereas the analytical favours statistical descriptions – with the result that 'ostensibly same information can lead to different choices depending on how the information is acquired' (106). Third, for reasons we shall see in a moment, the interplay of the two mechanisms gives rise to a systematic bias in decision-making: 'low-probability events generate less concern than their probability warrants on average, but more concern than they deserve in those rare instances when they do occur' (102).

To make matters worse, these problems interact badly with some related psychological phenomena surrounding risk. For one thing, Weber claims that there is a 'finite pool of worry': people have a limited capacity for the kind of worry that motivates action, so that an increase in concern about one risk tends to reduce concern about others (115). For another, there is an analogous limitation in people's responses to problems even when they are motivated to act. Decision-makers have a 'single action bias', such that they are 'very likely to take one action to reduce a risk that they encounter and worry about, but are much less likely to take additional steps that would provide incremental protection or risk reduction'. Moreover, this bias persists even if the single action taken is neither the most effective, nor suitably coordinated with other actors, since a single action alone is enough to reduce worry (115).

These two tendencies have a number of implications. First, the presence of a finite pool of worry suggests that we can expect political inertia even when people appreciate that a particular problem exists, if concern for that problem is 'crowded out' by other issues that seem more pressing. Second, given its dominance, failure to engage the affective mechanism is likely to result in a particular problem's being marginalized by other – perhaps objectively less important – concerns that do so engage (105). Third, even successful engagement is not enough, given the 'single action bias'. Hence, in cases where piecemeal, incremental policy-making is unlikely to work, it is vital not only to take major action when an issue has succeeded in grabbing the political spotlight, but also then to take all (or most) of the action necessary.

The relevance of these general claims to climate change seems clear. First, most of the available information comes from science and is both abstract and statistical. Hence, it engages the analytical system. However, given the dominance of the affective system, such engagement is liable to be ineffective by itself. Second, it is difficult to engage the affective system in the case of climate change because within that system 'recent personal experience strongly influences the evaluation of a risky option' (103) and 'personal experience with noticeable and serious consequences of global warming is still rare in many regions of the world'. (108) Third, given this, we should expect a communication problem. Weber claims that statistical information has a different impact on those who are used to employing their analytical systems and those who are not. Hence, she claims, there is likely to be a mismatch between the reactions of scientists and laypeople to the same information (108). Finally, concerns about the psychological limits of attention and action seem pressing. For one thing, empirical work suggests that many people see climate change as a real problem, but also rank it below many other concerns, particularly when it comes to voting behaviour (Jamieson, 2006: 101–2). For another, many political communities do seem to have suffered from a kind of attention-deficit disorder when it comes to climate change. Moreover, those efforts that have been made tend to be predominantly piecemeal and incremental. Even the current Kyoto agreement is routinely defended as 'merely a necessary first step'. But these may be dangerous tendencies given the single action bias.

What are the implications of all this psychology? Weber suggests that we must find a way of engaging the affective system, 'perhaps by simulations of [global warming's] concrete future consequences for people's home or other regions they visit or value' (103). But then she adds that invoking the gradualist paradigm is unlikely to work:

> To the extent that people conceive of climate change as a simple and gradual change . . . the risks posed by climate change would appear to be well-known and, at least in principle, controllable ('move from Miami to Vancouver when things get too hot or dangerous in Florida'). While some of the perceived control may be illusory, the ability or inability to take corrective action is an important component of vulnerability. (112)

Instead:

> It is only the potentially catastrophic nature of (rapid) climate change (of the kind graphically depicted in the movie 'The Day after Tomorrow') and the global dimension of adverse effects . . . that have the potential for raising a visceral reaction to the risk. (113–14)

In short, Weber claims that the abrupt paradigm has the capacity to engage the affective system in a way sufficient to motivate action. Given this, the growing scientific support for that paradigm is indeed good news in one respect. For it offers a potential way out of psychologically induced political inertia. Of course, Weber herself wants to go even further than this. For she asserts that *only* abrupt climate change – and truly global and catastrophic instances of it at that – which can help.

The Intergenerational Analysis

The third explanation of political inertia is, I confess, my own. This suggests that one root of the problem lies in its intergenerational structure. The basic idea can be illustrated (in a simplistic way) as follows.[2] Imagine a sequence of groups occupying the same territory at different times. Suppose, for the sake of simplicity, that each group is temporally distinct: no member of one group exists at the same time as any member of another group (i.e. there is no 'overlap' between the groups). Call each group so conceived a 'generation'. Suppose then that the preferences of the members of each group are 'generation-relative': they concern only things that happen within the timeframe of that group's existence. Finally, suppose that there are such things as temporally extended goods: goods that have benefits and costs that accrue in more than one generation. For current purposes, let us distinguish two kinds of such goods: those that have benefits in one generation and costs in later generations can be called 'front-loaded goods'; those that have costs in one generation and benefits in later generations can be called 'back-loaded goods'.

Other things being equal, in such a situation we would expect that if each group does exactly as it pleases it will consume as many front-loaded goods as possible, and eschew all back-loaded goods. But this observation appears to raise a basic problem of intergenerational fairness. Surely, the thought goes, there are situations in which a given group ought to forgo at least some front-loaded goods and invest in at least some back-loaded goods; presumably there are at least some constraints (of fairness, or justice, or some other such notion) on legitimate intergenerational behaviour. If this thought is correct, then we might expect that groups that are unaware of, or do not recognize, such constraints will tend to *overconsume* front-loaded goods, and *underconsume* back-loaded goods. In other words, each such generation will take advantage of its temporal position by *illegitimately passing on costs* to later generations for the sake of securing benefits for itself, and *illegitimately forgoing opportunities to benefit* later generations for the sake of avoiding costs to itself. Moreover, this problem will be iterated over time – since the incentives that generate the basic behaviour arise anew for each generation as it comes into existence – with the result that such buck passing is likely to produce cumulative effects on generations further along the temporal sequence. Hence, one can expect a systematic bias in overall decision-making across generations. Let us call this, 'the problem of intergenerational buck passing' (PIBP).

Elsewhere, I have argued that the PIBP is manifest in the case of climate change. On the gradualist paradigm, this looks especially likely. But might the abrupt paradigm help? Initially, it appears so, since the potential proximity of the relevant thresholds appears to undercut the intergenerational aspect of climate change. Consider, for example, the following statement by the (now former) British Prime Minister Tony Blair:

> What is now plain is that the emission of greenhouse gases, associated with industrialisation and strong economic growth from a world population that has increased sixfold in 200 years, is causing global warming at a rate that began as significant, has become alarming and is simply unsustainable in the long-term. And by long-term I do not mean centuries ahead. I mean within the lifetime of my children certainly; and possibly within my own. And by unsustainable, I do not mean a phenomenon causing problems of adjustment. I mean a challenge so far-reaching in its impact and irreversible in its destructive power, that it alters radically human existence. (Blair, 2004)

Blair's main claim appears to be that the impacts of climate change are both extremely serious, and coming relatively soon. (He does not mention abrupt climate change explicitly, but it is reasonable to assume that this is what he has in mind.) If this is right, it seems to give current people powerful reasons to act. Again, the abrupt paradigm appears to extinguish a major source of political inertia.

AGAINST UNDERMINING

At first glance, then, it appears, that the abrupt paradigm undercuts all three of the major explanations for political inertia we've considered. But I shall now argue that in the case of the last two explanations, this appearance is deceptive. Instead, it is plausible to think that the possibility of abrupt climate change will actually make the intergenerational problem worse, rather than better, and that the psychological problem will add to this sad state of affairs.

Let us begin with the intergenerational problem. Blair suggests that some impacts of climate change are serious enough to '[alter] radically human existence', 'within the lifetime of my children certainly; and possibly within my own'. A rough calculation suggests that this means possibly within the next 26 years, and certainly within the next 75 (or 58). At first glance, such claims do seem to undermine the usual intergenerational analysis. But this is too hasty. For the notion of proximity is made complicated in the climate change case by the considerable time lags involved – the same lags that give rise to the PIBP.

Consider the following. First, the atmospheric lifetime of a typical molecule of the main anthropogenic greenhouse gas, carbon dioxide, is often said to be around 200–300 years. This introduces a significant lagging effect in itself, but obscures the fact that around 25 per cent remains for more than a thousand years (Archer, 2005: 5). Moreover, many of the basic processes set in motion by the greenhouse effect continue to play out over thousands of years. Second, these facts have implications for the shape of the climate change problem. For one thing, the problem is *resilient*: once the emissions necessary to cause serious climate change have been released it is difficult – and perhaps impossible – to reverse the process. For another, the problem is *seriously backloaded*: at any given time the current impacts of anthropogenic climate change do not reflect the full consequences of emissions made up to that point. Finally, this implies that the full effects of current emissions are *substantially deferred*. Even if we are to reap some of what we sow, *we* will not reap all of it (Gardiner, 2006).

These points suggest that it is worth distinguishing two kinds of proximity: temporal and causal. When Blair claims that the impacts of climate change are coming soon, he means to speak of temporal proximity: the impacts are near to us in time. But claims about causal proximity are different: here the claim is that the point at which we effectively commit the earth to an abrupt change by our actions is close at hand. Given the presence of resilience, serious backloading and substantial deferral, temporal proximity does not always imply causal proximity, and *vice versa*; and this fact has important implications, as we shall now see.

Domino Effect

Consider first a scenario where we are in a position to commit humanity (and other species) to a catastrophic abrupt impact, but we ourselves won't suffer that impact because it will be visited on future generations. In other words, there is causal, but not temporal proximity. (Call this scenario, 'Domino Effect'.) Several of the most worrying impacts currently envisioned seem to fit this scenario. For example, even very rapid ice sheet disintegration is presumed to take place over centuries, such that its impacts are intergenerational (Hansen, 2004); similarly, the limited work that has been done on deposits of methane hydrate in the oceans suggest that the associated impacts would not arise for several centuries, if not millennia (Lenton et al., 2008; Archer and Buffett, 2005; Harvey and Huang, 1995). Hence, the real concern in these cases is with causal proximity: the worry is that by our actions we may commit future generations to catastrophic climate changes. However, such a scenario clearly raises, rather than undermines, the intergenerational analysis. So, we will have to look elsewhere for a challenge to the PIBP.

On the Cards

A second kind of scenario would involve temporal but not causal proximity. Suppose, for example, that we are already only a few years from crossing a major climate threshold, and that at this point we are already committed to doing so. The most obvious reason why this might be the case would be because, given the time lags, our past emissions make breaching the threshold literally inevitable. But it might also be that we are already committed because there are emissions that we are morally no longer going to be able to avoid, for example, because avoiding them would impose intolerable costs on current people and their immediate descendents. (Call this scenario, 'On the Cards'.)

If it turned out that *On the Cards* characterized our situation, and if we knew that it did so, then the implications of the abrupt paradigm for political inertia would be more mixed than the basic objection to the intergenerational analysis suggests. First, and most obviously, *On the Cards* might simply reinforce inertia. Suppose, for example, that a given generation knew that it would be hit with a catastrophic abrupt change no matter what it did. Might it not be inclined to fatalism? If so, then the temporal proximity of abrupt change would actually enhance political inertia, rather than undercut it. (Why bother?)

Second, and less obviously, *On the Cards* may provoke action of the *wrong kind*. For example, assume, for simplicity, that the two main policy responses for climate change are *mitigation* of future impacts through reducing the emissions that cause them and adaptation to minimize the adverse effects of those impacts that can or will not be avoided. Then, the following may turn out to be true of *On the Cards*. On the one hand, the incentives for the current generation to engage in mitigation may at least be weakened, and might disappear altogether. This is because, if a given abrupt change is, practically speaking, inevitable, then *it* appears to provide no incentive to a current generation with purely generation-relative motivations for limiting its emissions. Perhaps the current generation will still have reasons to engage in some mitigation, since this might help it to avoid further impacts (including abrupt impacts) after the given abrupt change. But the given abrupt change does no motivational work of its own. Hence, its presence does not help future generations. On the other hand, the incentives for the current generation to engage in adaptation might be substantially improved. If big changes are coming, then it makes sense to prepare for them (Alley, 2004). In itself, this appears to be good news for both current and future people. But there are complications. For it remains possible that the current generation's adaptation efforts may be unfair to the future. This point is important, so it is worth spending some time on it.

Let us consider three ways in which the improved motivation for adaptation provided by *On the Cards* may come into conflict with intergenerational concerns. First, considering only its generation-relative preferences, a current generation aware of an impending abrupt change will have an incentive to overinvest in adaptation *relative* to mitigation (and other intergenerational projects). That is, given the opportunity, such a generation will prefer to put resources into adaptation (from which it expects benefits), rather than mitigation (which tends to benefit the future). Moreover, even within the category of adaptation, the current generation will have an incentive to prioritize projects and strategies that are more beneficial to it (e.g. temporary 'quick fixes') over those that seem best from an intergenerational point of view.

Second, this problem is likely to be exacerbated by psychological effects. For example, Weber claims that proximity which brings with it engagement of the affective mechanism often leads to an overreaction – 'low-probability events generate

. . . more concern than they deserve in those rare instances when they do occur' (Weber, 2006: 103). Hence, those in the grip of an abrupt change are likely to over-invest in their adaptive responses.

Third, and most importantly, the proximity of the abrupt change may actually provide an incentive for *increasing* current emissions above the amount that *even a completely self-interested generation* would normally choose. What I have in mind is this. Suppose that a generation could increase its own ability to cope with an impending abrupt change by increasing its emissions beyond their existing level (e.g. suppose that it could boost economic output to enhance adaptation efforts by relaxing existing emissions standards). Then, it would have a generation-relative reason to do so, and it would have this *even if* the net costs of the additional emissions to future generations far exceed the short-term benefits. Given this, it is conceivable that the impending presence of a given abrupt change may actually *exacerbate* the PIBP, leaving future generations worse off than under the gradualist paradigm (or than they would be if the earlier generation had not discovered the falsity of that paradigm). Furthermore, just like the original PIBP, this problem can become iterated. That is, if the increased indulgence in emissions by earlier generations intent on adapting to a specific abrupt climate change worsens the situation for a subsequent generation (e.g. by causing a further threshold to be breached), then the later generation may also be motivated to engage in extra emissions, and so on. In short, under the *On the Cards* scenario, we may see the structural equivalent of an *Intergenerational Arms Race* surrounding greenhouse gas emissions. Abrupt climate change may make life for a particular generation hard enough that it is motivated to increase its emissions substantially in order to cope. This may then increase the impact on a subsequent generation, with the same result. And so it goes on.

At first, the possibility of an intergenerational arms race may seem outlandish, in at least two ways. For one thing, it may seem to envisage an impossible, or at least very remote possibility: that the proximity of abrupt climate change could motivate even more greenhouse gas emissions than are currently being generated. For another, it may seem to attribute to a generation a hopelessly immoral (and therefore utterly unrealistic) outlook.

The first objection seems to me implausible. Consider, for example, a substantial change in the ocean conveyor brought on by climate change. If the physical impacts in Europe were anything like the magnitude of the past events mentioned by oceanographers, then the social and economic impacts would likely be very large, and negative. Is it implausible to think that such impacts would cause a sharp change in energy and industrial policies in Europe? Is it unlikely that a Europe facing shortages of food, water and fuel (as the Pentagon report predicted) would abandon high energy taxes and clean burning technologies, seeking whatever aid additional energy could give it in fighting such problems? Moreover, is it likely that the rest of the world, witnessing such impacts, would stand by and stoically refuse to aid those in distress? Would they not relax their own standards, burning their own oil and coal in whatever ways might be helpful in alleviating such a tragedy? Such actions seem entirely natural. Moreover, they are likely to be exacerbated by the psychology of risk. If Weber is right that there is a finite pool of worry, and a single action bias, one would expect a current generation to be consumed with the immediate tragedies of a severe abrupt change at the expense of other, more long-term worries.

This brings us to the second objection. However likely people might be to act in these ways, wouldn't they have to be grossly immoral to do so? I'm not so sure. As the above scenario suggests, there may be something admirable about the actions of such a generation, even if there is also something tragic, in that such actions predictably harm future people. Indeed, such a generation may be *morally justified* in its actions. Considering a similar situation, Martino Traxler likens the case to one of self-defence:

Where the present harm from not emitting is conspicuous enough, we would be unrealistic, unreasonable, and maybe even irrational to expect present people to allow present harm and suffering to visit them or their kith and kin in order that they might avoid harm to future people. In these cases, we may with good reason speak of having so strong or so rationally compelling a reason to emit that, in spite of the harm these emissions will cause to (future) others, we are excused for our maleficence. (Traxler, 2002: 107)

We seem then to have uncovered a way in which abrupt climate change may lead to a form of the PIBP that is actually worse in several respects than the one suggested by the Gradualist Paradigm. First, abrupt climate change might increase the *magnitude* of intergenerational buck passing, by increasing the presence of front-loaded goods. If a current generation can protect itself more effectively against an abrupt change through extra emissions that harm the future, then it has a reason to do so. Second, a severe abrupt change may make taking advantage of such goods not simply a matter of self- or generation-relative interest (which might be morally criticized), but morally justifiable in a very serious way. Hence, abrupt change may make buck passing even harder to overcome.

Open Window

On the Cards shows that it is possible for abrupt change to make matters worse. But perhaps that scenario is too pessimistic. Hopefully, even though there is a sense in which the climate thresholds are close, it is not true that we are already committed to crossing one. Interestingly, this thought reveals a tension in the proximity claim that is supposed to undermine the intergenerational problem: to be successful, the threatened abrupt change must be temporally close enough to motivate the current generation, but distant enough so as not yet to be 'on the cards'. This tension suggests that the argument against the intergenerational analysis presupposes a very specific scenario: that there is an abrupt change that would affect the current generation, to which the planet is not yet committed, but to which it will become committed unless the current generation take evasive action very soon. (Call this scenario, 'Open Window'.)

Several issues arise about *Open Window*. The first, obviously enough, is whether there is such a window, and, if so, how big it is. These are empirical questions on which our information is sketchy. Still, the preliminary estimates are not particularly encouraging (cf. Lenton et al. 2008). Moreover, it is worth making some observations about the importance of the PIBP even if there is an *Open Window* for the current generation. Our second issue then is whether, if the window is open, this undermines the relevance of the PIBP. One concern is that generations might care less about the end-of-life abrupt climate change than earlier-in-life ones. Another is that even an open window severely restricts the relevance of future people's concerns. For *Open Window* to be effective, there have to be enough effects of present emissions that accrue within the window to justify the current generation's action on a generation-relative basis. But this ignores all the other effects of present emissions – that is, all those that accrue to other generations. So, the PIBP remains. Moreover, in light of the PIBP, there is a realistic concern that solutions that avoid a particular abrupt climate change will be judged purely on how they enable a present generation to avoid that change arising during their lifetime, not on their wider ramifications. In other words, each generation will be motivated simply to *delay* any given abrupt climate change until after it is dead. So, it may endorse policies that merely postpone such a change, making it inevitable for a future generation. Finally, sequential concerns may arise even under the open window scenario. Considering the PIBP, it would be predictable that earlier generations tend to use up most of any safety margin left to them. Given this, it may turn out that some later generation cannot help pushing over a given threshold, and using up most of the safety margin for the next.

The Self-Corrective Argument

If all of this is the case, the potential for the abrupt paradigm to undermine the intergenerational problem appears to be slim. But before closing, it is worth addressing one final argument. Weber suggests that the psychological problems she identifies may eventually take care of themselves:

> Failing these efforts, the problem discussed in this paper is ultimately self-corrective. Increasing personal evidence of global warming and its potentially devastating consequences can be counted on to be an extremely effective teacher and motivator. (Weber, 2006: 116)

The basic idea seems to be that, once realized, the impacts brought on by inaction on climate change are of a sort to engage the affective mechanism. Of course, as Weber recognizes, this may only happen once a substantial amount of damage is already done, and the planet is committed to significantly more. Still, the claim is that at least there is some kind of limit to inertia provided by the phenomena of climate change themselves.

Does the abrupt paradigm impose some limit on how bad climate change can get? Perhaps. But again the intergenerational problem rears its ugly head. If climate change is resilient and seriously backloaded, the effects on a present generation that experiences an abrupt change and knows these facts are unclear. If further bad impacts are already on the cards, or if the open window is only slightly ajar, then, if the present generation is guided by its generation-relative preferences, we may still expect substantial intergenerational buck-passing, and so more climate change. Experience of abrupt impacts may not teach and motivate, precisely because for such a generation the time for teaching and motivating has already passed – at least as far as its own concerns are implicated. Moreover, we should expect other factors to intervene. If a generation experiences a severe abrupt change, we might expect long-term concerns (such as with mitigation) to be crowded out in the finite pool of worry by more immediate concerns. We might also expect such a generation to be morally justified in ignoring those concerns, to at least some extent. In short, we might expect something akin to the beginnings of an intergenerational arms race.

CONCLUDING REMARKS

This chapter has considered three theses: that the possibility of abrupt change undermines the usual economic, psychological and intergenerational causes of political inertia; that it provides the current generation with positive motivation to act; and that it implies that there is some kind of fail-safe system that will limit humanity's on-going infliction of climate change on itself and other species. Against these claims, I suggested that although the real possibility of abrupt change does tend to undermine economic explanations for inertia (which were, however, not very strong anyway), it does not undercut either its psychological, or intergenerational roots. Instead, the abrupt paradigm threatens to make climate change an even worse problem than the gradualist model it is supposed to augment or supersede.

Abrupt climate change may actually increase each generation's incentive to consume dangerous greenhouse gas emissions, and may even cause at least some generations to have a moral license to do so.

I conclude that we should not look to the disasters of abrupt change – either the actual experience of them, or increasing scientific evidence that they are coming – to save us. One implication of this is that we should not waste precious time waiting for that to happen. If severe abrupt climate change is a real threat, the time for action is now, when many actions are likely to be prudentially and morally easier than in the future. Still, how effectively to motivate such action remains a very large practical problem, about which the psychologists have much to teach us. In my view, if we are to solve this problem, we will need to look beyond people's generation-relative preferences. Moreover, the prevalence of the intergenerational problem suggests that one set of motivations that we need to think hard about engaging is those connected to moral beliefs about our obligations to those only recently, or not yet, born. This leaves us with one final question. Can the abrupt paradigm help us with this last task? Perhaps so: for one intriguing possibility is that the prospect of abrupt change will engage intergenerational motivations. Indeed, Weber explicitly suggests as much in the full version of a passage quoted earlier:

> It is only the potentially catastrophic nature of (rapid) climate change (of the kind graphically depicted in the movie 'The Day after Tomorrow') and the global dimension of adverse effects *which may create hardships for future generations* that have the potential for raising a visceral reaction to the risk. (Weber, 2006: 113–14)

If Weber is right that the potential effects of abrupt change on future people can cause the needed psychological effects, then the psychology of abrupt climate change might turn out to be of profound importance after all, even taking the PIBP into account. Still, this would now be because such change helps to underwrite a solution to the intergenerational problem, not because it undermines its application. Hence, such a result would fit well with the main aim of this chapter, which has been to show that a solution to the intergenerational problem is still required, and that, given this, these are the relevant psychological and philosophical questions to be asking.

NOTES

1 This chapter is adapted from a paper that was originally published in *Journal of Social Philosophy,* Volume 40, Number 2, Summer 2009, edited by Carol C. Gould, pp. 140–62(23). Reproduced with permission of Blackwell Publishing Ltd.
2 The next two paragraphs are adapted from Gardiner (2003).

REFERENCES

Alley, R. (2004), 'Abrupt Climate Change'. *Scientific American* 68.

Archer, D. (2005), 'Fate of Fossil Fuel CO_2 in Geologic Time'. *Journal of Geophysical Research* 110.

Archer, D. and Bruce, B. (2005), 'Time-dependent Response of the Global Ocean Clathrate Reservoir to Climatic and Anthropogenic Forcing'. *Geochemistry. Geophysics. Geosystems* 6, Q03002 [doi: 10.1029/2004GC000854].

Berner, R. (2002), 'Examination of Hypotheses for the Permo-Triassic Boundary Extinction by Carbon Cycle Modeling'. *Proceedings of the American Academy of Sciences* 99 (7), 4172–7.

Barry, B. (2005), *Why Social Justice Matters.* Cambridge: Polity.

Blair, T. (2004), 'Climate Change Speech'. Available at: www.number-10. gov.uk/output/page6333.asp.

Broome, J. (2002), *Counting the Cost of Global Warming.* Isle of Harris, UK: White Horse Press.

Brown, D. (2002), *American Heat: Ethical Problems with the United States' Response to Global Warming.* Lanham, MD: Rowman & Littlefield, pp. 18–19.

Bryden, H. L., Hannah, R., Longworth, and Stuart A. Cunningham (2005), 'Slowing of the Atlantic Meridional Overturning Circulation at 25 Degrees North'. *Nature* 438 December 1, 655–7.

Ereaut, G. and Nat. Segnit (2006), *Warm Words: How Are We Telling the Climate Story and How Can We Tell It Better?* London: Institute for Public Policy Research.

European Environment Agency (2005), *The European Environment: State and Outlooks.* Copenhagen: European Environment Agency.

Gagosian, R. (2003), 'Abrupt Climate Change: Should We Be Worried?' (Woods Hole Oceanographic Institute), 12. Available at: www.whoi. edu/institutes/occi/hottopics _climate change.html.

Gardiner, S. (2003), 'The Pure Intergenerational Problem'. *The Monist,* 86 (3) July, 481–500.

—(2004a), 'The Global Warming Tragedy and the Dangerous Illusion of the Kyoto Protocol'. *Ethics and International Affairs* 18, 23–39.

—(2004b), 'Ethics and Global Climate Change'. *Ethics* 114, 555–600.

—(2006), 'A Perfect Moral Storm: Climate Change, Intergenerational Ethics and the Problem Of Moral Corruption'. *Environmental Values* 15, 397–413.

Hansen, J. (2004) 'Defusing the Global Warming Time Bomb'. *Scientific American* 290, 68–77.

—(2005), 'A Slippery Slope: How Much Global Warming Constitutes "Dangerous Anthropogenic Interference?"'. *Climatic Change* 68, 269–79.

—(2006), 'Can we still avoid dangerous human-made climate change?'. Talk presented at the New School University, Social Research Conference, 10 February, 2006, New York City.

Harvey, D. and Zhen Huang (1995), 'Evaluation of the Potential Impact of Methane Clathrate Destabilization on Future Global Warming'. *Journal of Geophysical Research* 100, 2905–26.

Houghton, J. (2004), *Climate Change: The Complete Briefing.* Cambridge: Cambridge University Press, 3rd edn, p. 184.

IPCC (1990), *Climate Change 1990: The Scientific Basis.* Cambridge: Cambridge University Press.

—(2001), *Climate Change 2001: The Scientific Basis.* Cambridge: Cambridge University Press.

—(2007), *Climate Change 2007: The Scientific Basis.* Cambridge: Cambridge University Press.

Jamieson, D. (2006), 'An American Paradox'. *Climatic Change* 77, 97–102.

Kristof, N. (2006), 'The Big Burp Theory of the Apocalypse'. *New York Times,* 16 April.

Laslett, P. and James Fishkin (eds) (1992), *Justice between Age Groups and Generations.* New Haven, CT: Yale University Press.

Lenton, T. et al. (2008), 'Tipping Elements in the Earth's Climate System'. *Proceedings of the National Academy of Sciences* 105 (6).

Lomborg, B. (2001), *The Sceptical Environmentalist.* Cambridge: Cambridge University Press.

Moore, F. (2008), 'Carbon Dioxide Emissions Accelerating Rapidly'. Earth Policy Institute. Available at: www.earth-policy.org/Indicators/CO$_2$/2008.htm

Oppenheimer, M. and Annie Petsonk (2004), 'Article 2 of the UNFCCC: Historical Origins, Recent Interpretations'. *Climatic Change* 73, 195–226.

Oreskes, N. (2005), 'The Scientific Consensus on Climate Change'. *Science* 3 December.

Parry, M. (2007), Quoted in David Adam, Peter Walker and Alison Benjamin, 'Grim outlook for poor countries in climate report', *The Guardian*, 18 September.

Schiermeier, Q. (2006), 'A Sea Change'. *Nature* 439, 19 January, 256–60.

Schwartz, P. and Doug Randall (2003), 'An Abrupt Climate Change Scenario and Its Implications for United States National Security'. Available at: www.grist.org/pdf/AbruptClimateChange2003.

Spash, C. L. (2002), *Greenhouse Economics: Value and Ethics.* London: Routledge.

Stern, N. (2006), *The Economics of Climate Change*. Cambridge: Cambridge University Press.
—(2008), 'The Economics of Climate Change'. *American Economic Review* 98 (2), 1–37.
Stouffer, R. J. et al. (2006), 'Investigating the Causes of the Response of the Thermohaline Circulation to Past and Future Climate Changes'. *Journal of Climate* 19, 1365–87.
Traxler, M. (2002), 'Fair Chore Division for Climate Change'. *Social Theory and Practice* 28, 101–34.
US National Research Council (2002), Committee on Abrupt Climate Change, *Abrupt Climate Change: Inevitable Surprises*, Washington D. C.: National Academies Press.
Vellinga, M. and Richard A. Wood (2002), 'Global Impacts of a Collapse of the Atlantic Thermohaline Circulation'. *Climatic Change* 51, 251–67.
Weber, E. (2006), 'Experienced-based and Description-based Perceptions of Long-Term Risk: Why Global Warming Does Not Scare Us (Yet)'. *Climatic Change* 77, 103–20.
Weitzman, M. (1998), 'Why the Far Distant Future Should Be Discounted at Its Lowest Possible Rate'. *Journal of Environmental Economics and Management* 36, 201–8.
Williams, Richard, S. and Jane, G. Ferrigno (eds) (1999), USGS Professional Paper 1386A. Reston, VA: USGS.

CHAPTER FIVE

LIVING IN UNCERTAINTY

ANTHROPOGENIC GLOBAL WARMING AND THE LIMITS OF 'RISK THINKING'

CHRISTOPHER GROVES

INTRODUCTION

All ethics is about the future, but not all futures are created equal. In considering what ethics is about, it is important to ask what *kind* of future is envisaged as its object. As such, ethics is inseparable from politics. In sociology, debates about phenomena such as 'the risk society' concern precisely how societies construct normative frameworks in response to their assumptions about the future. For example, since the 1960s or 1970s, public institutions have increasingly become dominated by certain prevalent interpretations of the ethical significance of uncertainty. Such developments have been represented by commentators as a transformation and extension of Weber's *Zweck-rationalität* into rational risk management (e.g. Habermas, 1971; Rose, 1999). Risk is in this sense more than a concept. It is a discursive and practical strategy for defining what is to count as *significant* uncertainty. It therefore reflects specific systems of value and normative assumptions, in which some aspects of uncertainty, such as calculable possible outcomes are foregrounded at the expense of others (Beck, 1992: 22).

The appropriateness of such definitional strategies (hereafter 'risk thinking', following Nikolas Rose) in the face of complex and long-term uncertainty is, as many have argued, questionable (e.g. Shrader-Frechette, 1993). One of the chief reasons for this is the short-termism of risk management practices that focus on calculability, in face of phenomena (like the production of persistent pollutants) that bring into focus questions about the nature of our longer term responsibilities to future humans, and indeed, non-humans. Perhaps the most pressing of these problematic phenomena is anthropogenic global warming (AGW). Faced with the possibility of radical temperature increases, and the prospect of associated social and ecological harm leading perhaps to the near-uninhabitability of the planet for human beings and many other species, the strategies for living with uncertainty embodied in risk thinking, with its emphasis on near-term calculation of probabilities, may appear particularly inappropriate.

Dale Jamieson has written that the roots of this inappropriateness lie in how risk thinking (or what he calls a 'management approach' to AGW) violates certain ethical criteria, and that they are thus inextricable from the framework of values which underlies risk thinking. A value framework 'specifies permissions, norms, duties and obligations; it assigns blame, praise and responsibility; and it provides an account of what is valuable and what is not' (Jamieson, 1992: 147). I argue below that the values behind risk thinking derive from deep-rooted social assumptions about the relationship between the present and the future, that these assumptions reflect a privilege accorded to certain forms of subjectivity, and that other forms of experience should be appealed to in beginning, as Jamieson puts it, 'a search for new values' and '[c]ollective moral change' (1992: 150, 151). Such a search, I suggest, has as its goal finding different ways to live in and with uncertainty.

THE PRESENT FUTURE OF AGW

Before we examine the assumptions on which risk thinking rests in more detail, let us review three aspects of how AGW confronts us with recalcitrant uncertainties, and challenges our ethical imagination.

(1) *Technological novelty*. The production of novel technological systems often creates situations where the kinds of knowledge which science views as its benchmark are no longer adequate. We are not in a laboratory situation in which probabilities of unwanted events can be assigned with high degrees of certainty. Instead, the use of technologies can often generate complex, singular situations whose broader

outcomes often remain very uncertain, yet may be highly hazardous (Kaiser, 1997: 201). The resulting situation is often one in which the capacity of a technology to produce harmful unintended consequences cannot be judged before its widespread use. This is true in two ways of AGW. First, AGW is a largely unpredicted side-effect of the widespread use of fossil-fuel technologies. Second, there is the role played by other technologies that introduce substances, such a chlorofluorocarbons, which do not exist in nature. In both cases, we are faced with having to assess the effects of processes of which humans have had no substantial past experience. This experience of novelty leads us to consider another aspect of uncertainty.

(2) *Simulation and knowledge.* How forms of knowledge evolve in response to novelty changes the relationship between knowledge and action. The role of scenario exercises in shaping planning for the future is increasingly familiar within business and public policy alike. Scenario or simulation-based planning first became an important strategic tool after World War II in relation to nuclear armaments. As a nuclear war could not be fought (it was hypothesized) without total destruction for both sides, planning had to make use of new methods. The use of computer simulations took on a vital role in such exercises, leading to huge investments in new technologies (Edwards, 1995). Just as with nuclear war, the prospect of climate change does not leave us the luxury of waiting until we can be certain about the exact shape of the future it might bring about before deciding to assign resources to some determinate path of action (Jamieson, 1992: 142). We have therefore to act on projected futures which contain a range of irreducible uncertainties because they are not based on past evidence and experience. The goal of simulation is therefore to produce general climate models (GCMs) which can at least reproduce the main features of recorded changes in climate. Despite the possibility of progressively reducing uncertainty, particularly where increased granularity of models may enable important regional impacts of climate change to be better assessed, inherent complexities of the climate system will remain outside even improved models (Harrison, 2008).

(3) *Invisible propagation*. Ulrich Beck notes that it is also characteristic of many novel technological interactions with nature that they 'typically *escape perception*' (Beck, 1992: 21). The detection of many chemical pollutants and radiation for example is impossible for humans without technological assistance. This imperceptible spreading of effects has been conceptualized as *naturalized technology*. Alfred Nordmann (2005: 3) introduces this idea to develop arguments advanced by earlier thinkers such as Gunther Anders and Hans Jonas about the irresponsibility which is inherent in the widespread everyday employment of advanced technologies. With sufficiently advanced technologies, it is impossible for us to accompany our experience of using them with an adequate imaginative representation of how they bring about their effects (unlike, for example, the use of a spade or a gun). In such circumstances, Nordmann suggests, it is impossible to act responsibly. As novel technologies potentially expand the consequences of our actions through synergistic unintended consequences across natural and social systems, we lose any imaginative grasp of the *reach* of what we do. Thus advanced technologies take on a new social significance: they appear like 'brute nature', and 'instead of knowing them, we merely know of them' (2006: 3). That such irresponsibility – more specifically, a structural deficit of responsibility from which we individually and collectively suffer – is related to a lack of imaginative and conceptual reach was, however, for Hans Jonas, characteristic of the 'timeprint' (Adam and Groves, 2007: 115–17) of technological societies as such and not simply of advanced technologies. Technologies which are capable of intervening at a deep level within the natural world need not be particularly advanced (such interventions can include the unintended consequences of burning fossil fuels, with CO_2 emissions being capable of remaining in the atmosphere for over a century). Nonetheless, their temporal reach gives us power over the future, in the sense that our acts may determine what conditions future beings will live under. But the intellectual capacities which lead to their development are not necessarily accompanied by an equally powerful capacity for developing appropriate ethical and political behaviour.

CONSTRUCTING THE FUTURE

Given these three aspects of the uncertain futures of AGW, we can ask how appropriate institutionalized decision-making processes are for dealing with them. We need to answer this question (i) in relation to the forms of knowledge and reasoning that inform decisions, and (ii) in relation to the values which guide these ways of knowing and thinking. First, however, we need to examine in more detail the sense in which the social significance of uncertainty is always a matter of interpretation, of selection, and prioritization, and to characterize how, in general, risk thinking does this.

The social meaning of an uncertain future requires extensive unpacking. Some important efforts at understanding the ideological and practical bases of different modes of social 'futuring' have been made, with the sociology of expectations (e.g. Brown et al., 2000) and the now extensive field of the sociology of utopia (e.g. Levitas, 1990; Jameson, 2005) all making notable contributions to understanding how various ways of constructing the future emerge within modernity. However, the additional step of positing some kind of essential connection between modernity and futurity as such is problematic, although it is often taken. The tendency to do so is evident if we compare, for example, Alexis de Tocqueville's description of the attitudes of Native Americans to the future with more recent writings on risk. Already in 1835, de Tocqueville was part of an established tradition of thinking when he wrote of 'that childish carelessness of the morrow which characterizes savage life' (1994/1835: 407). Recently, Antony Giddens (1999) ascribes to modernity an obsession with controlling the yet-to-come rather than as continuing to conserve the past. For other writers, the contemporary importance of concepts of risk is further evidence of this unique preoccupation of modernity with the future: 'risk is the integration of the future into the present' (Gaszo, 2009).

The separation here between modern and premodern epochs evokes that between culture and nature, identifying the traditional, like the natural, with a temporality keyed to cyclical repetition, while the modern opens out onto a linear progression into the future. The basis of this separation should, however, be questioned (Adam, 1995; 22–3). Not only does it over-simplify the temporalities of actual historical bodies of social practices, in which different ways of producing the future are always an at least implicit concern (Adam and Groves, 2007: 46–7), it also simplifies the temporality of nature itself, in which life as characterized by self-concern or *conatus* can be understood as already integrating adaptive and evolutionary futures into its living present (Jonas, 1982: 72–3). The idea of nature as 'without future' is a historical product (Adam and Groves, 2007: 61–4), as are representations of traditional societies as unconcerned with 'the morrow' that selectively ignore such significant counter-examples as the long-term promise-keeping embedded in the constitution of the Iroquois Confederacy, though to date from the twelfth century (Johansen, 1995).

Constructing the future through representation, ritual and repetition is common to 'traditional' and 'modern' societies, creating a 'horizon of expectations [*Erwartungshorizont*]' (Koselleck, 2002: 111), against which the future is made comprehensible, and action in the present possible. Futures can be avoided, propitiated, planned, predicted, accepted, cared for or insured against. In each case, a different configuration of knowledge, action and ethical life is implied, and with these, a different interpretation of the significance of what remains uncertain. With these interpretations come different forms of reasoning about the relationship between past, present and future and different 'habits of mind', through which experience is shaped.

The emergence of risk as a particular strategy for understanding uncertainty and shaping action in the present must be understood in this way, as an assemblage of social practices through which individuals and groups construct and orient themselves towards a specific horizon of knowledge, action and ethics. Critical histories and genealogies of risk attempt to show how shifts in social practices produce the future as calculable through the management of risk, and as a result produce new forms of experience, new subjectivities (e.g. Rose, 1999, 2001). These new forms, which Rose calls 'risk thinking' (Rose, 1999: 246–7) depend on particular codified forms of knowledge of the future. Whereas in traditional societies, knowledge of the future is seen as a gift of supernatural agencies to individuals, risk thinking is based on forms of depersonalized expertise, which can be applied in different places and different times (Giddens, 1990: 28).

This technical-rational character of risk thinking reflects specific assumptions about the relationship between present and future which often precede modernity but in which modern culture, industrial capitalist economies, and bureaucratic forms of authority are deeply rooted. The connection between experiment, deduction of natural laws and increased technical control of nature expressed by Baconian, Galilean and Newtonian natural philosophy was secured upon the assumption that the future of nature, independent of human activity, was an *abstract future* structured by bare repetition of regularities (Adam and Groves, 2007: 62–4). The Baconian project of technical control sought to harness the inherent predictability of nature. Via experiment, deduction and subsequent technological interventions, the laws of nature are redeemed from mere repetition, and are bent to 'higher' purposes. This interpretation of nature's futures also leads to the urge to understand the laws which govern the effects produced by the artefacts we make. In addition to their functional properties, over time it becomes desirable to fine-tune how artefacts operate and are operated. A steam engine, for example, might be designed both for efficient production of mechanical force, and for safety in the case of pressure vessel failure. Once safety becomes a concern, then social regulation follows, with, for example, codification of the proper operation of a steam engine feeding back into its design (Feenberg, 1999: 86–8). Formalization of knowledge and technical control gradually extend into social management (Macintyre, 1981: 25–6). The natural philosopher, scientist, and engineer are joined by the bureaucrat and social scientist as descendants of the shaman and diviner, privileged mediators between past and future.

Rather than inaugurating a historically novel engagement with the future as such, what risk thinking actually does is to reinforce a particular horizon of expectation, against which the future is viewed not merely as abstract but as *empty*. This horizon was one product of the separation of neo-classical economics from political economy in the nineteenth century (Adam and Groves, 2007: 69–75). 'Empty' here does not mean void or meaningless; on the contrary, the empty future is conceived as rich with possibility and potential for increased control and progress. It projects a horizon of expectation in which possibilities are conceived of in relation to measures of maximisation or at least optimality: the not-yet becomes exclusively an object of mathematical calculation. The totality of the future, encompassing both society and nature, is viewed as potentially within the grasp of rational management.

As the complexity of this object of knowledge and action became more evident throughout the twentieth century, probability-based management, utilizing the tools of decision theory and neo-classical welfare economics became more prevalent. Action may be hedged about with uncertainty, but insofar as it is uncertain, it is viewed as a carrier of determinate probable hazards, or *risks*. The emergence of risk thinking as a set of institutional habits of mind is therefore the projection of an empty future in which what constitutes optimal performance is judged against the background of uncertainties that are to be assessed as risks. What is uncertain falls – in principle – within the reach of mathematical instruments.

Systemic control and top-down power are still valorized. To make it possible to live with uncertainty, it must be reduced and domesticated. The interpretation of uncertainty in terms of risk establishes a standard for rational decision making, based on integrated analysis models (IAMs) of quantifiable inputs and outputs. Within such systems, the application of risk–cost–benefit analysis (RCBA) therefore plays a key role in assessing the rationality of a given policy. The assessment of different options, by integrating natural-scientific and economic analyses of the potential costs and benefits of each one, aims at working out how to achieve a future condition of maximal or optimal utility, which is held to be normative for decision making.

RISK THINKING AND AGW: METHODS AND ASSUMPTIONS

In this section, I will examine some of the methods and value assumptions which shape how risk thinking is employed in relation to AGW. I will briefly examine two case studies where risk thinking has been of crucial significance, and where its shortcomings are equally crucial. The reductiveness and value-dependence of risk thinking will be analysed in more detail, leading directly onto the next section, in which I will examine how the dominance of risk thinking, and its all-encompassing empty future horizon, might be undermined.

One of the primary ways in which public policy has tried to come to terms with AGW is by attempting to put a price on CO_2 emissions, based on an estimate of how much damage a given amount of CO_2 (or other greenhouse gas) might do, once released into the atmosphere. The aim is to incorporate the CO_2 emissions (and thus the environmental and social impacts) associated with a policy into cost-benefit analyses of its overall net benefit or cost. When such an assessment of the costs of CO_2 is undertaken, the problems of novelty, simulated knowledge and invisible propagation become central, particularly as CO_2 may remain in the atmosphere for a century or more. Given that any estimation of possible harm cannot be based soundly on past experience, how could policy makers arrive at a 'correct' quantitative estimate for the damage done by one tonne of CO_2? What might 'correct' mean in this context?

The meaning of 'correctness' here is derived from criteria embedded within the mathematical relationships between economic variables, and specifically, from criteria of optimal efficiency. In general, the normatively best future would therefore be one in which no further improvement in efficiency of allocation could be produced, no matter how resources are allocated. In the case of AGW, one influential and much-debated way of arriving at the appropriate figure has been the 'social cost of carbon' (or SCC). An optimal carbon price to reflect the SCC would be one at which no further reduction in harm done by CO_2 emissions would be possible without starting to reduce aggregate utility, where utility is understood as the satisfaction of preferences derived by individuals from consumption. The SCC therefore represents an optimally rational 'willingness to pay' on the part of the present generation to avoid harm to future generations when the effects of AGW kick in, and expresses an attempt to understand, in terms of determinate, quantitative risks, the 'permissions, norms duties and obligations' implied by the real world uncertainties which surround AGW.

It is important to understand that arriving at an optimal SCC also has to take into account uncertainties which fall outside the level of determinate risk. Estimating the damage done by each additional tonne of CO_2 requires a further judgement, concerning which of the different climate scenarios that general climate models have produced may be more plausible. This has to be done on the basis of how the global political and social 'climate' is expected to influence CO_2 emissions reductions over the next few decades. Consequently, how policy-makers interpret and react to the various aspects of uncertainty surrounding AGW itself becomes a factor. A 'business as usual' scenario, for example, may result in a CO_2 concentration of 700 ppm or more (not counting 'surprises' such as additional ice-cap melting and the release of methyl hydrates, etc.), with the result that each single tonne of carbon being emitted now has to be assigned a correspondingly higher potential for doing damage, and so a higher cost. At a lower level of future stabilized emissions the amount of damage done per tonne and thus the SCC will be lower.

Nonetheless, although the social interpretation of uncertainty (often referred to as the 'socially contingent impacts' of AGW) becomes a factor, the horizon of expectations here is still one against which the future is understood primarily in terms of the fate of a finite set of quantitative variables. We will now examine two important examples of practical policy consequences of this manifestation of risk thinking, followed by analyses of how they domesticate uncertainty in ways which are likely to have serious ethical and political consequences.

The Stern Review was widely represented as a decisive argument for a programmatic and concerted global approach to reducing GHG emissions. Nicholas Stern's team produced an IAM analysis of the economic justification for reducing emissions sufficiently to put the world on a 'pathway' to a stabilized concentration of 550 ppm CO_2e (CO_2 equivalent), based on a carbon. The reason for making 550 ppm a normative guide was the balance of marginal costs and benefits associated with this option as opposed to other stabilization levels within the range 450–650 ppm, together with a comparison between the costs to global GDP of 'business as usual' versus the costs of mitigation measures to achieve 550 ppm (Stern, 2006: 333–4). Achieving such a goal would be possible, Stern argued, on the basis of an SCC of £19/tCO_2e set for the year 2000 (with increases factored in year on year past this date).

Now to our second example. In early 2009, the UK Government decided to support the expansion of Heathrow airport, based on what were seen as the net economic benefits of providing a third runway to cope with future passenger demand, even after the costs of environmental damage from additional CO_2 emissions had been taken into account (UK Government, 2009a). The contribution of CO_2 emissions from additional air traffic to AGW was treated, within the IAMs on which the decision was based, as a monetized cost which could be offset by expected actual and notional economic benefits (UK Government, 2009b). A crucial element within this decision was what the Government nominated as the 'shadow price of carbon' or SPC (Price, R., S. Thornton, et al., 2007: 3–4), a modified version of the SCC designed, it was claimed, to take greater account of political and social 'contingencies' which might distort otherwise linear and predictable economic tendencies. In setting an SPC, it is thus necessary to specify which of the possible stabilization trajectories the world is now on.

In both the Stern Review and the use of the SPC as part of the justification for the Heathrow decision, it is possible to trace systematic distortions that are encouraged by risk thinking, and which represent reductive interpretations of uncertainty which then have serious ethical and political results. Consider the Heathrow decision. The SPC (time and inflation adjusted) of £25/tCO_2e used in the integrated assessments on which the Heathrow decision relied reflected an assumption that Stern's recommendations had been adopted globally, and that adjustments to global carbon emissions were *already on course* to achieve a future concentration of 550 ppm. As Paul Ekins (2008) notes, the effect of such an assumption is, however, to *lower* the SPC which is adopted in the present as normative. This in turn effectively reduces the present costs of high-carbon policies, thus making it more likely that a level of 550 ppm will *in fact* become unachievable. Ekins notes that using a higher SPC of around £123/tC (£33/tCO_2e) – still a long way short of Stern's higher business-as-usual level figure of £160/tC (£44/tCO_2e) – would make the net economic benefit of Heathrow expansion entirely disappear.

What this indicates is that, to produce a strictly quantitative assessment of the risk-benefit balance of different futures, it is already necessary to ignore a huge range of uncertain factors. The result is a circular argument. The supposedly normative criterion of optimality in pricing derives its force from two prior judgements: (i) a descriptive assessment of the uncertainties which surround global political action, and (ii) a normative judgement (after Stern) that a 550 ppm scenario is to be preferred. Accepting the optimality of the SPC is only possible if one accepts the broader interpretation of uncertainty implied by (i) and (ii). As Paul Baer and Clive Spash (2008: 5–7) argue, there is little in the Stern Review to justify on purely economic grounds a goal of 550 ppm, and indeed Stern himself has more recently (and on precautionary grounds, normatively distinct from an expected optimization of benefits) opted for a significantly stricter 450–500 ppm target (Stern, 2008: 49). It is evident that both (i) and (ii) rest on less-than-transparent value judgements.

How the SPC documentation and the Stern Review deal with uncertainty is very similar. In both, there is a mix of explicit analysis of 'hard numbers' and sometimes barely acknowledged foundational subjective assumptions. In a condition of uncertainty characterized by novelty, simulated knowledge, and invisible causal propagation of pollutants, risk thinking tends to prematurely domesticate by excluding unquantifiable factors in order to arrive at a quantitative decision model. The passage from deleting or smoothing out unquantifiables (which with AGW might include political action, social effects like mass migration, and/or non-linear catastrophic geophysical events like ice shelf collapse) to a 'sensitized' RCBA analysis has been characterized by Baer and Spash as a reduction of 'strong' to 'weak' uncertainty (2008: 16). This passage from strong to weak uncertainty in IAMs has been criticized in other contexts (e.g. Smil, 2003: 167–78) as an addiction to specious accuracy. John Adams vividly characterizes the reductiveness and value-blindness of this approach as that of 'the drunk looking for his keys, not in the dark where he dropped them, but under the lamp post where there was light by which to see' (Adams, 2007: 10).

With this misplaced 'clarity' comes a focus within risk thinking on the short-term visibility of results that reduces other dimensions of uncertainty to invisibility, and in doing so violates certain ethical intuitions by incorporating unquestioned value-judgements. I will mention here three examples. First, the normative assumption that benefits should be maximized or optimized tends to be accompanied by two other descriptive assumptions – that individuals, as rational optimizers, tend to prefer to put off costs and obtain benefits sooner, and that future people will benefit from an inexorably increasing level of consumption. Consequently, RCBA analyses tend to incorporate a 'pure rate of time preference', so as to discount future impacts. Where the timeprint of our actions is inherently long term, however, and the invisible propagation of their effects is assured and potentially catastrophic, arguments based on these assumptions will tend to be circular and lead to perverse consequences. If we assume everyone will be better off in the future, then there is no incentive to act responsibly now (cf. Baer and Spash, 2008: 7–10). Secondly, the assumption that we should aim to maximize or optimize benefits tells us nothing about the acceptability of the specific impacts of this policy upon individual humans, groups of humans or non-humans. It simply assumes that impacts across the board can be added up with no regard to their socially contingent unequal distribution between, for example, the poor and the rich. Thirdly and finally, the assumption that, once certain losses have been selected as significant, they can then all be counted within a single metric, that of monetary value, is highly questionable. To presume this is to assume that the social meaning of some values can effectively be translated into language which is typically used to understand others. As Joseph Raz notes (1986: 350–1), such acts of translation are not ethically or politically innocent. For example, treating friendship as having a price violates what is meant by friendship. It is this intuition to which objections to, for example, willingness to pay surveys of environmental values bear witness – refusing to put a price on a good may indicate, rather than irrationality, a rational refusal to consider that a particular good or harm should be treated as commensurable with others in the way that monetary valuation suggests it can be (e.g. O'Neill, 1993: 119–21; Rappaport, 1996: 70).

SYSTEMS OF VALUES, SOCIAL PRACTICES AND OPENINGS FOR CHANGE

Having examined some of the biases that shape risk thinking's ongoing colonization of the uncertainties surrounding AGW, we now need to consider how these might be remedied by a change in our 'system of values'. As Jamieson notes, values are not purely subjective; they have 'force for a range of people who are similarly situated' (1992: 147). Risk thinking, as an assemblage of institutionalized social practices, situates people as subjects of (and at) risk. It encourages individuals to map their own singular futures onto a generalized, empty future. If values are thought of as the coordinates around which the way we experience the world coalesces, then to change systems of values implies a shift in subjectivity.

Such shifts are not easy to accomplish. It is therefore true that without giving an account of how *practice* can contribute to the reformation of subjectivity, a philosopher's call for 'new values' will prove sociologically impotent. In this section, I make some general observations about what directions a shift in values and priorities appropriate to AGW might take. I also contribute some suggestions about practice. In neither case, importantly, is radical surgery in the sense of something like a 'transvaluation of all values' called for. Instead, it is necessary to draw attention to aspects of subjectivity which imply different future horizons, ones in which, for example, a plurality of interdependent yet irreducible values are recognized, rather than opposing to actuality something which 'merely ought to be, and is not actual' (Hegel, 1991/1830: §6).

With respect to the other future horizons that are implicated within subjectivity, we can draw on sociology and philosophy together to understand the *lived* and *living* futures that Barbara Adam and I have argued also provide horizons of expectation for subjectivity (Adam and Groves, 2007: 123–5). Where these horizons of expectation take us is not towards a concern with an abstracted, generalized future goal, but towards *care* for a plurality of singular values. In other words, what may be important as a starting point is to attempt to understand ethical motivation by exploring how people are affected by the fates of cared-for values. This may enable us to appreciate how we are always already, as socially embedded individuals, related to the future in ways which cannot be directly translated into the discourses and values which sustain empty futures.

Individuals, as subjects of care, are related to the future through others, and through their active capacities for 'taking care' (for more details, see Groves, 2009). Care has been a major concern for both phenomenological and feminist thought, in different senses. What nevertheless links these traditions of thinking about care is the temporality – and future-orientedness – they both ascribe to it. On the phenomenological side, the concept's heritage links it with the scholastic idea of *conatus*, and views interests as projects whose meanings are not fixed but possess instead a narrative structure. Feminist analyses of care begin from different foundations, but also describe human subjectivity as bound up with a temporally extended concern with the world, only here the world – along with the identity of the individual – is viewed as irreducibly socially mediated. Ethical life is seen as not being possible without connectedness, conceived of as an emotionally conditioned, active capacity for dedicating oneself to particular values, such as another person, a way of life, a moral principle or a particular project goal.

In becoming an ethically capable subject, we come to discover the significance of our acts through our affective, imaginative and cognitive connections with other concrete individuals, including non-human ones: animals, landscapes, institutions and ideals. We come to see these others as ingredients of the particular narratives that make up our lives. Our experiences of others to whom we are committed are therefore bound up with individuals who are *constitutively* valuable, insofar as their own flourishing is a necessary condition of our own lives being worth living (O'Neill, 1993: 24).

The future of care is therefore not 'empty'. It is always already being filled out, teeming with actual and potential significance, with the latent, singular fates of our commitments (Rolston, 1981: 124). As such, it is the source of the call our commitments make upon us, calling on us to extend our sphere of action in space and time, rather than to curtail it (Gilligan, 1982: 38). Care requires that we sensitize ourselves to what is needed in order that cared-for values can flourish. It needs an understanding of networks of social and ecological interdependence, and, beginning with singular futures, it calls on us to extend our imagination, emotion and reason in considering what conditions will continue to be necessary to allow constitutive values to flourish in the future. In this way, care induces us to tell stories, to connect ourselves through narrative with future generations of humans and non-humans, and to imaginatively extend our sense of connection to encompass the point of view of others who we will never meet, yet whose evaluation of our lives will contribute to determining their ultimate worth (O'Neill, 1993: ch. 3). It might be said that our 'fate' is in the hands of such others, just as much as theirs is in ours.

I have argued elsewhere that care thus leads towards two normative principles in the face of irreducible uncertainties: 'act so as to preserve and enhance the potential of what we find valuable, where 'valuable' means of value both to the flourishing of specific individuals living now and to the flourishing of individuals generally now and in the future', and 'act so as to preserve and enhance the capacities of future generations to care as such' (Groves, 2009: 27–8). In the face of these injunctions, it will be necessary to re-evaluate precautionary approaches to risk. Invoking the precautionary principle as a kind of decision rule is not sufficient. Precaution – or perhaps humility – considered as a *virtue* which enables us to recognize that we cannot *control* the singular futures we care about is arguably more appropriate. Forms of action which avoid the temptation to seek systemic control are necessary to effective care, along with the recognition that worst case scenarios and irreversible transitions gain a new priority when singular values are under consideration.

Having surveyed one alternative basis for a 'system of values', we now turn to the question of what practices and strategies may be useful to displace risk thinking. Using care as a basis for ethical argument will force implicit ethical commitments to the surface. This change of emphasis away from maximization or optimization and the privileging of predictive modelling may open up various approaches. I list here three possibilities in order of increasing concreteness.

First, towards a more differentiated precautionary attitude to mitigating and adapting AGW. A more explicit discussion of potential worst case scenarios for different emissions trajectories is necessary in order to examine the justifiability of lower targets for mitigation (e.g. aiming to keep future temperature increases under 2°C). Meanwhile, higher targets (e.g. 4°C plus) should be considered in order to guide global and regional adaptation strategies (cf. Anderson and Bows, 2008: 3880). In both cases, an approach oriented more to avoid ecosystem and social harm is possible.

Secondly, we have to recognize the dimension of equity: dispositions to care are equally distributed but unequally developed, and such inequality implies also unequal capacities to individually and collectively realize active and worthwhile lives (Young, 1990: 37). Consequently, approaches to per-capita emissions reduction limits and adaptation measures must be linked to provision for development in the global South, as in for example the Greenhouse Development Rights framework (e.g. Baer, Fieldman et al., 2008).

Thirdly, mitigation, adaption and development strategies have to be linked to localized and regional narratives which explore what may happen in the future to concrete objects of care. The global nature of AGW should not distract from the fact that its effects will be experienced in specific places, by individuals and collectivities with singular biographies, histories and futures. This takes us beyond debates focused on higher level values such as equity and towards other questions, such as how to live gracefully and flourish amidst the uncertainties of AGW. Here, the work of artists Newton and Helen Harrison is instructive. Their *Greenhouse Britain* (2007) is built around scenarios concerning the effects of rising sea levels on the Mersey Estuary and the Lea Valley in the United Kingdom. By working over an extended period of time with local people, planners, scientists and policy-makers who live and work in these areas, the Harrisons produce near-term science fiction scenarios that exploit local knowledge of connectedness to imagine how communities will change their ways of living. Further, their work re-injects human agency into this process through dialogue and collaboration. The goal is both to enable people to give voice to fears and offer them the opportunity to retrieve concrete hope in the face of uncertainty.

CONCLUSIONS

To put care at the heart of our understanding of 'permissions and obligations' in the face of AGW acknowledges that an element of non-reciprocal responsibility for the flourishing of values is an inevitable component of being human. While it acknowledges the fragility of constitutive values in the face of vast uncertainties, it also recognizes we have to respond in ways that are sensitized to preserving interdependence. Rather than assuming the existence of a common horizon of expectation that leads to conclusions which often do violence to ethical intuitions and human relationships alike, it seeks to establish different horizons of expectation which seek to preserve humility in the face of uncertainty, while still extending concern to encompass dimensions of a worthwhile life which are overlooked by the technocratic tendencies of risk thinking. A previous generation of green activists enjoined us to 'think global, act local'; an ethics of global and intergenerational care requires us to extend our circle of concern and connection out from our space and our time, to encompass those who we will never meet but whose fates are already inextricably bound up with our own.

REFERENCES

Adam, B. (1995), *Timewatch: The Social Analysis of Time*. London: Polity Press.

Adam, B. and Groves, C. (2007), *Future Matters: Action, Knowledge, Ethics*. Leiden, Brill.

Adams, J. (2007), 'Risk Management: It's Not Rocket Science – It's Much More Complicated Than That'. *Public Risk Forum*, May, 9–11.

Anderson, K. and Bows, A. (2008), 'Reframing the Climate Change Challenge in Light of Post-2000 Emission Trends'. *Philosophical Transactions of the Royal Society A* 366, 3863–82.

Baer, P., Fieldman, G. et al. (2008), 'Greenhouse Development Rights: Towards an Equitable Framework for Global Climate Policy'. *Cambridge Review of International Affairs* 21 (4), 649–69.

Baer, P. and Spash, C. L. (2008), 'Cost-Benefit Analysis of Climate Change: Stern Revisited'. CSIRO Working Paper Series 2008–07. Available at: www.csiro.au/files/files/pkec.pdf.

Beck, U. (1992), *The Risk Society: Towards a New Modernity*. London: Sage Publications.

Brown, N., Rappert, B. and Webster, A. (eds) (2000), *Contested Futures: A Sociology of Prospective Techno-Science*. Aldershot: Ashgate.

de Tocqueville, A. (1994/1835), *Democracy in America*. London, New York: Everyman.

Edwards, P. (1995), *The Closed World: Computers and the Politics of Discourse in Cold War America*. Cambridge, MA: MIT Press.

Ekins, P. (2008), 'Path of Least Resistance'. *The Guardian*, 13 February.

Feenberg, A. (1999), *Questioning Technology*. London: Routledge.

Gaszo, A. (2009), 'Risk Governance of Nanotechnologies'. Conference paper presented at *Size Matters 2009: Facing the Ethical Challenges of Nanotechnology*, 17–18 June, Schloß Saarbrücken, Germany.

Giddens, A. (1990), *The Consequences of Modernity*. Cambridge: Polity Press.

—(1999), 'Risk and responsibility'. *Modern Law Review* 62 (1), 1–10.

Gilligan, C. (1982), *In a Different Voice*. Cambridge, MA: Harvard University Press.

Groves, C. (2009), 'Future Ethics: Risk, Care and Non-Reciprocal Responsibility'. *Journal of Global Ethics* 5 (1), 17–31.

Habermas, J. (1971), *Toward a Rational Society: Student Protest, Science and Politics*. London: Heinemann Educational.

Harrison, N. and Mayer Harrison, H. (2007), *Greenhouse Britain: Losing Ground, Gaining Wisdom*. Available at: http://greenhousebritain. greenmuseum.org/.

Harrison, S. (2008), 'Climate Change and Regional Security: Assessing the Scientific Uncertainties'. *Royal United Services Institute Journal* 153 (3), 88–91.

Hegel, G. W. F. (1991/1830), *Encyclopaedia Logic*. Indianapolis, IN: Hackett.

Jameson, F. (2005), *Archaeologies of the Future: The Desire Called Utopia and Other Science Fictions*. London: Verso Books.

Jamieson, D. (1992), 'Ethics, Public Policy and Global Warming'. *Science, Technology and Human Values* 17 (2), 139–53.

Johansen, B. (1995), 'Dating the Iroquois Confederacy'. *Akwesasne Notes New Series* 1 (3), 62–3.

Jonas, H. (1982), *The Phenomenon of Life*. Chicago and London: University of Chicago Press.

Kaiser, M. (1997), 'The Precautionary Principle and Its Implications for Science'. *Foundations of Science* 9, 201–5.

Koselleck, R. (2002), *The Practice of Conceptual History: Timing History, Spacing Concepts*. Stanford, CA: Stanford University Press.

Levitas, R. (1990), *The Concept of Utopia*. Hemel Hempstead: Philip Allan.

Macintyre, A. (1981), *After Virtue: A Study in Moral Theory*. London: Duckworth.

Nordmann, A. (2005), 'Noumenal Technology: Reflections on the Incredible Tininess of Nano'. *Techne* 8 (3), 3–23.

O'Neill, J. (1993), *Ecology, Policy and Politics*. London: Routledge.

Price, R., Thornton, S. et al. (2007), *The Social Cost of Carbon and the Shadow Price of Carbon: What They Are, and How to Use Them in Economic Appraisal in the UK*. London: DEFRA.

Rappaport, R. A. (1996), 'Risk and the Human Environment'. *Annals of the American Academy of Political and Social Science* 545, 64–74.

Raz, J. (1986), *The Morality of Freedom*. Oxford: Clarendon Press.

Rolston, H. (1981), 'The River of Life: Past, Present and Future', in *Responsibilities to Future Generations*, ed. E. Partridge. New York: Prometheus Books.

Rose, N. (1999), *The Powers of Freedom: Reframing Political Thought*. Cambridge: Cambridge University Press.

—(2001), 'The politics of life itself'. *Theory, Culture and Society* 18 (1), 1–30.

Shrader-Frechette, K. (1993), *Burying Uncertainty: Risk and the Case Against Geological Disposal of Nuclear Waste.* Berkeley, CA: University of California Press.

Smil, V. (2003), *Energy at the Crossroads.* Cambridge, MA: MIT Press.

Stern, N. (2006), *The Stern Review: The Economics of Climate Change.* London: HM Treasury.

—(2008), *Key Elements of a Global Deal on Climate Change.* London: LSE.

UK Government (2009a), *Adding Capacity at Heathrow: Decisions Following Consultation.* London: Department for Transport. Available at: www.dft.gov.uk/pgr/aviation/heathrowconsultations/heathrowdecision/ decisiondocument/decisiondoc.pdf.

—(2009b), *Adding Capacity at Heathrow Airport: Impact Assessment.* London: Department for Transport. Available at: www.dft.gov.uk/pgr/ aviation/heathrowconsultations/heathrowdecision/impactassessment/ ia.pdf.

Young, I. M. (1990), *Justice and the Politics of Difference.* Princeton, NJ: Princeton University Press.

PART III

ACTION/INACTION

CHAPTER SIX

BRINGING HOPE 'TO CRISIS'

CRISIS THINKING, ETHICAL ACTION AND SOCIAL CHANGE

SARAH S. AMSLER

INTRODUCTION

The spectre of crisis now casts an urgent but oddly bearable shadow on everyday life. It appears through documentaries on the science of climate change and video footage of melting ice; we manage it with recycling bins and reusable bags. The spectre of the economic crisis also permeates social consciousness via graphs of capitalist class decline that, while they feel like our own, remain weirdly disconnected from the human 'calamities of capitalism' (Lichtman, 2009: 20). And then there is the steady stream of notifications about more peripheral crises, all in need of urgent resolution: flashpoints in conflict situations, social welfare, migration, diplomacy and health. The erstwhile extraordinary experience of being in crisis punctuates everyday public discourse as something very ordinary indeed (Krznaric, 2008).[1]

And yet, many political activists and critical theorists still regard crisis as the basis for critique and as a precondition for radical social change – or at least a situation in which it might be made possible. These 'crisis thinkers', many of whom follow a line of thinking that stretches back to Hegel, claim that the experience of crisis is both an objective form of immanent critique and a subjective source of motivation for action.[2] For, it is argued, if people can *feel* the social contradictions and inequalities that are visible through rational analysis, they will be spontaneously motivated to act upon them. But what does it mean when they do not? Under what conditions do threats of ecological, economic or personal crisis *not* function as mobilizing forms of social critique? And when might crisis thinking shift from being a progressive politics of hope into a reactionary politics of fear?

Although the problem of climate change puts these questions into a difficult new context, and I will argue later even into crisis, they are not peculiar to our time or place. Philosophers, perplexed by any lack of critical moral consciousness in the face of insufferable experiences of alienation, exploitation and injustice, have long sought to identify the conditions that motivate emancipatory action. For some time, it was assumed that material, existential crisis was the one universal experience that could 'point to the contradictions of the present and . . . encourage the emergence of needs, patterns of interaction, and struggle which point the way towards a new society' (Benhabib, 1986: ix). However, by the early twentieth century and particularly in the work of Antonio Gramsci and the Frankfurt School theorists, it was clear that the systemic inequalities of capitalism 'no longer articulated themselves as social crisis' and that this was due 'not to economics alone, but transformations in culture as well' (Benhabib, 1986: 176). A new crisis emerged in crisis thinking: the crisis of the negation, suppression or incorporation of crisis itself.

This chapter departs from this point to consider whether and how crisis thinking contributes to practices of affirmative critique and transformative social action in late-capitalist societies. I argue that different deployments of crisis thinking have different 'affect–effects' and consequences for ethical and political practice.[3] Some work to mobilize political action through articulating a politics of fear, assuming that people take most responsibility for the future when they fear the alternatives. Other forms of crisis thinking work to heighten critical awareness by disrupting existential certainty, asserting an 'ethics of ambiguity' which assumes that the continuous production of uncertain futures is a fundamental part of the human condition (de Beauvoir, 2000). In this chapter, I hope to illustrate that the first deployment of crisis thinking can easily justify the closing down of political debate, discouraging radical experimentation and critique for the sake of resolving problems in a timely and decisive way. The second approach to crisis thinking, on the other hand, has greater potential to enable intellectual and political alterity in everyday life – but one that poses considerable challenges for our understandings of and responses to climate change.

I thus begin by considering how crisis thinking is deployed in political campaigns to change social attitudes and behaviours towards global climate change, as the frequent use of apocalyptic narratives in this context highlights the distinctions between these different types of crisis thinking. I focus in particular on the proposition that there could one day be a 'world without us' (Weisman, 2007) to explore the different kinds of critique and future imaginaries that this form of crisis thinking might engender. Finally, I consider how practices of 'disclosing critique' (Kompridis, 2006; Honneth, 2007) and 'bringing things to crisis' (Spivak, 1988, 1990) can help inform a critical pedagogy of crisis in everyday life.

THE 'CRISIS OF HOPE' AND ENVIRONMENTAL (IN)ACTION

There are two prominent narratives of crisis in contemporary environmental politics. One is rooted in fears of ecological catastrophe, and the other in a sort of anthropological pessimism that human beings lack the will or capacity to prevent it. The problem of global climate change is often articulated as an apocalyptic narrative of species self-destruction; a 'ticking time bomb' discourse of catastrophic ecological crisis which can – perhaps – only be averted through revolutionary cultural, political and economic change. James Speth, for example, writes that 'it is now an underestimation to say we are running out of time. For such crucial issues as climate change, deforestation and loss of biodiversity, we ran out of time quite a while ago' (2008: 19). The website for Al Gore's (2006) film *An Inconvenient Truth* asserts boldly that 'we have just ten years to avert a major catastrophe that could send our planet into a tail-spin of epic destruction'. And the UK Crisis Forum (2008) explains there is a 'high probability that unless we drastically change our global political and economic practice, the human species may not survive into the foreseeable future'.

Crisis is deployed here as an affective and cognitive call for revolutionary change. Interestingly, however, it is also situated against a concern that neoliberal society has become so radically dehumanizing that the forms of 'human nature' which would make such change possible are already suppressed.[4] For many critical theorists, this is an impasse to the development of an emancipatory politics; some even suggest that it constitutes a 'crisis of hope' (Binde, 2001; Bauman, 2004; Jameson, 2004; Browne, 2005; Smith, 2005; Kompridis, 2006: 245; Davis and Monk, 2007). The crisis of hope is twofold. For social theorists, it implies that systemic changes in economy, politics and culture are closing down spaces for radical freedom. In everyday life, however, it is experienced more symptomatically as a sense of individual powerlessness in the face of uncontrollable and often nebulous forces including climate change, irrational markets of global capital, spiritless regimes of new bureaucratic management and opaque processes of political decision-making that appear unresponsive to traditional forms of democratic opposition. It is argued that many people living in neoliberal societies now 'experience change as a symptom of our powerlessness rather than as the product of our own agency' (Kompridis, 2006: 247), or in other words, that the experience of history and world-making has become one of neither crisis nor purposeful direction, but rather one of disempowered 'drift' (Sennett, 1999).

The stripping of opportunities for social self-determination is of course not unique to neoliberal space and time. Powerlessness, loneliness and hopelessness have long been tragic realities for all but the privileged in every society. Now, however, it is the levelling of these experiences and the increasing sense of despair that anything can be done to alleviate them that is of particular concern. This new expression of social despair has a deep, ontological dimension, which presumes there is something peculiar about the cultural and affective organization of neoliberal societies that damages human feeling and imagination, muffles and distorts compassionate relationships, stunts capacities of self-reflection, and devalues future ethics. In other words, there is a concern that the totality of our prevailing social practices negates the human desire for both transcendence and connection. There is a suspicion that we may be losing or have lost, not only as Theodor Adorno once put it 'the capacity to imagine the totality as something entirely different' (quoted in Daniel and Moylan, 1997: vii), but in some cases the deeper desire to do so – and where reality seems really intractable, the will to even try.

It is important to understand that this is not just a generalized critique of neoliberalism, but one that follows a very particular form of theorizing as well. Critical theorists refer to such explanations as diagnoses of 'social pathology'; accounts of systematic 'misdevelopments' or crises in individual character and social structure which are believed to undermine the very foundations of ethical will formation and social change (Habermas, 1987; Honneth, 2007: 4). In certain situations – climate change being an obvious, but not the only example – these 'misdevelopments' are regarded as potentially lethal rather than simply as undesirable. This type of crisis thinking can be illustrated with a classical example that is sometimes evoked in contemporary climate change discourse: Erich Fromm's critique of the 'paralysis of criticism' in advanced industrial societies. In his writing on the topic of nuclear armament during the mid-twentieth century, Fromm communicated an acute sense of desperation about what he considered to be widespread political apathy towards the threat of nuclear violence. 'The unbelievable fact', he wrote, was that

> no serious effort is made to avert what looks like a final decree of fate. While in our private life nobody except a mad person would remain passive in the view of a threat to his total existence, those who are in charge of public affairs do practically nothing, and those who have entrusted their fate to them let them continue to do nothing. How is it possible that the strongest of all possible instincts, that for survival, seems to have ceased to motivate us? (Fromm, 1978: 19)

For Fromm, the 'peaceful production of the means of destruction' was an example of irrational economic and technological development, historical myopia and the arrogant complacency of the privileged and powerful; it was a social problem. The 'pathological' contradictions that made this into a *crisis*, however, were affective and ontological in nature: could radical social change be possible if people were not moved even by, as Fromm saw it, the actual threat of death?[5] If the experience of crisis is necessary to alert people to the wrongness of present conditions, what happens when it becomes effectively managed, contained, suppressed or eliminated? How can alternative futures be imagined if the future itself is not a matter of care and concern?

There are important parallels between Fromm's theory of the necessity of crisis and some contemporary discourses on environmental attitudes. Critical ecologists, policy-makers and environmental activists often criticize 'blasé attitudes' towards what they consider to be the self-evident crisis of climate change, and are demoralized by the lack of a spontaneous compulsion towards collective response.[6] For example, Joel Kovel has argued that

> irresistible [economic] growth, and the evident fact that this growth destabilizes and breaks down the natural ground necessary for human existence, means . . . that we are doomed under the present social order, and that we had better change it as soon as possible if we are to survive. One wants to scream out this brutal and plain truth, which should be on the masthead of every newspaper . . . but it is nothing of the kind. Yes, endless attention is paid to the crisis, a great deal of it useful, some of it trivial, and some plainly harmful. But where is the serious, systemic reflection of the brutal truth – that humanity is in the hands of a suicidal regime, which scarcely anyone thinks is either possible or desirable to fundamentally change? (Kovel, 2002: 5)

Kovel's consciousness of crisis is acute, but not shared or acted upon – at least at the same intensity – by anything resembling a critical mass. The interpretive gap between what he acknowledges to be an 'obdurate set of facts' about discrete environmental events, on the one hand, and the subjective judgement that would enable an individual to interpret them as constituting a holistic, life-threatening ecological crisis, on the other, gives rise to a crisis of hope in the human capacity for change itself. 'Something', concludes Kovel, must have 'gone terribly wrong in the relation between humanity and nature' for this type of alienation to be possible (2002: 12).

He is not alone in drawing this conclusion. It has long been argued that the reconstruction of human–nature relationships can only be accomplished 'in the context of . . . the rise of a new consciousness [. . .] major cultural change and a reorientation of what society values and prizes most highly' (Speth, 2008: 199). In the late 1970s, philosopher Hans Jonas even argued that the rise of the technological society had already altered the nature of human action so considerably that a complete reworking of human ethics was required (Jonas, 1984). However, when the objective failures of environmental and human degradation are combined with a fear that we lack an adequate ethos for addressing them, the rhetoric of crisis can become a 'discourse of catastrophe' that produces a paralyzing sense of imminent peril. Some critics have thus argued that instead of being a catalyst for mobilization, this kind of crisis thinking is 'in danger of tipping society into a negative, depressive and reactionary trajectory' (Hulme, 2006).

For social scientists and activists alike, this raises a number of important questions. Can crisis be a catalyst for psychological and cultural revolutions? Are they within the human remit to *create*, or must they emerge through the convergence of historical forces? What practices or conditions, what experiences or sensibilities, might 'tip' moral and political consciousness from despair to hope, from imaginaries of 'presents' and 'ends' to visions of alternative futures, and from the depression of powerlessness to the hope of collective empowerment? Can crisis thinking actually be a form of affirmative critique; one that is intimately connected with, but not reducible to, human action?

CRISIS THINKING AS 'INVOLUNTARY ENLIGHTENMENT'

One answer to these questions is that we are only effectively mobilized by the corporeal experience of catastrophe itself. According to Ulrich Beck, phenomena such as extreme weather events, mass extinctions, economic collapse and acts of extreme violence can function as moments of 'involuntary enlightenment', which, if they fail to destroy, are 'wake-up calls' that compel the reordering of priorities and beliefs (Beck, 2006; Speth, 2008: 211). Indeed, the possibility that we can *imagine* what it *would* be like to *have* experienced something catastrophic and thus be motivated to try to alter this course of coming events seems to be what many narratives of ecological crisis seek to evoke.[7] This is one version of the theory that crisis is most transformative when it is materially 'lived', or when, in the words

of critical theorist Jürgen Habermas, people 'experience structural alterations as critical for continued existence and feel
their social identity threatened' (cited in Benhabib, 1986: 232).

Experiences of 'involuntary enlightenment' are certainly pedagogical, insofar as they shape subjectivities. But for those who
seek to create a critical consciousness of crisis – we might even
say to cultivate a habit of attuning oneself to latent tendencies of
crisis in everyday life – this exploitation of crisis to motivate
unreflective action is precisely the problem. It is an unlikely road
to political hope, for instead of exposing the indeterminacy
of futures this approach recommends a sort of materialist fatalism in which catastrophic phenomena are regarded as naturally
occurring, with predictable and uniform effects on an undiffer-
entiated mass of subjects. There is no room here for a theory
of political time, of a temporality which assumes the openness
of the future, reconstruction of the past or power of human and
nonhuman intervention to shape the world (Brown, 2005).

Relying on 'involuntary enlightenment' to mobilize transformative action more significantly reduces people to immanent,
one-dimensional beings who are ultimately motivated either by
extreme and proximal suffering, or by the need to protect material and corporeal self-interest. While this may not be an entirely
post-human imaginary, it is certainly one that abandons hope in
the possibility of human agency. And in the context of political
movements to transform environmental attitudes and actions,
the question is not how to capitalize most effectively on others'
catastrophic experiences, but how to imagine them *in absentia*
and cultivate new ways of *being in* crisis in everyday life.

CRISIS THINKING AS THEORETICAL 'TRANSLATION'

The problem of educating critical sensibility has thus been a
longstanding preoccupation for political and cultural activists,
particularly those who believe that transformations of consciousness can be accomplished by 'translating' the objective,
structural crises of capitalist societies into subjective feelings
of alienation, domination and exploitation. In more practical
terms, many anti-capitalist and environmental struggles hinge
on the belief that while the system is ultimately untenable in the
long term, the worst forms of suffering can be averted if people
learn to interpret their personal problems as consequences of

structural injustice. In the critical philosophies that often inform these activities, there is a deep hope in the transformative power of crisis which is grounded in, as Simon Clarke explains it, an 'emphasis on the *necessity* of crisis as an essential and ineradicable feature of the capitalist mode of production, that defines the objective limits of capitalism and the necessity of socialism' (1994: 7).

However, this theory is itself prone to continual crisis, for unless we *feel* the effects of social and economic contradictions we are unlikely to experience them as 'crises', and unless we experience crisis we will remain unmoved to address the structural contradictions of our lives. It has even been argued that 'in periods that are not periods of crisis, or in individuals bent upon avoiding crisis at all cost, there can be all kinds of approaches to [the social], but there can be no [insurgency]' (de Man cited in Spivak, 1988: 197). If there is a disjuncture between 'systemic' crises and 'lived' experiences – as I argue is almost inevitable for complex problems like climate change and capitalism – energy is focused on finding ways to mediate the 'contradictions, malfunctioning and disturbances of social systems' with the 'experienced needs, demands, feelings and dissatisfactions that the social structure generates in individuals', on the other (Benhabib, 1986: 12). This, in the classical tradition of critical theory, is the role of critique.[8]

However, this form of crisis theory has spawned a number of paralyzing tautologies in which a dysfunctional system produces both its own contradictions *and* its own anti-venom against their poisonous effects. From Werner Sombart's inquiry into 'why there was no socialism in the United States' (1906/1976) to Marcuse's 'society without opposition' (1964) and the disappointments of the European Left in the 1970s (Clarke, 1994: 8), theoretical faith in the transformative potential of crisis is often compromised by the realization that this promise can be lost in translation.

CRISIS THINKING AS COUNTER-HEGEMONY

The practice of translating systemic crises into lived ones, of helping people 'read the world' through their own experiences, has thus become regarded as something of a political art. The creation of compelling crisis narratives is in fact often considered a fundamental element of effective political mobilization; the concern being to

> mobiliz[e] perceptions of the crisis that will find and construct resonance with individuals' fragmented experiences and individuated exposure to the symptoms of state and economic failure, thereby unifying them, giving them political inflection and relating them to a vision of the alternative. (Hay, 1995: 74)

The production of crisis narratives in popular culture can therefore be viewed as a way to frame problems, ideological resolutions and instructions for action in order to mobilize and coordinate mass levels of social activity (Hay, 1999: 333). It is consciousness-raising, but of an ideological sort that does not require – and indeed, may obscure – a deep understanding of existing social conditions. In fact, within this framework, attempts to produce a *sense* of crisis may be disarticulated from existing material conditions, and any set of failures and contradictions can become a 'context providing the material conditions capable of sustaining a variety of conflicting constructions or "narratives" of crisis' (Hay, 1995: 64, 77). The interpretation and explanation of climate change through geological, theological, Gaia, indigenous, technological, teleological and cyclical narratives is a particularly illustrative example of this.[9] Popularizing such crisis narratives, therefore, is a way to evoke emotive political responses from a mass of individuals and 'topple the counter-stories in one's culture' that contribute to political division, fragmentation and resignation (Garner in Speth, 2008: 213).[10] Crisis thinking here functions less as a practice of critique and more as a discursive strategy in a cultural war of position (Gramsci, 1988). As Gramsci argued, 'crisis forms the context within which the ideological struggle to impose a new trajectory (a transformatory unity) on the structures of the state takes place' (cited in Hay, 1995: 74).

However, this counter-hegemonic form of crisis theory bears uncomfortable resemblance to various expressions of the populist politics of fear. For example, it was the creation of 'a coherent and simple discourse of crisis capable of finding and constructing resonance with individuals' experiences . . . of the economic and political context' – not some sort of radical transformation of social consciousness – which empowered the British New Right during the late 1980s (1995: 65). More recently, it has been argued that 'the success of right-wing governments and sentiments lies in reworking hope in a negative form', or in other words, in their capacity to articulate narratives of crisis which evoke fear (Zournazi, 2002: 15; see also Ahmed, 2004; Davis and Bertrand Monk, 2007). This is possible because crisis is affectively double-edged: radical rupture may be both liberating and terrifying at the same time. Crisis narratives can be specifically formulated to exploit the desire for certainty that emerges from experiences of ambiguity and insecurity, reducing the experience of crisis to a rhetorical catalyst for social reaction by posing what Henry Giroux has called the 'false choice between being safe or being free' (2005: 3).

This sort of crisis thinking may be particularly likely in the context of climate change, where the balance of emotion is often tipped far more in the direction of powerlessness or uncertainty than towards agency and confidence. According to Colin Hay, for example, a counter-hegemonic crisis narrative is most effective under three conditions: first, that it concerns something people assume can be acted upon; second, that they are in a position to act upon it; and third, that the conceptual construction of crisis resonates somehow with their lived experiences (1995: 64). In the case of climate change, instead of the threat of conceivable suffering, we encounter – often from incongruous situations of comfort and security and in highly mediated ways – the unfathomable possibility of collective nonexistence, wrought by a confluence of human and non-human factors, unfolding somewhere out of our control, and happening in an unspecified future. This is a different species of 'crisis' altogether: not individualized, material and lived, but inter-subjective, ethical and imagined. 'Translating' such structural phenomena into personal concerns becomes problematic; it requires a rethinking of crisis thinking altogether.

The 'involuntary enlightenment', 'translation' and 'counter-hegemony' models of crisis thinking illustrate how the experience of crisis has been variously theorized as a catalyst for action by critical theorists and political activists alike (Spivak, 1990a; Kompridis, 2006; Honneth, 2007). However, these examples also demonstrate that there is nothing intrinsically transformative or ethical about crisis thinking; that like pure 'thought', pure 'action' is not a value *sui generis*. And while activist versions of crisis thinking are often presented as being the most socially progressive – 'doing nothing' is precisely the problem – we must also ask whether these practices sometimes have the counterintuitive effect of closing down spaces of possibility by fetishizing action and devaluing the practices of reflection, analysis and imagination that can emerge in periods of critical ambiguity. Beyond simply asking *whether* crisis narratives 'influence' people's attitudes and actions, therefore, we must ask what *kinds* of ideas and actions are enabled by different forms of crisis thinking.

WHAT'S IN A CRISIS?

But is it possible to distinguish between these different forms of crisis thinking in normative terms? The answer to this question does not lie in the definition of the term 'crisis' itself, which has been characterized as 'illusive, vague, imprecise, malleable, open-ended and generally unspecified' (Hay, 1996: 421). This ambiguity is a good thing; it means we can make crisis mean something other than what it often seems to be. In everyday talk, crises are often understood as autopoietic moments of 'intense difficulty or danger' or times 'when a difficult or important decision must be made'. This is particularly clear in medical contexts, where a crisis is 'the turning point of a disease when an important change takes place, indicating recovery or death' (OED, 2005). The objectivism and activism in these definitions is striking, particularly as the term *crisis* was originally associated, through its Greek root *krisis*, with cultural practices of critique, judgement and deliberation (Benhabib, 1986; Brown, 2005; Kompridis, 2006). In illness, for example, a person's condition was not considered 'critical' simply because it could go either way, but because the direction of any change depended upon the impact of judicious human intervention (Brown, 2005: 6). Crisis was not a matter of fate, but the name for a moment at which those involved in a situation come to understand they cannot go on as they have before.

The medical definition of crisis is not wholly appropriate for theorizing social experience; there are few instances in which a form of social life could be presumed to 'live' or 'die' in totality. Its importance is rather that it defines crisis phenomenologically, referring less to an objective moment of decision into which we are thrown and more to a subjective realization that we must make new sense of our circumstances and possibilities. In this view, dangers, difficulties, decisions and changes are not objectively existing things that we can simply recognize through observation and then make rational judgements about. Our distinctions between 'intense' and 'relaxed' moments, or 'difficult' and 'easy' decisions are themselves the results of processes of critical, inter-subjective judgement. They are narrated through cultural explanations, mediated through emotional rules, and situated within a complex frame of social, political and psychological conditions. Our experience of emotions of joy and pain 'involves the attribution of meaning through experience' (Ahmed, 2004: 23), and even our 'intentional action is linguistically mediated' through a web of cultural meaning (Benhabib, 1986: 135). Crisis narratives do not simply allow us to *identify* or *communicate* structural crises, but to *define* complex social situations as critical moments of possibility, and to articulate the necessity of alternatives within a normative critique of existing conditions. They are ways of explaining 'how we go on' once we decide that we cannot go on as before (Benhabib, 1986; Spivak, 1988; Hay, 1995; Kompridis, 2006: 248; Lear, 2006). And, in the case of climate change, where the establishment of thresholds and tipping points is particularly political, they are also ways of *asserting* that we cannot.

Crisis thinking must therefore be understood as a cultural and emotional practice as well as a subjective experience or objective condition. A critical consciousness of crisis can create an intensified engagement with space and time in which we feel particularly responsible for reflecting critically on how we reproduce, reject or transform the cultural practices that shape our world. When crisis can be experienced in this way, it provides openings for critique, for a reflective practice that not only allows us to consider 'the proportion of continuity and discontinuity in the forms of life we pass on', but that also frames this reflection as an ethical and political responsibility (Habermas cited in Kompridis, 2006: 11). Kompridis thus makes a clear distinction between thinking of crisis as a moment of decision that resolves a conflict and seeing it as a moment of decentring which produces or discloses one. On the one hand, we may read crisis as an urgent call to decisive action; a moment of truth in which we fatefully intervene (or not) to alter the course of history. On the other hand, we can understand crisis as a space of reflexive self-critique in situations where 'you feel that your presuppositions of an enterprise are disproved by the enterprise itself' (Spivak, 1990b).[11] In this latter view, the political value of a crisis experience is not that it allows us to impose order onto uncertainty by expediently cutting out the elements that create contradiction. The value is that it brings these elements to the centre of consciousness, making it necessary for us to question the rules of order themselves, and the limitations and possibilities of our own agency, according to these alternative logics.

The transformative potential of crisis in this approach emerges from the experience of being disrupted or 'decentred' in ways we neither choose nor control; they are unpredictable, spontaneous and surprising. Feeling out of place, uncomfortable, unrecognizable, regarded as a threat to sacred normalities – or as Nietzsche once wrote, the 'bad conscience' of one's own time and society (cited in Kompridis, 2006: 5) – can provoke a state of heightened reflexivity in which we realize that our bodies, truths and ways of being do not fit the contours of a dominant reality (Ahmed, 2004: 152). It exposes, in Kompridis' terms, 'breaks and punctuations' in everyday life that 'open up spaces for reflection and critique, and that give meaning and shape to everyday life' (Kompridis, 2006: 114). The experience of crisis is thus ultimately a moment in which possibility is made possible, 'when the "not yet" impresses upon us in the present, such that we must act, politically, to make it our future' (Ahmed, 2004: 184). However, contrary to the 'translation' and 'counter-hegemonic' theories of crisis, this experience cannot be deliberately produced *for* oneself or others; 'discomfort is not simply a choice or decision . . . but an effect of bodies [or ideas and practices] inhabiting spaces that do not take or "extend" their shape' (Ahmed, 2004: 152, my words in brackets). This being-outsideness, which is a condition of crisis experience, cannot be communicated linguistically from one person to another through rational argumentation. Rather, it must be disclosed through encounters with radically disruptive realities and imaginations that expose our own as partial and situated.

But given that people deal with the experience of crisis in different ways, often by seeking to avoid or abort it, to what extent can crisis thinking be offered as an 'inducement to thought' in practice? (Spivak, 1988: 197; Kompridis, 2006: 3). Within critical theory, there is sometimes an implicit suggestion that it should be possible to live in contradiction to everything and everyone, and to make one's own 'consciousness of crisis' into a moral virtue. But individual pre-orientations to crisis are as contingent as the experience of crisis itself. Crisis may be experienced as fear or hope, and even the ostensibly radical position of 'productive unease' (Spivak, 1990a) is not necessarily affirmative in a psychological sense. Ulrich Beck (2006) has pointed out that in risky situations people do often engage in transformative action, but they also enter into states of denial or withdraw altogether. So what are the affective and ethical conditions of bringing things to productive crisis in the first place? What makes it possible for a person to experience situations of ambiguity, insecurity and uncertainty as spaces where they can engage in difficult processes of self-transformation and world-making? Are such situations *necessarily* transformative, and – thinking particularly about the nature and scale of climate change – do individuals or collectivities always have the capacity to influence their trajectories? And is it possible for us to *cultivate* such a sensibility, rather than either seeking to impose it or abandoning the project to individualized choice and experience?

CRISIS THINKING AS CRITICAL PEDAGOGY

It is possible to argue, of course, that we are continually cultivating our political and ethical sensibilities, our ideas and beliefs and relationships, in one direction or another. In other words, life is always – already pedagogical: even non-action teaches us something about our relationship to the world, and our educational experiences implicate us in both hegemony and resistance (Giroux, 2000). The question is perhaps thus not whether we can or should try to cultivate a more critical sensibility of crisis, but what this might mean in practice.

We have already seen that crisis theory has well-developed pedagogical arms. In socialist and environmentalist politics, theories of crisis offer a framework for translating systemic crises (such as global climate change and/or capitalist injustice) into lived experiences, in order to instruct people in how they can most effectively transform or create the circumstances in which they live. There are many versions of this, from the instrumental manipulation of crisis narratives as studied by Colin Hay (1996, 1999) to the establishment of communities aimed at creating alternative environments rather than seeking to simply capitalize on the emotional volition of crisis experience (see, for example, Himmelweit, 2009, on the new Transition Towns). In one sense, however, these disparate engagements with crisis can be considered part of what Hegel once referred to as an 'ancient vision of moral education, according to which political activity was the cultivation and education of virtuous human characteristics' (cited in Benhabib, 1986: 26). Although Hegel's philosophy of education is beyond the scope of this chapter, it is this faith in the pedagogical role of crisis that matters here. As Allen Wood has pointed out, Hegel conceived of *Bildung* as a 'process of liberation achieved only by means of initial frustration, struggle and an altered conception of oneself' (1998: 304). This belief, which is itself a specified expression of crisis thinking, filters through different traditions of critical education. Early American pragmatists, for example, argued that learning is only accomplished through cognitive crisis and struggle (for an interesting look at how this was applied to educational practice, see Weeks 1914). Paulo Freire's (1970) revolutionary popular education relied heavily on the value of collectively struggling through the cognitive and ultimately social transformation of 'limit situations'. More recently, work in 'border pedagogy' and 'liminal education' have re-asserted the importance of what we might call crisis experience as site of transformative learning (Giroux, 2005; Fassbinder, 2006).

From these pedagogical perspectives, crisis provides a space for being able to learn and for alterity as much as it creates a need for particular ideas and acts. The transformative power that is often ascribed to crisis is here rooted in the political sensibilities that the experience is assumed to generate or necessitate. Openness to the future. A critical relation to time. Awareness of material limitations and possibilities. Sensitivity to the contraction and expansion of possibility. Recognition of one's being in the world, and of being with and for others. Empathy. Existential responsibility. Tolerance of ambiguity. Hope. If crisis has a role in mobilizing political consciousness, therefore, the problem is not whether we can evoke extraordinary crisis experiences, but whether we can learn to experience crisis in this way in our everyday lives, and to create environments in which this might be possible.

It is here that Kompridis' theory of crisis offers some practical direction. For while he defines crisis as an 'extraordinary' experience in philosophical terms, he also sees it as ubiquitous in everyday life. Working from the argument that crisis is 'normal' in late-capitalist societies, he suggests that we must therefore 'account for the degree to which modern individuals are saddled by the obligation to criticise *and* innovate if they are to ensure the continuity and renewal of their cultural traditions' (2006: 30). Crisis need not only refer to an extraordinarily difficult moment of decision or to 'life-and-death' in the literal or even rhetorical sense. It can also name experience of needing to make decisions about how to imagine and act towards uncertain and undetermined futures. Being-in-crisis, for Kompridis, is thus an *ethical* and *political* condition rather than an existential act; a practice of framing experience in ways that enable us to more consciously reproduce, reject or transform the cultural practices that shape our world (Kompridis, 2006: 30). It is a pedagogical activity, an 'inducement to thought' through which we may explore, reflect on and create new ways of being.

The emphasis on learning is significant in situations where social change seems so urgently overdue and unlikely that thinking, particularly open-ended processes of reflection, is dismissed as inefficient, irresponsible, or – in the words of Wendy Brown – 'untimely' (2005). Theodor Adorno once argued that in situations where the possibility of effecting radical change is very circumscribed or uncertain – and climate change may be an example *par excellence* – it is possible that 'one clings to action because of the impossibility of action' (1991: 199). In other words, action becomes valuable in and of itself simply because it keeps open the possibility of future action. I disagree with Adorno that such action is therefore illusory, an example of 'misguided spontaneity' or self-serving 'pseudo-action'. But even this brash and oversimplified critique of activism makes the important point that 'repressive intolerance toward a thought not immediately accompanied by instructions for action is founded in fear' (Adorno, 1991: 200). We need not conclude from this that urgent problems of climate change should be framed in 'sweet and patient' tones, or that 'thinking them through' is enough (Moser and Dilly, 2004: 37). But nor must we conclude that their urgency means theorizing them cannot also be a kind of political action, or that people *must* experience them *as* a crisis in order to engage. For, following Adorno, 'when the doors are barricaded, it is doubly important that thought not be interrupted' (1991: 200).

The association of crisis with critical thought as well as critical action recommends a different form of crisis thinking and definition of activism, one that emphasizes the radical possibilities of *being in* crisis as well as *responding to* it, and that places the radical transformation of self, others and environments at the centre of this experience. By seeking new ways to go on where we cannot as before, we remake ourselves; for '"problem solving" fully involves and affects not only our rationality but also our sensibility, our subjectivity' (Kompridis, 2006: 174). This notion of problem solving is pedagogical rather than technocratic; focused less intently on when we will solve the problems of climate change and more on attuning ourselves to the new understandings and possibilities that might emerge in the struggles – perhaps even the unsuccessful ones – to do so. In other words, 'as a reflective process of self-clarification, getting ourselves "right" involves a learning process that demands a complex cognitive and affective engagement with our forms of life and cultural traditions' (Kompridis, 2006: 8).

This shifts the pedagogical orientation of crisis thinking from a didactic model of learning in which people are instructed in the dangers of a particular crisis and the methods of its appropriate resolution, towards a dialogical model in which it is 'brought to crisis' in the everyday (Spivak, 1988, 1990b). The traditional aim of 'mediating' between lived and structural crisis presumes that people must learn to 'feel' functional contradictions or 'rationalize' their experiences of emotional disruption. Bringing something to crisis, on the other hand, evokes discomfort not in order to change *what* people think, but rather *how*; it is a 'calculated attempt to change the preconditions under which a society conducts evaluative discourse on the ends of common action' (Kompridis, 2006: 261; Habermas in Honneth, 2007: 58). In addition to trying to 'make climate change hot', for example, there must also be ways of talking about whether we care if it is or not, and why (Moser and Dilly, 2004). These projects may be neither one and the same, nor comparable in political import-ance. This form of crisis thinking disrupts the dichotomous view of systemic and lived crises: they are not separate kinds of crisis but different modes of knowing the social world (Benhabib, 1986: 123).

The value of this kind of crisis thinking lies in the fact that it requires both a radical openness to ambiguity and a critical affection for messiness, awkwardness and contradiction in every-day life. However, it is precisely this quality that brings climate change and critical philosophy into crisis with one another. Can 'untimely critique' be justified even in the face of environmental catastrophe; is it ethically responsible to experience climate change as *that* sort of crisis? In a world that seems to celebrate both Marcuse's nightmare of a 'society without opposition' and the populist politics of fear, should we be cultivating a kind of crisis thinking that privileges critical reflection as much as rapid response? I argue that we should. In her book *Edgework*, Wendy Brown (2005) makes a compelling argument that the closing down of crisis through reformist problem-solving, supposedly for the greater good, often works to mask deeper injustices and contradictions. As she argues, 'critical theory is essential in dark times not for the sake of sustaining utopian hopes, making flam-boyant interventions, or staging irreverent protests, but rather to contest the very senses of time invoked to declare critique untimely' (2005: 4).

The challenge for critical theorists and political activists alike is that crisis narratives of climate change – like the nuclear threat before it, and on a lesser scale like the spectre of global terrorism – can be easily deployed to justify this sort of closing down. In this chapter, I have argued that creating simplistic narratives of complex problems that aim to mobilize a mass of atomized individuals through either rational argumentation or emotional panic are neither straightforwardly effective nor transformative. I have also argued that, in addition to theories of crisis which place faith in the possibility that fear, the personalization of abstract forces or hegemonic power will first evoke and then resolve the painful disruptions of crisis experience, there is an alternative theory of crisis that celebrates them as spaces of freedom. The political hope of crisis thinking need not lie only in the power of crisis experience to mobilize transformative action; indeed, this is to hope for too much and too little all at once. The hope of crisis thinking may rather lie in the more humble possibility that it disrupts the flow of historical time and consciousness enough to make space for criticism, encounter and alternative imaginaries. These imaginaries, of course, cannot be ours to determine. They may be fearful or hopeful, enervating or energizing. The critical pedagogy of crisis, therefore, cannot simply be a matter of learning to recognize crises in everyday life or to extrapolate them in more abstract terms. Rather, it is a matter of creating environments where we can cultivate an ethics of ambiguity that will enable us to engage with experiences of crisis in more critical ways.

NOTES

1 For more on the concept of the 'extraordinary ordinary', see Kompridis (2006).

2 Proponents include Theodor Adorno, Hannah Arendt, Seyla Benhabib, Ernst Bloch, Martin Heidegger, Immanuel Kant, Reinhart Koslleck, Axel Honneth, and Nikolas Kompridis –although none would necessarily categorize themselves as 'crisis thinkers' (Kompridis, 2006: 27, 64). The discussion of critical philosophy as 'crisis thinking' is beyond the scope of this chapter; Kompridis traces it to Hegel, for whom the need for transformative thought and action emerges from 'the consciousness of "diremption", of division or breakdown (*Entzweiung*), that is, the consciousness of crisis' (Kompridis, 2006: 18, also p. 275). Although Hegel did not theorize the relationship between crisis experience, thought and action in the ways discussed here, his belief that such experiences necessitate the development of a philosophy that can envisage the ultimate reunification of dialectically conflicting tendencies has provided fertile ground for others to theorize the role of crisis and crisis thinking. Benhabib, for example, has argued that 'whereas for Hegel the purpose of critique is to further the integration of the autonomous individual into an ethical community, Marx views critique as crisis theory, the main function of which is to point to the contradictions of the present and to encourage the emergence of needs, patterns of

interaction, and struggle which point the way toward a new society' (1986: ix).

3 The term 'affect–effect' is borrowed from Jane Bennett, who uses it to explain how feelings and sensory experiences can work to *effect* the world, and to explore how psychological, material and social conditions shape transgressive experiences as either enchanting or scary (Bennett, 2001: 30).

4 'Neoliberalism' is a highly contested and flexible concept (Nonini, 2008). Beyond naming a certain ideal-type of 'post-Fordist, "disorganized", transnational' capitalism (Fraser, 2009: 98), it also evokes the decline of organized collective action, the stripping away of basic social security, the rise of new-right politics and cultures, the de-democratization of the public sphere (Gindin and Pantich, 2000; Harvey, 2000), the marketization of social institutions such as education, science and medicine (Bauman, 2004: 65–5; Giroux, 2004), the ascendance of bureaucratic forms of power which minimize public deliberation and debate (Fromm, 1998; Laclau and Mouffe, 1976), and the delegitimization of utopianism as a cultural practice (Jameson, 2004, 2005).

5 For further comparison of the 'motivational crises' of the Cold War and contemporary climate change, see Speth (2008: 17–18). The comparison suggests that the failure of apocalyptic discourses, many of which 'appear to do little to bring about a sense of moral transformation or re-awakening', is not a recent phenomenon (Skrimshire, 2008). This raises questions less about why the impact of apocalyptic and utopian imaginaries has declined, and more about the conditions under which they become meaningful in the first place.

6 The 'blasé attitude' is a concept used by Georg Simmel to characterize a condition of alienation produced through affective and sensory overstimulation and/or by the commodification of things. 'Whereas the cynic', he argued, 'is still moved to a reaction by the sphere of value, even if in the perverse sense that he considers the downward movement of values part of the attraction of life, the blasé person – although the concept of such a person is rarely fully realized – has completely lost the feeling for value differences. He experiences all things as being of an equally dull and grey hue, as not worth getting excited about, particularly where the will is concerned. The decisive moment here – and one that is denied to the blasé – is not the devaluation of things as such, but indifference to their specific qualities from which the whole liveliness of feeling and volition originates' (Simmel, 1982: 256).

7 This sort of anticipatory consciousness is framed in the future anterior tense; a looking-back-from-the-future-in-the-present. Both Bloch's (1995) and Lacan's (1981) work are useful for understanding the political role of future-anterior-tense narration.

8 As Benhabib argues, 'social critique must show crises not only to be objectively necessary but experientially relevant as well. In the final analysis, it is the success of the theory in translating the

functional language of crisis into the experiential language of suffering, humiliation, oppression, struggle and resistance, which bestows upon it the name of "critical theory"' (1986: 142).
9 Many thanks to Stefan Skrimshire for this observation.
10 From the perspective of William Connolly's recent work on 'body/ brain processes', this can also be understood as a 'technology of collective mobilization' that works on non-conscious levels of experience (2006: 74). While intriguing, the development of this idea is beyond the scope of this chapter.
11 Kompridis offers an insightful illustration of how these two interpretations overlap in the Heideggerian concept of 'resoluteness' (*Entschlossenheit*), which is generally translated as 'decisiveness'. However, it can actually be interpreted in two ways. If the emphasis is on the first part of the word (*Entscheidung*) it translates into 'decision'; the sort of decision in which one *un*closes a sword from a sheath in a moment of swift and decisive action. If the second half of the word is emphasized, however, (*Erschlossenheit*) the meaning changes to '*dis*closure', which means to open up or reveal something that is hidden or not yet existing (Kompridis, 2006: 58). This nuanced translation points to potentially deep connections between these radically different ways of understanding the concept of crisis.

REFERENCES

Adorno, T. (1991), 'Resignation', in J. M. Bernstein (ed.), *The Culture Industry*. New York and London: Routledge.
Ahmed, S. (2004), *The Cultural Politics of Emotion*. New York and London: Routledge.
Bauman, Z. (2004), 'To Hope Is To Be Human'. *Tikkun* 19 (6), 64–7.
Beck, U. (2006), 'Living in a World Risk Society', public lecture given at the London School of Economics and Political Science, 15 February. Available at: www.libertysecurity.org/ IMG/pdf_Beck-2006.pdf.
Benhabib, S. (1986), *Critique, Norm and Utopia: A Study of the Foundations of Critical Theory*. New York: Columbia University Press.
Bennett, J. (2001), *The Enchantment of Modern Life: Attachments, Crossings and Ethics*. Princeton, NJ: Princeton University Press.
Binde, J. (2001), 'Toward an Ethics of the Future', in A. Appadurai (ed.) *Globalization*. Durham, NC: Duke University Press.
Brown, W. (2005), *Edgework: Critical Essays on Knowledge and Politics*. Princeton, NJ: Princeton University Press.
Browne, C. (2005), 'Hope, Critique and Utopia'. *Critical Horizons* 6 (1), 63–86.
Clarke, S. (1994), *Marx's Theory of Crisis*. London: St. Martin's Press.
Connolly, W. (2006), 'Experience and Experiment'. *Daedalus* 135 (3), 67–75.
Daniel, J. and Moylan, T. (1997), *Not Yet: Reconsidering Ernst Bloch*. London: Verso.
Davis, M. and Bertrand Monk, D. (2007), *Evil Paradises: Dreamworlds of Neoliberalism*. New York: The New Press.

de Beauvoir, S. (2000), *The Ethics of Ambiguity*. New York: Citadel.

Fassbinder, S. (2006), 'Interfering with Capitalism's Spell: Peter Mclaren's Revolutionary Liminality'. *International Journal of Progressive Education* 2 (3), 9–20.

Freire, P. (1970), *Pedagogy of the Oppresed*. New York: Continuum.

Fromm, E. (1978), *To Have or To Be?* London: Abacus.

Gindin, S. and Pantich, L. (2000), 'Rekindling Socialist Imagination: Utopian Vision and Working-Class Capacities'. *Monthly Review* 51 (10). Available at: www.monthlyreview.org/300gind.htm

Giroux, H. (2000), 'Public Pedagogy as Cultural Politics: Stuart Hall and the "Crisis" Of Culture'. *Cultural Studies* 14 (2), 341–60.

—(2004), 'When Hope Is Subversive'. *Tikkun* 19 (6), 38–9.

—(2005), Introduction to *Border Crossings: Cultural Workers and the Politics of Education*. 2nd edn. New York and London: Routledge.

Gramsci, A. (1988), 'War of Position and War of Manoeuvre', in Forgacs, D. (ed.) *A Gramsci Reader*. London: Lawrence and Wishart.

Habermas, J. (1987), *The Philosophical Discourse of Modernity: Twelve Lectures*. Cambridge, MA: MIT Press.

Harvey, D. (2000), *Spaces of Hope*. Berkley, CA: University of California Press.

Hay, C. (1995), 'Rethinking *Crisis*: Narratives of the New Right and Constructions Of Crisis'. *Rethinking Marxism* 8 (2), 60–76.

—(1996), 'From Crisis to Catastrophe? The Ecological Pathologies of the Liberal-Democratic State Form'. *Innovation: The European Journal of Social Sciences* 9 (4), 421–34.

—(1999), 'Crisis and the Structural Transformation of the State: Interrogating the Process of Change'. *British Journal of Policy and International Relations*, 1 (3), 317–44.

Himmelweit, S. M. (2009), 'Transitioning the financial crisis'. *Red Pepper*, 28 June. Available at: www.redpepper.org.uk/Transitioning-the-financial-crisis (accessed 21 July 2009).

Honneth, A. (2007), *Disrespect: The Normative Foundations of Critical Theory*. Cambridge: Polity Press.

Hulme, D. (2006), 'Chaotic world of climate truth'. *BBC News*, 4 November. Available at: http://news.bbc.co.uk/1/hi/sci/tech/6115644.stm (accessed 28 June 2009).

Jameson, F. (2004), 'The Politics of Utopia'. *New Left Review* 25, 35–54.

—(2005), *Archaeologies of the Future: The Desire Called Utopia and Other Science Fictions*. London: Verso.

Kompridis, N. (2006), *Critique and Disclosure: Critical Theory between Past and Future*. Cambridge, MA: MIT Press.

Kovel, J. (2002), *The Enemy of Nature: The End of Capitalism or the End of the World?* London: Zed.

Krznaric, R. (2008), 'Empathy and climate change: proposal for a revolution of human relationships', unpublished paper. Available at: www.romankrznaric.com/Publications/Empathy%20and%20Climate%20Change%20Krznaric.pdf (accessed 19 July 2009).

Lacan, J. (1981), *The Language of the Self: The Function of Language in Psychoanalysis*. Trans. A. Wilden. Baltimore, MD: John Hopkins University Press.

Laclau, E. and Mouffe, C. (1976), *Hegemony and Socialist Strategy*. New York: Verso.

Lear, J. (2006), *Radical Hope: Ethics in the Face of Cultural Devastation*. Cambridge, MA and London: Harvard University Press.

Lichtman, R. (2009), 'Myths of the Marketplace: The Terrible Violence of Abstraction'. *Capitalism, Nature, Socialism* 20 (2), 14–21.

Marcuse, H. (1964), *One Dimensional Man: Studies in the Ideology of Advanced Industrial Society*. Boston, MA: Beacon Press.

Moser, S. and Dilling, L. (2004), 'Making Climate Change Hot'. *Environment* 46 (10), 32–46.

Nonini, D. (2008), 'Thinking about Neoliberalism As If Specificity Mattered'. *Focaal: European Journal of Anthropology* 51, 151–4.

The Oxford Dictionary of English (revised edition). Ed. Catherine Soanes and Angus Stevenson. Oxford University Press, 2005. *Oxford Reference Online*. Oxford University Press. Available at: www.oxfordreference.com/views/ENTRY.html?subview=Main&entry=t140.e17807

Sennett, R. (1999), *The Corrosion of Character: Personal Consequences of Work in the New Capitalism*. New York: W. W. Norton.

Simmel, G. (1982), *The Philosophy of Money*. Oxford: Blackwell.

Skrimshire, S. (2008), 'Curb Your Catastrophism'. *Red Pepper*, June/July.

Smith, N. (2005), 'Hope and Social Theory'. *Critical Horizons* 6 (1), 45–61.

Speth, J. G. (2008), *The Bridge at the End of the World: Capitalism, the Environment, and Crossing from Crisis to Sustainability*. New Haven, CT and London: Yale University Press.

Spivak, G. (1988), 'Subaltern Studies: Deconstructing Historiography', in *In Other Worlds: Essays in Cultural Politics*. New York and London: Routledge.

—(1990a), 'Rhetoric and Cultural Explanation: A Discussion with Gayatri Spivak'. Interview by P. Sipiora and J. Atwill. *Journal of Advanced Composition* 10 (2), 293–304.

—(1990b), 'Negotiating the Structures of Violence' with R. Dienst, R. Kennedy, J. Reed, H. in Spivak, G. and Harasym, S. (eds) *The Post-Colonial Critic: Interviews, Strategies, Dialogues*. New York and London: Routledge.

Weeks, A. (1914), 'The Crisis Factor in Thinking'. *The American Journal of Sociology* 19 (4), 485–90.

Weisman, A. (2007), *The World without Us*. New York: Macmillan.

Wood, A. (1998), 'Hegel on Education', in Rorty, A. O. (ed.) *Philosophers on Education: New Historical Perspectives*. New York and London: Routledge.

Zournazi, M. (2002), *Hope: New Philosophies for Change*. Annandale, NSW: Pluto Press.

CHAPTER SEVEN

EMPATHY AND CLIMATE CHANGE

PROPOSALS FOR A REVOLUTION OF HUMAN RELATIONSHIPS

ROMAN KRZNARIC

A PASSAGE TO INDIA

Jenna Meredith can empathise more than most with the 4.5 million people made homeless by flooding in South Asia after her home in Hull, UK, was hit by flooding earlier this year. She travelled to Orissa in eastern India with Oxfam to meet families who have lost their homes.

This story appeared on the Oxfam website in August 2007. In June that year, the worst flooding in Britain in 60 years had destroyed Jenna's home. Not only had she and her two daughters lost their worldly possessions, but due to financial pressures, she had stopped paying her house insurance six months earlier. Jenna became a spokesperson for local residents on her housing estate who felt that the government was doing too little to help them. When she made a comment in a radio interview about how the people of Hull were living like refugees in the Third World, she was contacted by Oxfam, who invited her to discover what life was like for poor villagers who had recently faced flooding in India.

'It was heartbreaking', she said, after returning from her one-week trip. 'I have been flooded out and lost everything so I know what it is like for the people in India. But in comparison I feel lucky. We can go and buy food from the shops, but the people I've met have lost their crops. They haven't got anything.' One person she spoke to was Annapurna Beheri, whose home and small family shop selling biscuits and tobacco were washed away. 'Annapurna was incredible. Her life has been turned upside down and now she has been reduced to living in a corrugated shack. I cried when the floods hit Hull, but she has nothing left and the family barely have enough food.'

Jenna was overwhelmed by her face-to-face meeting with the villagers in Orissa. 'Until you go to see a country like that for yourself, it's impossible to comprehend what's really happening. I know I can't walk away from this. I am determined to continue the campaign not only to get aid to those in need, but also to try to do whatever we can to reduce the effect of global warming. I have had a life-changing experience. I'll do everything I can to make a difference.'[1]

EMPATHY AND THE CLIMATE GAP

How can we close the gap between knowledge and action on climate change? Millions of people in rich countries know about the damaging effects of climate change and their own greenhouse gas (GHG) emissions, yet relatively few are willing to make substantive changes to how they live. They might change a few light bulbs but they do not cut back on flying abroad for their holidays nor do they want to pay higher taxes to confront global warming.[2]

One common approach to closing the climate gap is to argue that it is economically beneficial for us to do so: if we don't act now, climate change will become an increasing drain on national income as we try to deal with the damage, and individuals will face a reduction in living standards, for instance due to higher food and energy prices. A second major approach, based on ideas of justice and rights, is to argue that we have a moral obligation not to harm the lives of others through our excessive GHG emissions.

So far economic, moral or other arguments have not been enough to spur sufficient action. I believe that a fundamental approach has been missing: empathy.

Individuals, governments and companies are currently displaying an extraordinary lack of empathy on the issue of climate change, in two different ways. First, we are ignoring the plight of those whose livelihoods are being destroyed today by the consequences of our high emission levels, particularly distant strangers in developing countries who are affected by floods, droughts and other weather events. That is, there is an absence of empathy *across space*. Second, we are failing to take the perspective of future generations who will have to live with the detrimental effects of our continuing addiction to lifestyles that result in emissions beyond sustainable levels. Thus there is a lack of empathy *through time*. We would hardly treat our own family members with such callous disregard and continue acting in ways that we knew were harming them.

In this chapter I wish to suggest that generating empathy both across space and through time is one of the most powerful ways we have of closing the gap between knowledge and action, and for tackling the climate crisis. The problem is that, until now, empathy has been largely ignored by policymakers, non-governmental organizations and activists. Oxfam's idea of taking a British flood victim to witness the effects of flooding in India is an exception. It is time to recognize that empathy is not only an ethical guide to how we should lead our lives and treat other people, but is also an essential strategic guide to how we can bring about the social action required to confront global warming.

To begin this interdisciplinary journey, I will discuss exactly what empathy means, then show that there is strong historical evidence that it is possible to generate empathy on a large scale and for it to bring about major social change. Following this I will explain in more detail what it would mean to promote greater empathy on climate change across space and through time, and suggest concrete ways of doing so.

Tackling climate change requires nothing less than a revolution of the empathetic imagination.

WHAT IS EMPATHY?

If you pick up a psychology textbook and look up the meaning of 'empathy' you will usually find that two types are described.[3]

Empathy as Shared Emotional Response

The first form is the idea of empathy as a shared emotional response, sometimes called 'affective' empathy. For instance, if you see a baby crying in anguish, and you too feel anguish, then you are experiencing empathy – you are sharing or mirroring their emotions. This idea is reflected in the original German term from which the English word 'empathy' was translated around a century ago, 'Einfühlung', which literally means 'feeling into'.

However, if you see the same anguished baby and feel a different emotion, such as pity, then you are experiencing sympathy rather than empathy. Sympathy refers to an emotional response which is not shared. One of the reasons people often confuse the two is historical. Up until the nineteenth century, what used to be called 'sympathy' is what we mean today by empathy as a shared emotional response. Thus when Adam Smith begins his book *The Theory of Moral Sentiments* (1759) with a discussion of 'Sympathy', he is actually referring to a concept closer to the modern idea of affective empathy.

Empathy as Perspective-taking

A second definition of empathy is the idea of empathy as 'perspective-taking', which the psychology literature refers to as 'cognitive' empathy. This concerns our ability to step into the shoes of another person and comprehend the way they look at themselves and the world, their most important beliefs, aspirations, motivations, fears and hopes. That is, the constituents of their internal frame of reference or 'worldview' (*Weltanschaung*, as the sociologist Karl Mannheim called it). Perspective-taking empathy allows us to make an imaginative leap into another person's being. This approach to empathy became prominent in the 1960s through the work of humanist psychotherapists such as Carl Rogers.

The way we do this quite naturally is evident in common phrases such as 'I can see where you're coming from' and 'Wouldn't you hate to be her?'. Although we can never fully comprehend another person's worldview, we can develop the skill of understanding something of their viewpoint, and may on that basis be able to predict how they will think or act in particular circumstances. Perspective-taking is one of the most important ways for us to overcome our assumptions and prejudices about others. For example, dozens of psychological studies show how perspective-taking exercises can be developed to help challenge racial and other stereotypes, by encouraging people to imagine themselves in the situation of another person, with that person's beliefs and experiences. Hence many empathy researchers, including Daniel Goleman and Martin Hoffman, consider perspective-taking as an essential basis for individual moral development. With perspective-taking, the emphasis is on understanding 'where a person is coming from' rather than on sharing their emotions, as with affective empathy.

While these two kinds of empathy are related, in this chapter I will focus on the perspective-taking form, since this is the one that is most susceptible to intentional development and has the greatest potential to bring about social change. But what is the evidence that an apparently 'soft skill' like empathizing can not only shape how we treat people on an individual level, but also have a mass social impact and be effective in tackling the hard realities of the climate crisis?

EMPATHY AND SOCIAL CHANGE

One of the great failures of policy-makers and others engaged in confronting global warming is to recognize that developing empathy can bring about major changes in human behaviour and contribute to social transformation.[4] There is compelling evidence that some of the most significant shifts that societies undergo cannot be fully explained without taking empathy into account, and that if governments and civil society organizations wish to promote certain forms of change, they should engage in generating empathy on a mass scale. The historian Theodore Zeldin argues, for instance, that learning 'to empathise with people different from ourselves' is one of the 'the most effective means of establishing equality' that modern societies possess.[5] Similarly, the educational thinker Alfie Kohn writes: 'Perspective taking offers a deep way of taking account of others when making decisions with them or for them. But it also offers a way of detoxifying the poisonous We/They structure of nationalism' (Kohn, 1990: 158–9). Empathy is thus not just a psychological phenomenon but also a political tool.

An historical example demonstrating the power of empathy can be found in the struggle against slavery and the slave trade in Britain in the late eighteenth century. In the early 1780s slavery was an accepted social institution. Britain presided over the international slave trade and some half-million African slaves were being worked to death growing sugarcane in British colonies in the West Indies. But within two decades an unprecedented social movement had arisen that turned a large proportion of the British public against slavery, such that the trade was abolished in 1807. Recent research shows that standard explanations for this shift have failed to take into account the critical role of empathy. According to Adam Hochschild, there was a 'sudden upwelling' of empathy for the suffering of slaves due to factors such as public talks being given by former slaves, the use of posters and reports that educated people about their plight, and connections made between the pervasive practice of forced impressment of men into the British navy and the denial of liberty faced by slaves. Hochschild concludes that the success of the anti-slavery movement was based on the fact that, 'The abolitionists placed their hope not in sacred texts, but in human empathy' (Hochschild, 2006: 5, 222, 366).

There are many other instances where empathy has brought about social transformation.[6] They illustrate how taking the perspective of others through a leap of the empathetic imagination erodes our ability to dehumanize strangers and treat them as being of less worth than ourselves. Empathy has the potential to create a microcosmic and personal form of social change, altering the way that people behave towards one another. That is, if we want change, we do not need a revolution of institutions or economic incentives: we need a revolution of human relationships.

Empathetic shifts are not just an historical phenomenon. In the past two decades there has been a significant growth of projects and policies that are designed specifically to generate empathy as a way of tackling social problems. They build on the work of psychologists, sociologists and economists who have shown that not only do we often act on the basis of empathy, but that it is possible to increase our propensity to do so. They also provide an important guide for how we might design an appropriate empathetic response to the challenge of climate change.

Some of the most innovative and successful empathy development is taking place in schools. In countries such as Canada, the United Kingdom and the United States, children at both the primary and secondary level are now explicitly being taught empathy skills as a way of helping to reduce aggressive behaviour, boost academic achievement and create community cohesion. In England, the government's Social and Emotional Aspects of Learning (SEAL) programme (present in around three-quarters of primary schools) provides role plays, thought experiments, imaginative writing exercises and other methods for fomenting empathy. In Canada, the Roots of Empathy programme regularly brings a baby into the classroom to develop perspective-taking skills as a method of experiential learning.[7]

Empathy is also the guiding principle of 'immersion programmes' that have been established by several international NGOs and inter-governmental development agencies for their staff since the early 1990s. The World Bank, for example, has a 'Grass Roots Immersion Program' (GRIP) and a 'Village Immersion Program' (VIP), in which international staff spend up to a week living with a poor family in a rural or urban area in a developing country. The participants often help with tasks such as cooking or crop harvesting, and have opportunities to discuss daily life with their host families. According to one participant in a programme for the UK's Department for International Development (DFID), the immersion helped create the 'ability to put into words the perceptions of poorer people and more ability to empathise with their perspective' (Irvine et al., 2004: 6–10).

We can draw three lessons from these historical and contemporary examples. First, that empathy can be generated on a large scale and can have major social impact. Second, that empathy is now taken seriously as a policy tool around the world (even if it has barely infiltrated strategic thinking about climate change). Third, that there are three key methods for actively generating empathy: through educational learning, by creating conversations between people and by offering direct experience.

But before sketching out my suggestions for how to design empathy projects that will bring about action on climate change, I want to explore in more detail the two human realms where such climate change projects and policies need to be targeted: building empathy with people distant through time; and with people distant across space.

THE CHALLENGE OF DISTANCE THROUGH TIME

Climate change poses the fundamental problem of motivating us to act, and make sacrifices, on behalf of future generations – people whose lives are distant from us through time. We need to cut our carbon emissions right now for the benefit of individuals who do not yet exist and whom we shall never meet. While we are aware of some impacts of global warming today, the reports of the Intergovernmental Panel on Climate Change predict with strong certainty that the problems will get worse for future generations. Even if we take concerted action immediately, we are already locked into major and damaging climate impacts, even under the most conservative projections.

But why do we find it so hard to make policies that will benefit future people? A primary reason is because our political systems generally trap us in short-term electoral cycles (of usually four or five years), so politicians are largely unwilling to push for costly reforms that will only have an impact 50 years from now. In Japan in the eighteenth and nineteenth centuries, by contrast, the authoritarian Shogunate system encouraged political rulers to engage in visionary long-term policies such as mass tree planting to deal with extreme deforestation and soil erosion. These were leaders who wanted to preserve the nation for their own descendents, who they believed would inherit their political power.[8] Although I am not an advocate of authoritarian hereditary rule, it is clear that liberal democratic systems have a bias towards the present.

A second important reason for our short-term thinking is that not everybody is our progeny. We tend to care most for the people closest to us, especially those to whom we are biologically related. We worry about the welfare of our children and grandchildren. But the bonds start becoming weaker with respect to our great-grandchildren, and become almost completely absent when we consider the prospects for people a century from now to whom we are not related. This point is illustrated by a remark apparently made in the pub by the evolutionary biologist J. B. S. Haldane, who said that he would happily die for three of his children or six of his grandchildren (Glantz and Jamieson, 2000: 878). Added to this is the fact that we are not even particularly proficient at considering our own future welfare, illustrated by the case of smokers who seem willing to gain the pleasures of a nicotine rush today, even though they know that it may result in lung cancer and death in the future.

Economists have offered an extremely unethical solution to the problem of thinking about future generations in the context of climate change, which is known as discounting. Studies such as the Stern Review propose that we should 'discount' the future costs of climate change impacts, giving greater weight to costs incurred in the present.[9] For instance, using a discount rate of 5 per cent, it would be worth spending only US$9 today to avert an income loss of US$100 caused by climate change in 2057. With no discount, it would be worth spending up to US$100. A high discount rate can consequently generate a strong cost-benefit case for deferring or limiting mitigation efforts. Yet if we believe all human beings are equal, we cannot morally justify deciding not to act today because future generations should be expected to pay more of the costs of climate change. Even Ramsey, the founding father of discounting, observed (in 1928) that discounting was 'ethically indefensible and arises merely from the weakness of the imagination'.[10]

This suggests a second way of approaching the issue of future generations, which is to argue that we have a moral obligation to act on their behalf to prevent climate change as a matter of social justice and in compliance with the idea of universal human rights. Philosophers have got themselves into knots thinking about this, wondering about how we can ascribe rights to unborn beings, how we can take into account the uncertainties of the future, and how to deal with the ethical dilemmas of allocating scarce resources between those who are in need today and those who will be in need in the future.[11] It is certainly true that ethical arguments based on justice and rights can have political force (as they did in the US civil rights movement, for example) and might encourage individuals and governments to take action to cut carbon emissions. But there is little historical evidence that human beings will undertake major efforts for unborn generations on moral grounds.

We need something more than moral or economic arguments to generate social action on climate change. We need to create an empathetic bond between the present and the future. We must become experts at imagining ourselves into the lives and thoughts of our great-grandchildren, and of strangers in distant times. When we fill our car with petrol or fly from London to New York, we need not only to believe that this is morally wrong or that it will have long-run economic costs. We also need to be able to feel that future generations are watching us, to consider what they might think, to put ourselves into their shoes. Such an empathetic connection may stir us into changing how we live and what we do.

But how do we actually go about generating empathy for future generations? What methods and strategies are open to us? One option is what might be broadly called 'education', by which I mean using films, novels, non-fiction books, web-based reports and other secondary forms of information to encourage people today to step imaginatively into the shoes of individuals who are distant in time and confronting the expected impacts of climate change. The spate of climate change disaster movies that have been released in recent years appear, at first glance, to fit into this category. One prominent example is *The Day After Tomorrow* (2004), where the world faces a new ice age, snow appears in New Delhi, and Los Angeles is destroyed by tornadoes. The problem with this and other global warming blockbusters is that they usually emphasize the special effects and melodrama much more than offering a complex portrayal of individual characters adjusting to new realities, which limits our ability to look through the eyes of future generations. A film with more serious empathetic intent is *The Age of Stupid* (2009), in which the story is told from the perspective of an old man living in the devastated world of 2055, looking back at 'archive' footage and asking, 'Why didn't we stop climate change when we had the chance?'. This is the kind of film that can make us stop and think about how our carbon crimes might be perceived by future generations, which helps us make the psychological leap of empathetic imagining.

Some of the most effective educational and cultural forms that take us into the minds of future people put a clear emphasis on psychological exploration rather than the spectacle of apocalyptic disasters. The novelist J. G. Ballard described his science fiction as being about 'inner space' rather than 'outer space'. Works such as his prophetic novel *The Drowned World* (1962), set in 2145 when London has been flooded due to the effects of solar radiation, and global temperatures are rising with cata-strophic effects on human life, stand as models for generating empathy through time. They focus less on the disaster than on how it affects human relationships, and the emotions, priorities and mental landscapes of the protagonists. By personalizing the future, such 'inner space' fiction can help take us empatheti-cally into distant lives. A contemporary example is Cormac McCarthy's post-apocalyptic novel *The Road* (2006). There has been some kind of disaster (we are never told what caused it) leading to the destruction of American society, acute food scar-city and a Hobbessian war of all against all among the few survivors. The empathetic power of the book comes from its almost total focus on the two main characters – a father and a son – and how they understand themselves and one another in this barren and frightening world.

Too much dwelling on dystopian scenarios might induce an excessive sense of despair which dampens efforts to rouse people to take action on climate change. So we also need to produce utopian visions of how people might adjust to a climate-changed society, inspiring a greater sense of hope. Here the fictional models are books such as Ernest Callenbach's *Ecotopia* (1975), which the author described as 'a protest against consumerism and materialism' in American life, and which pictures how an ecologically sustainable society might function. A more subtle example is Ursula Le Guin's *The Dispossessed* (1974), which depicts an anarchist society on a drought-stricken planet, where there is a mixture of individual freedom and social control, reflecting the book's original subtitle, 'an ambiguous utopia'.

Education – whether as novels, films or in other forms – is most likely to expand our empathetic imaginations when it explores psychological inner space, and provides a mixture of utopian and dystopian possibilities. As I will discuss below, education needs to be combined with strategies based on con-versation and direct experience to generate the shift in empathy required to confront climate chaos.

THE CHALLENGE OF DISTANCE ACROSS SPACE

Climate change is as much a problem across space as it is one through time. Studies by development agencies demonstrate that weather events that are either caused by climate change, or closely resemble those that are likely to become increasingly common due to it, are already devastating the lives of some of the world's poorest people, who usually live in far away countries about which we know little. From floods in West Bengal to drought in Kenya to rising sea levels in Tuvalu, global warming is already having major human impacts and is forcing people to protect their livelihoods with new flood defences, faster-maturing crops and other emergency measures. Oxfam estimates that the cost of adapting to climate change in developing countries will be at least US$50bn each year, every year (Raworth, 2007: 3).

So we need to take action to help alleviate the difficulties faced by people today whose lives are threatened with a severe development reversal caused by excessive GHG emissions in rich countries. Unfortunately rich countries have a poor record of coming to the assistance of those who are distant across space, especially people from developing countries or whose cultures are very different from their own. In 1970 wealthy nations committed to contribute 0.7 per cent of their annual gross national incomes as development aid. Today, the average figure is just 0.28 per cent, with the United States providing only 0.16 per cent (Norway and the Netherlands are among the few countries to have achieved the target). We sometimes pour money into major emergency situations, as has occurred on multiple occasions since the Biafra crisis of the late 1960s, but our staying power is limited and we are easily distracted by other matters closer to home. By the end of April 2008, rich nations had paid only $92m into a UN fund to help the least developed countries with their most urgent and immediate adaptation needs, which is less than what Americans spend on suntan lotion each month (Oxfam, 2007: 1).

Why don't we do more to help? There are major academic industries in politics, sociology and cultural studies that attempt to answer this question. Some people argue that it is due to racial prejudices and the legacies of colonialism. Others, that nationalism prevents us looking beyond borders, or that we maintain ourselves in a state of collective psychological denial about the lives of the poor and our responsibility for their plight.

There are those who believe that we have become anesthetized to the images of poverty and destitution we see on television, or who suggest that most people feel that whatever they can give is too little to make any real difference so they do not bother. And there are analysts who claim we are simply too selfish to give a damn.

The most significant explanation, I believe, is simply that these people live far away and we don't know them. They are strangers to us. We cannot really imagine who they are and what their lives are like, let alone how the impacts of our carbon emissions affect them. Jenna Meredith's experience of meeting Annapurna Beheri was an exact counter to this kind of ignorance. If we personally knew people who had been flooded in Bangladesh we would be far more likely to do something about it than if we did not. That is the undeniable power of human relationships and the empathetic bond. When the Asian Tsunami struck at the end of 2004, the unprecedented humanitarian response can be explained not only by the scale of the disaster and its proximity to Christmas, but because there were so many Western holiday-makers among the victims. Tens of thousands of Europeans were sending text messages to check if friends or relatives abroad had been killed or injured. And even if their loved ones were safe, people could easily envision how one of their close friends or children travelling around Asia on a gap year might have lost their lives. The aid that went to countries such as Sri Lanka and Thailand was, to a significant degree, an empathetic reaction. Suddenly Asia was not full of distant strangers but rather friends or people just like us.

I believe that we should be supporting communities in developing countries to adapt to climate change on purely ethical grounds. We must, as a matter of justice, take responsibility for problems caused in poor countries by our own carbon emissions. We must recognize that these emissions are effectively violating human rights, and we need to avoid undermining other people's rights, whether they live around the corner or in a corrugated shack in Orissa.[12] But such beliefs are not sufficient to sustain practical action on the behalf of people in distant lands. Something more is needed. And that something is empathy. Whenever we hear of floods in India, we should picture individuals like Annapurna Beheri and try to imagine what she is feeling at that very moment. Whenever we joke about how climate change is giving us a lovely warm summer, we need to imagine that drought-struck farmers in Kenya can hear us chuckling in the sun.

EMPATHY PROPOSALS FOR THE ERA OF CLIMATE CHANGE

I would like empathy to become the watchword of a new era of policies, social movements, cultural projects and individual action on climate change. How can we encourage this empathetic revolution of human relationships? What exactly might it look like?

We need to generate empathy in three different ways. First, through educational initiatives, such as the documentary film *The Age of Stupid* discussed above. We must also expand our empathetic imaginations through new forms of conversation and direct experiences that can shift our worldviews. The following are a few ideas for conversational and experiential projects for generating empathy both across space and through time, which could be undertaken by governments, organizations in civil society and individuals.

Proposals to Generate Empathy Across Space
Climate Comrades
The old-fashioned idea of pen pals could be revived for the age of climate change. People living in rich countries could engage in one-to-one conversations with those living in poor countries suffering from the effects of global warming, using cheap technologies such as Skype, Facebook, email and webcams. This might be organized through existing or newly forged links between schools, church groups or twin town programmes, with some coordinating help from development agencies like Oxfam or ActionAid. So a teenager in Edinburgh could have regular video conversations with another teenager in Uganda, whose rural community is being hit by drought. Your Climate Comrade would hopefully become a friend for life, opening you up to a new empathetic understanding of what climate change means for people's livelihoods, and encouraging you to take political action.

Climate Corps

The Peace Corps established as a federal agency in the United States in the early 1960s has given hundreds of thousands of young people the opportunity to experience the realities of living in poverty in a developing country, especially in Latin America. I would like the European Union to establish a similar programme called the Climate Corps. Young people would go on placements for a year to live with a community in a poor country hit by climate change. They would work on adaptation projects such as helping build flood defences, or engage in other work of use to their hosts, such as teaching English to village children. In EU countries with military service, Climate Corps should be offered as an alternative option. With the right marketing, joining the Climate Corps could become a rite of passage for young people as popular as back-backing for a year before university. One of the rules of Climate Corps is that you must travel to and from your destination without exceeding a carbon emission limit, which would force you to avoid travel by plane.

Proposals to Generate Empathy Through Time

Climate Banquets

In nineteenth century France there were conversation banquets that brought together people from different classes to help bridge social divides. We need something similar for climate change. But those who we must bring together are young people and adults. Policy-makers and politicians are more interested in talking with each other than with the children and youths whose lives will be most affected by global warming, and whose views represent the perspectives of future generations more than any other group in society. So I propose that every major city holds a cross-generational Climate Banquet, which invites a thousand young people to sit down opposite a thousand older people to discuss the future impacts of climate change, in order to develop empathy through time. Among the adults would be politicians, oil company executives, convinced climate change sceptics and people who take regular short haul plane flights for their holidays. Just picture a mile-long line of trestle tables snaking through the city streets, with a thousand conversations happening at once.

The Climate Futures Museum

Without a time machine, it is impossible to give people direct experience of the future. But we can find ways to simulate the projected realities of every day life a century from today. That is why cities around the world should establish a Climate Futures Museum. The purpose of a Climate Futures Museum would be to provide experiential learning designed to develop our empathy with future generations who will have to live with the impacts of climate change if we fail to take concerted action in the present. The museum would not contain standard informational displays behind glass cases or on computer screens. Instead, it would house experiential exhibitions that allow visitors to understand in reality what it would be like to have their homes flooded, to be faced by drought, or to experience a hurricane. You might have to put on a life jacket and be tossed around in a dinghy in a wave machine. Creative minds would be needed to design an empathetic experience that would be etched in your memory for ever.

EMPATHY AND FUTURE ETHICS

There is no doubt that forging a new empathy-based ethics to create political action on climate change faces considerable barriers to its success. Political vision remains excessively short-term, the media can ignore or distort the threats of climate change, advertisers continue to lure us into luxury consumption, and many people remain locked in their personal psychologies of denial about the realities of global warming and its destructiveness.[13] Yet is it worth remembering that all social revolutions have had major obstacles to overcome: few people at the time believed that those who led the movement against slavery and the slave trade in the late eighteenth century had even a remote chance of success. There are more cracks in history through which we can glimpse possibilities for change than we generally imagine.

Sceptics might object that we should not put excessive faith in empathy since building it on a mass scale will take too much time, and given the urgency of the situation we should focus more of our efforts on immediate strategies, such as direct action, which have greater likelihood of shifting the international climate change agenda in significant ways. I agree that direct action and other forms of grass-roots mobilization are absolutely necessary to shake us out of our self-destructive slumber, but I believe they should be accompanied with a radical empathy strategy. Why? First, because empathy will make them stronger and more sustainable. Social mobilization usually follows a wave pattern: there are peaks and troughs of activity, with social movements booming then often weakening as passions die down and organizational difficulties emerge. But we cannot allow such waves to occur with action on climate change; empathy has the power to keep the flame of political action alive. Second, because the struggle against climate chaos will be a long one, ongoing over several decades, just like the civil rights struggle in the United States. Empathy is one of the most fundamental tools we have to shift attitudes and beliefs at the deepest levels. Without it, the demands of protesters will forever fall upon deaf ears.

We must always keep in mind the challenges of our ethical futures. It is quite likely that in coming decades the effects of climate change – such as food and water shortages, and waves of environmental refugees – will put massive pressures on social cohesion. The result may well be serious levels of social breakdown and conflict as we compete over increasingly scarce resources. If this eventuates, generating empathy today will be even more important for our future ethics. Empathetic recognition of other people's humanness is the most basic necessity for preventing the worst forms of cruelty and violence. According to Martha Nussbaum, the Holocaust was ultimately possible because it derived from an ideology that was blocking empathy:

> In short, empathy does count for something, standing between us and a type of especially terrible evil – at least with regard to those for whom we have it. The habits of mind involved in this exercise of imagination make it difficult to turn around and deny humanity to the very people with whose experiences one has been encouraged to have empathy. Thus the Nazis went to great lengths (as did German culture more generally) to portray Jews as a separate kind, similar to vermin or even inanimate objects . . . When, unexpectedly, empathy did arrive on the scene – whether through desire or through some personal experience that tapped its roots – the result was a

breakdown in the mental mechanism that sustained moral denial. (Nussbaum, 2003: 334–5)

Empathy may be the bulwark we need against the possible threat of social disintegration that could result from future climate catastrophes. It is an insurance policy with the potential to guard us from causing extreme harm to one another, and to help maintain the social bonds that are necessary for communities to survive and thrive.

Tackling climate change urgently requires an empathetic revolution, a revolution of human relationships where we learn to put ourselves in the shoes of others and see the consequences of global warming from their perspectives. The result will be an expansion of our moral universes so we will take practical measures to help those who are distant through time or distant across space. If we fail to become empathetic revolutionaries, the gap between climate knowledge and action will never be closed. Each of us needs to carve into everything we do, the empathetic credo, 'You are, therefore I am.'

NOTES

1 This section draws on information available at: www.oxfam.org.uk/get_involved/campaign/climate_change/engelique_video.html; http://www.oxfam.org.uk/applications/blogs/pressoffice/?p=961; Yorkshire Post 31/7/7, http://www.yorkshirepost.co.uk/features?articleid=3093143.
2 Many thanks to the following for their advice and suggestions for this essay: George Marshall (Climate Outreach and Information Network), Kate Raworth (Oxfam), Stefan Skrimshire (University of Manchester) and Kevin Watkins (UNESCO).
3 The text in this section, and part of the following one, has been adapted from Krznaric (2010).
4 See Krznaric (2007a) for a more detailed analysis of the relationship between empathy and social change.
5 See Zeldin's extensive work on how empathy and human relationships can create social change (1999a, 1633; 1999b, 3; 1995 236–55, 326).
6 For some examples, see Krznaric (2010).
7 I have discussed empathy education extensively in Krznaric (2008).
8 I have explored this case in Krznaric (2007b).
9 It should be noted that the Stern review is known for breaking with mainstream economic approaches by proposing a low discount rate. Yet it still incorporates discounting into its methodology.

10 United Nations Development Programme 2007, 62–3. See also Glantz and Jamieson (2000: 877).

11 For some of the philosophical debates, particularly with respect to Rawlsian conceptions of justice and utilitarianism, see Glantz and Jamieson (2000: 878) and Kymlicka (2002: 34–5).

12 See Raworth (2008) for an analysis of how rich-country carbon emissions are violating human rights.

13 For an excellent discussion of denial around climate change, and how to overcome it, see Marshall (2007: 86–138). For analysis of other barriers to action, see Kollmuss and Agyeman (2002).

REFERENCES

Glantz, Michael and Dale Jamieson (2000), 'Societal Response to Hurricane Mitch and Intra-Versus Intergenerational Equity Issues: Whose Norms Should Apply?'. *Risk Analysis* 20 (6), 869–82.

Goleman, Daniel (1996), *Emotional Intelligence: Why It Can Matter More Than IQ*. London: Bloomsbury.

Hochschild, Adam (2006), *Bury the Chains: The British Struggle to Abolish Slavery*. London: Pan.

Hoffman, Martin (2000), *Empathy and Moral Development: Implications for Caring and Justice*. Cambridge: Cambridge University Press.

Irvine, Renwick, Robert Chambers and Rosalind Eyben (2004), 'Learning from Poor People's Experience: Immersions'. Lessons for Change Series No. 13, Institute of Development Studies, University of Sussex.

Kohn, Alfie (1990), *The Brighter Side of Human Nature: Altruism and Empathy in Everyday Life*. New York: Basic Books.

Kollmuss, Anja and Julian Agyeman (2002), 'Mind the Gap: Why Do People Act Environmentally and What Are the Barriers to Pro-Environmental Behaviour?'. *Environmental Education Research* 8 (3), 239–60.

Krznaric, Roman (2007a), 'How change happens: interdisciplinary perspectives for human development', an Oxfam Research Report, Oxford: Oxfam GB.

—(2007b), 'Food coupons and bald mountains: what the history of resource scarcity can teach us about tackling climate change', Occasional Paper 2007/63, Human Development Report Office. New York: United Nations Development Programme.

—(2008), 'You are therefore i am: how empathy education can create social change', an Oxfam Research Report, Oxford: Oxfam GB.

—(2010), *Empathy*. Durham, UK: Acumen.

Kymlicka, Will (2002), *Contemporary Political Philosophy: An Introduction*. Oxford: Oxford University Press.

Marshall, George (2007), *Carbon Detox: Your Step-By-Step Guide to Getting Real About Climate Change*. London: Gaia.

Nussbaum, Martha (2003), *Upheavals of Thought: The Intelligence of Emotions*. Cambridge: Cambridge University Press.

Oxfam (2007), 'Financing adaptation: why the UN's Bali climate conference must mandate the search for new funds', Oxfam Briefing Notes 4 December 2007. Oxford: Oxfam International.

Raworth, Kate (2007), 'Adapting to climate change: what's needed in poor countries, and who should pay', Oxfam Briefing Paper 104. Oxford: Oxfam International.

—(2008), 'Climate wrongs and human rights: putting people at the heart of climate change policy', Oxfam Briefing Paper. Oxford: Oxfam International.

United Nations Development Programme (2007), *Human Development Report 2007/2008: Fighting Climate Change: Human Solidarity in a Divided World*. Basingstoke and New York: Palgrave Macmillan.

Zeldin, Theodore (1995), *An Intimate History of Humanity*. London: Minerva.

—(1999a), 'How Work Can Be Made Less Frustrating and Conversation Less Boring'. *British Medical Journal* 319, 18–25 December, 1633–5.

—(1999b), 'The Future of Work'. Available at: www.oxfordmuse.com/museideas/futurework.htm.

CHAPTER EIGHT

ARE WE ARMED ONLY WITH PEER-REVIEWED SCIENCE?

THE SCIENTIZATION OF POLITICS IN THE RADICAL ENVIRONMENTAL MOVEMENT

ANDREW BOWMAN

Someone once said that it is easier to imagine the end of the world than to imagine the end of capitalism. We can now revise that and witness the attempt to imagine capitalism by way of imagining the end of the world.[1]

Fredric Jameson (2003: 76)

INTRODUCTION

In late August 2007 it seemed a radical climate change movement had truly burst onto United Kingdom's political scene. Thousands attended the second Camp for Climate Action, established under the noses of police on the site of a proposed third runway for Heathrow airport. Not least because of the 'mass direct action' protest promised by organizers, the event captured media headlines. Subsequently, direct action against major polluters deemed responsible for climate change has grown markedly – runways have been occupied, power-stations stormed and coal trains hijacked. Spokespersons and supporters have placed these protests within the lineage of past radical social movements. Alter-globalization, anti-roads camps of the 1990s, civil rights and even the Zapatistas, are cited as co-travellers (Camp for Climate Action, 2008a: 10 – 11). One of the more recent manifestations, Climate Rush, involves participants dressing up as Suffragettes at demonstrations to ram home the message.[2] Rallying around slogans such as 'social change not climate change' and 'government and corporations are not the answer', radical climate activists have posited the climate crisis as an opportunity to create a more just and equitable future society.

This chapter will examine the relationship between radical climate activism and climate science. It is focused specifically on the politics of climate change rather than environmentalism more broadly, and differentiates 'radical' climate activism from more mainstream politics of climate change by its more counter-systemic, antagonistic tendencies: favouring direct-action and other protest tactics external to legal political channels; antagonistically challenging the role of state, corporations and the capitalist mode of production in precipitating the climate crisis; employing discourse which encompasses calls for far-reaching social change as well as simple emission reductions.

If this radical politics of climate change is embodied by a social movement, then it is extremely small – but growing – and loosely bound together through a number of organizations and networks, perhaps actively involving no more than a few thousand people. It is predominantly composed of people who are young, white and university educated. The most prominent organizations – some of which are discussed more fully below – are derived from green anarchism and pressure group politics, and include anti-aviation group Plane Stupid, the environmental network organizations Rising Tide and Earth First!, Climate Rush and the Camp for Climate Action. This latter organization is particularly significant for the expression of radical climate politics. For the past four years it has held annual camps and other major events which, in both organization and participation, draw together activists from around the country, and project messages through the national media to a broad audience.

Utopian visioning, open resort to law-breaking and denouncements of corporate power should place these protests well outside the prevalent post-political form of governance, where climate change is a matter for consensually agreed technical arbitration rather than political and ideological contest (see Mouffe, 2005; Swyngedouw, 2007; Žižek, 2007). However, other features of these emergent protest groups do quite the opposite, creating contradictions between the urge to create a more just, equitable society through confrontation with existing systems of power, and the pragmatism of action within the time-frame imposed by scientific understandings of climate change. The warning that 'time is running out' is frequently voiced alongside claims that there may only be '10 years left to prevent run-away climate change', or that any temperature rise above 2°C will entail certain catastrophe (MSNBC, 2006). These dire pronouncements often add weight to arguments and justification to actions, but can also form a political strait-jacket which limits the scope of action and imagination, encouraging accommodation with existing systems of power.

Despite the tactical illegality and flirtation with revolutionary rhetoric, radical climate politics enjoys a high level of elite support compared to other folk devils of radical protest. This situation has much to do with an increasingly problematic relationship between radical climate politics and the science of climate change. As a phenomenon inaccessible to unassisted sensual perception, un-knowable outside of computer models and aggregated statistics, and dependent upon expert knowledge, climate change has induced a high degree of scientism in environmental politics.[3] Science is, as Ulrich Beck observes, frequently implicated as cause, medium of definition and source of solution to the environmental crisis (Beck, 1992: 155). Large environmental NGOs such as Greenpeace and Friends of the Earth were propelled from the margins to the mainstream by departing from the 'wild cries of moral outrage . . . development of alternative cosmologies and counter-systemic utopian experiments' of contemporary environmentalism's embryonic period in the 1960s and 1970s (Szerszynski, 1996: 105). In the smaller, more recently formed radical climate action campaigns organizations which are the focus of this essay, orientations have been progressively steered towards emphasizing cool rationalism and clear scientific evidence as a basis for action. As such, it is increasingly science, or at least a particular rendering of it, that is invoked to shape political priorities.

Some consequences of this are immediately apparent. Spokespersons for these campaigns tend to perform impeccably in media debates with prestigious adversaries from fossil fuel dependent industries because of their grasp of 'the facts'. In a society that hasn't quite given up the idea that it should be governed rationally according to expert knowledge, this approach wins respect, and with it political battles. The question is, by adapting to this language of power, to what extent is this nascent movement transformed by it? This chapter will explore the consequences of scientism within radical climate change politics. The argument set out is not an attempt to purge science from politics, nor a relativistic interrogation of the veracity of the science of climate change. It is an attempt, however, to highlight a potentially dangerous, almost unconscious tendency that allows science to be mobilized in order to constrain certain types of politics, while masking others.

THE UNRELIABLE FRIEND[4]

With so-called 'climate deniers' becoming increasingly irrelevant during the first decade of the twenty-first century – as even the oil giants began to acknowledge, verbally at least, the threat of climate change – climate science began to occupy an ever more important role in environmentalism. As consensus over the interpretation of the science of climate change was established among (nearly) all the people that mattered,[5] the politics of climate change began to revolve not around the opposition of 'deniers' vs 'believers', but the multifaceted struggle over who could most effectively claim to be acting on behalf of 'the science'. Climate politics has become primarily a matter of who is best at counting the carbon, and forcing through the necessary reductions. Even among the more radical elements of the loosely defined 'climate change movement', this has created what is best described as a 'post-political' approach to climate change.

The post-political condition is defined by attempts to do away with the universal political and ideological antagonisms which defined past forms of oppositional politics, particularly between socialism and capitalism (Mouffe, 2005). Divisions and tensions are ironed out in favour of points of agreement, turning contested government into consensual governance by enlightened technocrats (Žižek, 2007: 198–204). In the case of climate change, the political consensus is built around the scientific consensus. Climate change campaigners avoid making 'unrealistic' or 'divisive' political or economic arguments, but simply focus on what everybody already agrees on – the science stipulating that a dramatic reduction in CO_2 emissions must be brought about immediately. The grounds for protest thus often become discordance between 'the science', and the actions of major polluters and their regulators. Correspondingly, the targets of protest become those who, in continuing to produce large volumes of this particular gas, have either ignored or failed to fully understand 'the science'. In 2007, protestors blockaded the Department for Transport because of their failure to appreciate the significance of aviation to overall CO_2 emission levels (Camp for Climate Action, 2007a). In the same year, the staff of BAA, the United Kingdom's largest airport owner, were locked in their offices with a pile of scientific reports thrown in by protesters wielding a 'read the science' banner and refusing to release them until they complied (Plane Stupid, 2007). And in 2009, the street in front of the London Carbon Exchange was occupied by thousands to express dissent against a government that would 'defy science' by introducing carbon trading (Camp for Climate Action, 2009).

Rather than political goals for the future being informed by science, compliance with science has often become the political goal in itself. The choice of locations and protest targets for the Camp for Climate Action is a good example. In the first year, 2006, it was situated next to Drax coal-fired power-station in Yorkshire, because this was the largest single point-source of CO_2 emissions in the United Kingdom (Camp for Climate Action, 2007b). In the second year, Heathrow airport was chosen first because 'the effect of Heathrow's planes on the climate is equivalent to 31 million tonnes of CO_2 emissions per-year', and secondly because aviation is the single fastest growing source of CO_2 emissions in the United Kingdom (ibid.). In the third year, Kingsnorth coal power station in Kent was chosen, 'firstly because it emits 10 million tons CO_2 a year', and secondly to oppose the new station being built there, highlighting coal as the most carbon-intensive form of power generation (Camp for Climate Action, 2008b).

Fittingly, the main march of the 2007 Camp left under the banner, 'We are armed only with peer-reviewed science.' Behind, protesters marched with pages of a Tyndall Centre report on aviation held above their heads (Indymedia, 2007). The moment encapsulated a key strength of this protest, but also a key weakness. Being 'armed only with peer-reviewed science', suggests a weak arsenal of political, economic and ethical arguments.

The power of science to mobilize mass support tends to be exaggerated. Scientific statements might *appear* to be taken at face value, but the reality of public understanding of and responses to science is more complex. Being dependent upon complex technology and adhering to the advice of scientists doesn't imply a 'scientific' manner of being in and understanding the world. Numerous scientific scandals – most notably in recent years over genetically modified crops, BSE and the MMR vaccine – demonstrate that science and scientists, far from being implicitly trusted and revered may come to be an 'alien and inadequate tacit model . . . imposed on lay publics' by distant experts working in relative secrecy and speaking in esoteric terms (Wynne, 1996: 59).[6] Jerome Ravetz points out that 'in spite of professions of democratic sentiment, science is still part of elite culture. The very language of science . . . requires a style of thinking that is almost totally restricted to those with a lengthy (and expensive) education' (Ravetz, 2006). Furthermore, and arising in part from this, stems the 'contradiction between the democratic pretensions of contemporary science and its actual elitist role in a still very unequal society' (ibid.).

Alienation experienced from scientific authority may not be solely due to the socio-cultural factors distancing laypersons from scientific experts. Most issues confronted by radical climate activism are necessarily abstracted from the world of day-to-day lived experience – for those living in complex, urbanized and industrialized societies, there is no real way of identifying or understanding climate change without a vast scientific infrastructure. To confront the issue, climate campaigners have to protest against events separate from, or even contradictory to, direct experience: invisible gasses, global shifts occurring over the course of decades, and catastrophic events which have yet to take place (Szerszynski 1996: 162; Ingold, 2000: 209–18).

It is, as climate change activists have discovered, hard to create meaning for a world one does not inhabit (Ingold, 2000: 173). The environment we relate to and understand in terms of embodied knowledge and practises is the one that surrounds us rather than the one presented to us in abstract scientific discourse. Knowledge of this world does not simply consist of representations in the mind, cognitive maps received through exposure to certain discourses – such as statements of scientific fact (ibid.: 200–17). If it did, nurturing public understanding of climate change would be a simple matter of saturating public discourse with scientific statements. This is, however, the general approach taken by campaigners, replicating what is known in science communication studies as the 'deficit model' of public understanding. According to this understanding, the public respond uncritically to scientific information, which is communicated in a linear fashion from experts to lay persons. Negative responses arise only as a result of a deficit in knowledge or understanding, to which the remedy is simply to increase exposure to scientific statements (Gregory and Miller, 1998). Negative public judgments over the reliability of scientific knowledge are, however, not based purely on 'ignorance', 'cognitive dissonance' or susceptibility to 'bad science'. They are also, as sociologist Brian Wynne states, 'a judgment of the quality of the institutions which are the proponents of that knowledge, and which appear utterly unwilling to render that knowledge-culture accountable to public discussion of its limitations' (Wynne, 2001: 447). Campaigning methods which reproduce the deficit model of the public understanding of science reinforce elite power–knowledge relations, encouraging the distancing of scientists from both public trust, and standards of accountability.

The process by which scientific knowledge is produced can also be inherently unhelpful to those seeking to create consensual 'certainty' on an issue for political ends. As the history of science has shown, even when experimental conditions are perfect, falsehoods have been created with precisely the same methods as acknowledged facts.[7] Science – at least in the idealized sense – is based upon continual uncertainty, doubt and questioning. Attempts to establish certainty must grapple with the paradox of 'infallible truth and permanent progress' (Sardar, 2001: 128). As sociologist of science Bruno Latour observes, this creates a Janus-faced science. One side facing towards the public and the social and political contest which scientific claims become embroiled in, where science appears 'ready-made' and based around certainty. The other facing inward to the scientific community, where science is continually in the making, claims are contested, fragile and subject to constant uncertainty

(Latour, 1987). The leak of private email correspondence from climate scientists at the University of East Anglia in November 2009 demonstrated this tension forcefully. In 'issue driven science' such as that of climate change, where, as Funcowitz and Ravetz put it, 'typically facts are uncertain, values in dispute, stakes high and decisions urgent', there is a tendency to revert to the former, positivist position (Funcowitz and Ravetz, 2008). Subsequently, uncertainties become erased, or are assumed a distraction: the work of mischief makers.

Climate science remains essentially an unprecedentedly complex experiment taking place in real time. Establishing authority on an issue often becomes a matter of persuasion over whose scientists are the most trustworthy. For example, NASA scientist Jim Hansen's vocal support for protest movements in the United Kingdom against coal power have made him a frequently cited and eulogized figure. With numerous different climate change commentators simultaneously claiming that 'the science' leaves no solution but theirs, science comes to be not so much a means of informing debates around political problems, but of shutting them down and ensuring the triumph of one political argument over another as more scientific. As Mike Hulme, founding Director for the Tyndall Centre for Climate Change Research points out, climate science here 'is being used to justify claims not merely about how the world is . . . but about what is or is not desirable – about how the world *should* be' (Hulme 2009: 74). Besides the damage done to political debate, in the process of such squabbles, trust in scientific knowledge itself may be seriously damaged (Yearley, 2005). Oil industry efforts in the 1990s to keep the metaphorical climate change ball in the long grass succeeded through successful exploitation of the above issues (Monbiot, 2006: 20–43). Ultimately this is a struggle for what Ulrich Beck has called, 'the means of definition', that is, the ability to define the nature of environmental problems, and their solutions (Beck, 2009: 31–3).

Radical climate politics showcases the science of climate change principally through mass-media coverage of audacious 'direct action' protest.[8] In these media encounters, and the pamphlets, publications and workshops aimed at convincing the deniers at large, it is to elite institutions that activists turn to for legitimacy. A common refrain to be heard goes along the lines of, 'Don't believe me? How about the Inter-Governmental Panel on Climate Change and the consensus opinion of thousands of the world's best scientists? How about the government's (ex) chief scientific advisor David King (Sir David to you), who has called Climate Change "a bigger threat to society than terrorism?"' (BBC, 2004).

Even if this tactic of 'science as bludgeon' were to be successful, in the long term these elite scientific institutions and individuals are questionable friends of movements pursuing radical social change. They may converge on physical science, but elsewhere interests are markedly different. The IPCC is an excellent illustration. When campaigners use the IPCC to win political arguments, it is usually the report of Working Group One, 'The Physical Science Basis' (Solomon et al., 2007) However, take the report of Working Group 3, 'The Mitigation of Climate Change', and one finds many of the demons currently plaguing climate activists with an eye towards environmental justice: biofuels, pricing mechanisms for conventional fuels which would exclude the poor, and a range of 'market mechanisms' (Metz et al., 2007).

There is a tendency in radical climate activism to treat science in the most idealized enlightenment fashion, as apolitical knowledge for knowledge's sake, independent of the conditions of its production. Negative consequences could well follow from this failure to recognize that all knowledge is produced to influence a certain social reality and is inextricably bound with the operation of power. Scientism in radical climate change politics has bolstered the grip of elite scientific institutions over the means of definition. Paradoxically, given the stress upon direct action and grass-roots movement building, much radical climate activism veers towards strengthening the power of established social elites over what is deemed legitimate knowledge.

THE SCIENTIZATION OF POLITICS

The politics of climate change outlined above can be termed *scientized*. This scientization is foreclosing political options within – as well as external to – climate change campaign organizations. One of the principle political uses of science is, in Latour's words, to 'bring order to [society] with incontestable findings that will silence the endless chatter of the mob' (Latour, 2004: 11). 'Science' invoked as infallible objective knowledge of 'nature' eliminates uncertainty and with it the moral and political contestation of an issue, especially when this knowledge is fully available only to a minority of experts in society. In climate politics, science is used in this manner to rule out certain areas where, it is adjudged, 'science says' there's nothing to contend. These appeals to truth in nature have often been effective in paralysing those who wish to debate matters such as whether car manufacturers' interests are more important than melting icecaps. 'The time for debate over climate change' it is often said, 'is over'. But, ultimately, what aspects of the climate change debate does this refer to? The depoliticization process – the arbitrary transformation of 'matters of concern' into 'matters of fact' – is at work within the climate change movement as well as upon denialist opponents.[9] That which cannot be quantitatively measured, numerically expressed and thus presented as 'scientific fact', loses political value in this scientized politics of climate change.

Political, ethical and moral arguments are eclipsed, as campaigns come to revolve around CO_2 measurements. Influential climate change campaigners positively revel in this situation. Joss Garman, for instance, co-founder of the influential anti-aviation direct action group Plane Stupid, columnist for *The Ecologist* and Greenpeace employee, revealingly refers to the 'carbon movement' when discussing the wave of direct action protest around climate change (Garman, 2009). Responding to suggestions that current environmental protests are no more than a new manifestation of a long running tradition of dissent among young people, Garman said:

They say the Sixties was the anti-war decade; the Seventies saw marches against racism at home and apartheid abroad; if it's the Eighties it must be Ban the Bomb and Maggie Out; the Nineties was roads and anti-globalisation; and the Noughties, this decade, is about climate change. We'll soon be on to something else, right? Wrong . . . this isn't about ideals so much as hard science . . . We know how this story ends, but not because we've read obscure economic treatises or dense theories from Friedman and Hayek or Hobsbawm and Marx.

We know because scientists are providing measurable objective evidence that the high-carbon economic model has an
in-built self-destruct mechanism. (ibid.)

While many people – including no doubt a few within the
'carbon movement' – might consider it complimentary to be
compared to these movements, in the scientized politics of
climate change, it is in some respects a slur. Any basis for
political action that does not come from objective, quantifiably
measured Nature, is merely blind idealism. Any imagining of
a future society beyond the correct level of parts-per million
carbon dioxide, is Utopian dreaming.

George Monbiot, a prominent media commentator and activist
granted a place by camp organizers on the main plenary of the
2007 and 2008 camps (and treated with almost messianic levels
of reverence from much of the audience), shares this sentiment.
For Monbiot, and many others, allowing challenges to capitalism
and state-corporate power to encroach on the pragmatism of
meeting emissions targets by any means necessary means 'putting politics first and facts second' (Monbiot, 2008). The result
of this influential strand of thought is, however, simply a different mixture of facts and politics (which ultimately no amount
of purification can ever fully separate), a different interpretation
of what kind of solutions will solve climate change, and what it
would ultimately mean to 'solve' climate change. If warming
were kept just below a 2°C limit at the expense of the exclusion
of the world's poor majority from energy consumption, and the
continued ravages of preventable disease and under-development,
would this be better than higher warming in a world of greater
fairness and equity? Even when sticking to the facts, it's almost
impossible to avoid mixing in politics; in claiming to have
removed it, dangerous blind spots are created. The entire politics
of the climate, and human suffering in the present and future,
become contained in CO_2, as do solutions (Swyngedouw, 2007:
33). This scientized politics is reflected in action. Take the
occupation of Stansted Airport runway by Plane Stupid activists in December 2008. The Plane Stupid website reads:

> 6:00am update: BAA have confirmed that the first flights
> out of the airport have been delayed. The average flight

out of Stansted has a climate impact equivalent to 41.58 tonnes of CO_2.

8:10am update: At least 39 people have been arrested and the runway re-opened. BAA are claiming that 21 flights have been cancelled. Every minute the airport emits around 4 tonnes of CO_2.

10:20am update: The Press Association reports that 57 people have been arrested, and 56 Ryanair flights cancelled. That's one flight per protester, meaning each personally stopped 41.58 tonnes of greenhouse gas equivalent (Plane Stupid, 2008).

Joss Garman justified the action as follows:

Plane Stupid chose to close Stansted because the government approved the expansion of capacity at the airport by 10 million passengers a year, despite scientists saying that aviation is Britain's fastest growing source of emissions . . . With each activist preventing about an average of 41.58 tonnes of CO_2 equivalent each, they truly achieved something – the beauty of direct action as opposed to mere protest. That's important given that the mantra of the godfather of climate science, Professor Hansen of NASA, that 'every ton of carbon counts'. (Garman, 2008)

Carbon counting comes to eclipse other forms of political dissent – even when it comes to bank bailouts and war. The Royal Bank of Scotland has been the target of repeated protests over the past year – not because of its role in the financial crisis, or its absorption of taxpayers' billions, but because of its investment in carbon intensive industries (Camp for Climate Action, 2008c).[10] Military air bases have been targeted not because of the function they perform, but because the function could be more energy efficient. A spokesperson for one such protest stated that regardless of what was thought about war,

there is still the large amount of unnecessary flying. Often the planes will do 'touch and goes' [sic.] where they land and then take off several times. These are needless emissions of carbon dioxide. (Earth First! Action Reports, 2008)

In scientized environmentalism, the radical, oppositional tactic of direct action becomes confused with radical, oppositional politics. Protests operate more as a means of communicating with elites than forming alternate forms of social power. Scientized environmentalism is about 'sending a message to the government' that they have been insufficiently technocratic, having failed in their carbon counting, and failed to reign in greedy consumers. It reinforces notions that important decisions should be taken only by minorities with sufficient levels of professional expertise or moral conviction, and not left to the ignorant masses. Rather than a serious attempt to rethink the way our society operates in response to ecological crisis, it represents more a plea for efficient governance within existing systems: ways of killing hundreds of thousands of people that use less carbon dioxide, giant financial organizations carrying out their relentless exploitation on a more energy efficient basis.

At a workshop during the 2007 camp, veteran environmentalist Mayer Hillman exclaimed, to much applause, that democracy itself was an obstacle to action on climate change. Though most environmentalists would place corporate lobbying power as the primary hindrance, they will be well aware of opinion polls demonstrating the unpopularity of green taxation and limits on consumption (Brown, 2008). Referendums on city centre congestion charging have met with clear rejections,[11] and were it not for the recession, consumption levels would still be soaring. Many direct actions therefore implicitly play the role of punitive measures against the population which the state is as yet not prepared to take. With a message usually amounting to little more than 'cut the carbon', and more effort put into questions of 'how much?' than 'how?', campaigners' concerns may in time not so much be accepted as co-opted, providing leverage for agendas antithetical to the emancipatory movements which climate activists position themselves alongside.

There are signs that this is underway already, with Climate Change Minister Ed Milliband following the Climate Camp's call for a mass protest mobilization at the December 2009 UNFCCC in Copenhagen (Hinsliff and Vidal, 2009). Following the financial crisis and growing governmental preferences for a more interventionist state and a 'green stimulus' packages to get capitalism back on its feet, there is increasingly little to differentiate the rhetoric of 'radical' greens from their supposed foes in government. For both, the true enemy is externalized in CO_2, the pathology of environmental destruction a matter for technical reconfiguration rather than systemic change (Swyngedouw, 2007: 33). The recent targeting of carbon-trading is an encouraging step towards considering processes rather than point sources. However, carbon trading becomes a problem principally because, drawing again on James Hansen, it is deemed 'ineffectual' (Camp for Climate Action, 2009). Where will this lead? Perhaps, as critical philosopher Slavoj Zizek observes, if ecological politics becomes devoid of the political antagonism between rich and poor, included and excluded, 'we may well find ourselves in a world where Bill Gates is the worlds' greatest humanitarian fighting against poverty and diseases, and Rupert Murdoch the greatest environmentalist mobilizing hundreds of millions through his media empire' (Žižek, 2007).

THE FUTURE ISN'T WHAT IT USED TO BE[12]

As a result of the process of scientization, a contradiction now runs through the radical climate action movement. On one side, there are those who see the action as part of a broader struggle to create a more just, equitable society in the future, with climate change being one facet of a larger problem. On the other, the pragmatists who want to stay focused on the carbon, and let the task of creating this society wait until the world has been saved from catastrophic climate change. Scientism has in large part created this tension.

Because political action in the present is firmly tied to science, so too are imaginings of the future. Staunch opponent of green politics Brendan O'Neill certainly has a point when he observes of the Climate Camp, 'If; possibly; perhaps; risk . . . all these caveats are expunged by the protestors who declare simplistically "the science says we have 10 years to SAVE THE WORLD!"' (O'Neil, 2007). With current interpretations of climate science among campaigners being that major emissions reductions must be made within the next decade, the radical propositions that have energized so many participants involved in environmental protest, become simply unthinkable. To quote Monbiot again,

Everyone in this movement knows that there is very little time: the window of opportunity in which we can prevent two degrees of warming is closing fast. We have to use all the resources we can lay hands on, and these must include both governments and corporations . . . The facts are as follows. Runaway climate change is bearing down on us fast. We require a massive political and economic response to prevent it. Governments and corporations, whether we like it or not, currently control both money and power. Unless we manage to mobilise them, we stand a snowball's chance in climate hell of stopping the collapse of the biosphere . . . Yes, let us fight both corporate power and the undemocratic tendencies of the state. Yes, let us try to crack the problem of capitalism and then fight for a different system. But let us not confuse this task with the immediate need to stop two degrees of warming, or allow it to interfere with the carbon cuts that have to begin now. (Monbiot, 2008)

The apocalypse now has a fairly precise date in the very near future (as discussed previously, these expressions commonly include 10 years, 100 months, the point at which we reach 2 degrees of warming). In the time-frame the science prescribes, it truly is easier to imagine the end of the world than the end of capitalism. This vision of fast approaching civilizational collapse guaranteed by the world's finest scientific minds narrows the scope of political action and imagination. Indeed, as Jameson says, this imagining of apocalypse has become a way of imagining capitalism (Jameson, 2003: 76). Paralyzed by apocalypse, the imagination falls back to means of technically reconfiguring existing social forms rather than radically changing them (Swyngedouw, 2007: 13–19). Green political movements of all varieties now lead the charge to revitalize capitalist accumulation through variants of the 'green new deal'.

As well as peer-reviewed science, climate campaigners are armed with fear – specifically fear of the future – to spur action among those comfortable in the present. Resource wars, 'environmental refugees', frequent extreme weather events and full ecological collapse are all frequently presented as near inevitabilities if action is not taken immediately. Radical environmentalism embodies the contradictions between a desire for change, a deep, over-powering fear of the future and yearning for an idealized past where the relation between humanity and nature was apparently stable and blissfully enjoyable. This passage from the Camp for Climate Action's newspaper is exemplary:

> There was a kind of certainty to our lives, there was little doubt that we, our friends, our families would have a future, probably brighter than the past. But for the first time in human history the ability of our planet's ecosystems to sustain future generations can no longer be taken for granted. Throughout the world, researchers, scientists, farmers and indigenous people, those who are in touch with their land base, those who have the knowledge and take the time to really look and listen to the natural world, to notice the weather, the state of the soil, the sea and forests, are showing us the evidence of a colossal collapse. They are warning us that we are entering an era of great uncertainty, that it is not a bright future that lies on the horizon, but catastrophe.
>
> And yet as the horizon advances something extraordinary is happening, we realise that within the crisis is a chance of a life time, a chance to radically change our way of life. Not long ago we knew the best time for planting seeds, we knew when we could start picking apples in the orchard, when the leaves would turn deep orange, when to look forward to building snowmen. Things like the cuckoo's dependable call would be a sign that spring had come. But the cuckoos are disappearing and it seems all the patterns of the world are being scrambled. Of course there were always exceptions, nature's surprises – a flash flood every few decades, unexplained droughts, unexpected hurricanes. But they were blips in a constant natural heartbeat. (Camp for Climate Action, 2008a)

Within these ecologies of fear, deeply conservative tendencies can be nurtured. Alongside vague, unspecific references to the need to 'radically change our way of life', action drifts towards largely technical measures that ultimately means that society remains the same, in lower carbon form (Swyngedouw, 2009).

The justification for this approach is, of, course compelling. Were run-away climate change to become a reality, much of the work towards the general improvement of humanity could be rapidly undone. The destruction of a habitable climate as a consequence of the ceaseless drive for expansion of surplus value is perhaps the greatest historical case of what Harvey calls 'accumulation by dispossession' (Harvey, 2005). However, the question most infrequently addressed within scientized climate politics is this; in 'saving the world', what kind of world is being saved? Whose world?

Control of the 'means of definition' will largely determine when exactly climate change is generally agreed to be 'solved' or 'under control'. Just as with the struggle waged by environmentalists to ensure widespread consensus that anthropogenic climate change is real, theories and objects gain the solidity of recognized truth through the amount of supporters amassed behind them, not their intrinsically truthful qualities (Latour, 1987). A compelling vision of future struggles for the means of definition as regards climate change is provided by the arguments over whether isolated catastrophes such as hurricane Katrina are a direct result of climate, or whether Darfur represents the world's first 'climate change war' (Darfur Integrated Regional Information Network, 2007; Young, 2007). With ever more state and corporate institutions recognizing climate change as an opportunity rather than a threat, control over the means of definition regarding climate change will almost certainly be wrested from environmentalists and scientists – if indeed it was ever with them in the first place. Hoffman and Woody (2008) exemplify this change of heart in the starkest imaginable terms, encouraging business leaders to see climate change as a market transition rather than an environmental problem. It could be argued that the consensus around the reality of climate change is principally a result of corporate interest in the matter rather than the triumph of science (Jankovic and Bowman, 2009). Environmentalism's 'greenwash' frame for understanding capitalist approaches to climate change is increasingly outdated. As the terrain of the struggle shifts, scientized climate politics may draw some unlikely allies. The fixation with ecological catastrophe dovetails neatly with emergent state security agendas and justifications for inequality and exclusion.[13] Localized, self-contained communities become exclusionary national or supra-national formations, with militarized borders to keep 'climate refugees at bay' (Wright, 2007). The ethics of personal restraint and individual moralization of carbon emissions, become legitimation for increased bio-political state management – to forcibly protect the masses from themselves. The most severe manifestation of this trend is the Optimum Population Trust, who seek to forcibly control human reproduction and freedom of movement, particularly in the majority world.[14] Sustainable development becomes a disciplinary measure against ascendant majority world nations. The Kyoto protocol's Clean Development Mechanism already exhibits elements of this: richer countries are essentially allowed to pay poorer nations to maintain a lower level of energy consumption.[15] The necessity of urgent action becomes a suspension of democracy, and the eradication of attempts to envisage life beyond capitalism. Individual motivations may be far from those described above, but power can operate through people's actions independently of motivations, with the ultimate effects being far-removed from original intentions. Scientized climate politics create blindspots to this dystopian green-future.

CONCLUSION

There is no *necessary* opposition between science and politics. Far from science necessarily destroying politics, it can throw it wide open again by bringing to light new matters of concern just as readily as it erases them (Latour, 2004). Despite the revolutionary facade, Monbiot's assertion that preventing runaway Climate Change is no place for counter-systemic politics, has been explicitly recognized in the actions and rhetoric of scientized climate campaigns. Perhaps the place for a truly radical, grassroots movement around the issue of climate change is not the focus on technocratic aspects of simple emissions reduction. Mainstream environmental organizations and government and corporate agencies are aware of these issues, and best placed to tackle them. Forcing home the latest facts and figures on atmospheric CO_2 concentrations and rates of Arctic melt are necessary but increasingly insufficient aspects of campaigning. An environmentalism that engages more thoroughly with the political, economic and ethical aspects of climate change is needed to make sure that the solutions being tabled are just, and the low-carbon world still worth striving for. Can the future once again be a projection of the improvement of humanity as well as simply survival? As this essay hopes to have demonstrated, scientism hinders this engagement, depriving us, as Latour puts it, 'of both autonomous knowledge and independent morality' (Latour, 2004: 4). The only way to move around this problem is to acknowledge the radical uncertainty of the futures faced – an uncertainty which seems all the stronger the closer one looks at the science. With uncertainty comes a choice between different paths taken, and with this choice values, ethics and politics. It's time that these began taking centre stage.[16]

DISCLAIMER

This chapter comes out of some inspiring years of participation in environmental politics. Without some faith in the worth and relevance of most of the protest organizations discussed above, this chapter would never have been written. It is intended as constructive criticism, and indeed self-criticism!

NOTES

1 Jameson (2003) pp. 76.
2 www.climaterush.co.uk
3 Scientism is, put simply, the tendency to treat scientific knowledge as superior to all other ways of understanding the world, particularly political ideals and moral frameworks. It implies a relatively uncritical, positivistic stance towards the social relations of scientific knowledge. From this stem technocratic impulses.
4 This term is taken from Yearley (1992).
5 I refer primarily to those elites in the overlapping spheres of business, politics and science. The general public are an entirely different matter, with polls showing a majority remaining unconvinced that human activity is causing climate change. See Jowit (2008).
6 See also Smith, 2006 and Allan, 2002.
7 Kuhn (1962/1996) was the first to open science to this form of historical and sociological interrogation. Further landmark texts include Bloor (1976), Latour (1987) and Pickering (1995).
8 Direct Action is a contested term within radical environmentalism. It is generally taken to mean, based upon an anarchist tradition, a political intervention made to prevent a harmful process taking

place, based upon the legitimacy of autonomous action rather than an appeal to a higher authority to act on ones behalf. Examples could include sabotage of foresting machinery, or blockading road construction workers. Many 'direct action' protests now self-consciously aim more at producing a dramatic symbolic event, or spectacle, that will attract media attention, with the purpose of raising public awareness and putting pressure on the legislative process.

9 Latour is here building on earlier work (1994) in which he describes the 'modern constitution' used to order western societies, in which objects and issues are arbitrarily divided between 'human' and 'natural' categories – the former being 'matters of concern', the latter 'matters of fact'. Latour instead suggests we should view all as quasi-objects, neither entirely human, nor entirely natural.

10 See also www.oyalbankofscotland.com.

11 Manchester is the most striking example. A referendum on the Transport Innovation Fund gave citizens of the metropolitan district a chance to choose between a dramatically expanded public transport network in return for charges for city centre car use, or business as usual. The latter was chosen by two thirds of voters.

12 One of the Camp for Climate Action's (2008a) more recent, and most apt, slogans.

13 See Webb (2007) for a summary of some of the plans underway. 'Climate refugees' is an entirely spurious concept, the reductionism of which obscures the questions of economic development and societal resilience that determine whether or not climatic fluctuations force people to migrate.

14 See www.optimumpopulation.org

15 This has attracted opposition, see Trans National Institute (2008).

16 For this insight I am highly indebted to Silvio Funcowitz and Jerome Ravetz (see particularly 2008 and 1999) and their development of the concept 'Post Normal Science'.

REFERENCES

Adam, D. (2009), 'Leading Climate Scientist: "democratic process isn't working"'. *The Guardian,* Wednesday 18 March.

Allan, S. (2002), *Media, Risk and Science.* Buckingham and Philadelphia, PA: Open University Press.

BBC (2004), 'Scientist Renews Climate Attack'. 31 March 2004. Available at: http://news.bbc.co.uk/1/hi/uk_politics/3584679.stm

Beck, U. (1992), *Risk Society: Towards a New Modernity.* London: Sage.

—(2009), *World at Risk.* Cambridge: Polity Press.

Bloor, D. (1976), *Knowledge and Social Imagery.* London: Routledge.

Brown, C. (2008), 'Green Tax Revolt: Public "will not foot bill to save planet".' *The Independent,* 2 May 2008.

Camp for Climate Action (2007a), 'Climate Activists Blockade Department for Transport to Stop Airport Expansion'. Available at www.earthfirst.org.uk/actionreports/node/4872

—(2007b), 'Last Year Drax. This Year Heathrow: Camp for Climate Action Announces This Year's Target'. Press release 24 May 2007. Available at: www.climatecamp.org.uk/themes/ccamptheme/files/pressrelease24_05_07.php

—(2008a), 'You Are Here'. Available at: http://climatecamp.org.uk/themes/ccamptheme/files/paper.pdf

—(2008b), 'Thousands to Take Direct Action against Kingsnorth Power Station'. Press Release 19 June 2008. Available at: www.climatecamp.org.uk/themes/ccamptheme/files/pr19-06-08.pdf

—(2008c), 'Royal Bank of Scotland Targeted by Climate Camp Activists for the Second Day Running'. Press release 8 August 2008. Available at: http://climatecamp.org.uk/node/430

—(2009), Climate Campers to Target the Carbon Market, 'because nature doesn't do bail outs'. Press Release 05 February 2009. Available at: http://climatecamp.org.uk/themes/ccamptheme/files/pr5-2-09.pdf

Climate Rush (2009), Available at: www.climaterush.co.uk/who.html

Earth First! Action Reports (2008) Climate Campaigners target Military Base Available at: www.earthfirst.org.uk/actionreports/node/21212

Funcowitz, S. and Ravetz, J. (1999), 'Post-normal Science – an Insight Now Maturing'. *Futures* 31, 641–6.

—(2008), 'Post-normal Science'. *Encyclopedia of Earth*. Available at: www.eoearth.org/article/Post-Normal_Science

Garman (2008), 'Today's Protestors, Tomorrow's Saviours'. *The Guardian*, 8 December 2009.

—(2009), 'This Is Not Youthful Rebellion. We See the Catastrophe Ahead'. *The Observer*, 8 March 2009.

Global Climate Campaign (2009), 'Global Day of Action: Call for International Demonstrations on Climate Change December 12th 2009'. Available at: www.globalclimatecampaign.org/

Gregory, J. and Miller, S. (1998), *Science in Public: Communication, Culture and Credibility.* New York: Plenum.

Harvey, D. (2005), *The New Imperialism.* Oxford: Oxford University Press.

Hinsliff, G. and Vidal, J. (2009), 'Miliband Calls for Populist Push in Battle Against Climate Change'. *The Observer*, 26 April 2009.

Hoffman, A. J. and Woody, J. G. (2008), *Climate Change: What's Your Business Strategy?* Boston, MA: Harvard Business Press.

Hulme, M. (2009), *Why We Disagree About Climate Change: Understanding Controversy, Inaction and Opportunity.* Cambridge: Cambridge University Press.

Indymedia (2007), 'Day 6: Climate Camp's 24 hours of Direct Action'. Available at: http://indymedia.org.uk/en/2007/08/378854.html

Ingold, T. (2000), *The Perception of the Environment: Essays in Livelihood, Dwelling and Skill.* London: Routledge.

Integrated Regional Information Network (2007), 'Sudan: Climate Change – Only One Cause among Many for the Darfur Conflict'. Available at: www.irinnews.org/Report.aspx?ReportId=72985

Jameson, F. (2003), 'Future city'. *New Left Review* 21. May to June.

Jankovic, V. and Bowman, A. (2009), 'Show me the money: climate change and the economy'. Unpublished paper.

Jowit, J. (2008), 'Poll: Most Britons Doubt Cause of Climate Change'. *The Guardian*, Sunday 22 June.

Kuhn, T. S. (1962/1996), *The Structure of Scientific Revolutions.* Chicago: The University of Chicago Press.

Latour, B. (1987), *Science in Action.* Cambridge, MA: Harvard University Press.

—(1994), *We Have Never Been Modern.* . Cambridge, MA: Harvard University Press.

—(2004), *The Politics of Nature: How to Bring the Sciences into Democracy.* Cambridge, MA: Harvard University Press.

Lynas, M. (2007), *Six Degrees: Our Future on a Hotter Planet.* London: Fourth Estate.

Metz et al. (2007), *Climate Change 2007: Mitigation of Climate Change. Contribution of Working Group III to the Fourth Assessment Report of the Intergovernmental Panel on Climate Change.* Cambridge: Cambridge University Press.

Monbiot, G. (2006), *Heat: How to Stop the Planet Burning.* London: Penguin.

—(2008), 'Climate Change Is Not Anarchy's football'. *The Guardian,* 22 August.

Mouffe, C. (2005), *On the Political.* London: Routledge.

MSNBC (2006), 'Warming Expert: Only Decade Left to Act In Time "We have a very brief window of opportunity", NASA Scientist Says'. Available at: www.msnbc.msn.com/id/14834318/.

O'Neil, B. (2007), 'Let the Puritans Protest'. Available at: www.spiked-online.com/index.php?/site/article/3682/.

Pickering, A. (1995), *The Mangle of Practise: Time, Agency and Science.* Chicago: University of Chicago Press.

Plane Stupid (2007), 'Climate Activists Mark 10 years of Blair'. Available at: www.planestupid.com/actions.

—(2008), 'Plane Stupid Shuts Down Stansted Airport'. Available at: www.planestupid.com/actions

Ravetz, J. (2006), The maturing of the structural contradictions of modern European science. An exploratory sketch. Draft for Comment.

Said, E. (1979), *Orientalism.* London: Penguin.

Sardar, Z. (2001), 'The Science Wars: A Post Colonial Reading', in *After the Science Wars* (Ashman, Keith M. and Barringer, Philip S. eds). London: Routledge.

Shift Magazine (2009), *Shift Magazine Issue 6.* Available at: www.shiftmag.co.uk

Smith, M. (2006), 'Lessons from History'. *Postnote,* January 2009, Number 323. Parliamentary Office of Science and Technology. Available at: www.parliament.uk/documents/upload/postpn323.pdf

Solomon et al. (2007), *Climate Change 2007: The Physical Science Basis: Contribution of Working Group I to the Fourth Assessment*

Report of the Intergovernmental Panel on Climate Change. Cambridge: Cambridge University Press.

Stop Climate Chaos Coalition (2009), 'Why is 2 Degrees C So Important?' Available at: www.stopclimatechaos.org/why-2-degrees-C-so-important.

Swyngedouw, E. (2007), 'Impossible "sustainability" and the Post-Political condition', in *The Sustainable Development Paradox: Urban political Economy in the United States and Europe* (Krueger, R. and Gibbs, D. eds). New York: Guilford Press.

—(2009), 'Trouble with Nature: "Ecology as the New Opium for the Masses." Forthcoming in *New Challenges for Planning Theory* (Healey, P. and Hillier, J. eds). London: Ashgate.

Szerszynski, B. (1996), 'On Knowing What To Do: Environmentalism and the Modern Problematic', in *Risk, Environment and Modernity: Towards a New Ecology* (Lash, S., Szerszynski, B. and Wynne, B. eds). London: Sage.

The Cole Hole (2009), 'Direct action'. Available at: http://thecoalhole. org/about/action/.

The Guardian (2009), Liberty Central's Civil Liberties Hero of the Week: The Lib Dems' G20 Observers. Available at: www.guardian. co.uk/commentisfree/libertycentral/2009/may/15/civil-liberties-g20-police-assault-ian-tomlinson.

Transnational Institute (2008), 'Clean Development Mechanism: Dump It, Don't Expand It'. Available at: www.tni.org/detail_page.phtml? act_id=18988&username=guest@tni.org&password=9999& publish=Y.

Webb, D. (2007), 'Thinking the Worst: The Pentagon Report', in *Surviving Climate Change: The Struggle to Avert Global Catastrophe* (Cromwell, D. and Levene, M. eds). London: Pluto Press.

Weber, M. (1970), *Essays in Sociology*. London: Routledge.

Wright, S. (2007), 'Preparing for Mass Refugee Flows: The Corporate Military Sector', in *Surviving Climate Change: The Struggle to Avert Global Catastrophe* (Cromwell, D. and Levene, M. eds). London: Pluto Press.

Wynne, B. (1996), 'May the Sheep Safely Graze? A Reflexive View of the Expert-Lay Knowledge Divide', in *Risk, Environment and Modernity: Towards a New Ecology* (Lash, S., Szerszynski, B. and Wynne, B. eds). London: Sage.

—(2001), 'Creating Public Alienation: Expert Cultures of Risk and Ethics on GMOs'. *Science as Culture* 10 (4).

Yearley, S. (1992), 'Green Ambivalence about Science: Legal-Rational Authority and the Scientific Legitimation of a Social Movement'. *The British Journal of Sociology* 43 (4), 511–32.

—(1993), 'Standing In for Nature: The Practicalities of Environmental Organisations Use of Science', in Milton, K. (ed.). *Environmentalism: The View From Anthropology*. London: Routledge.

—(2005), *Cultures of Environmentalism*. Basingstoke: Palgrave Macmillan.

Young, E. (2007), 'Climate Myths: Hurricane Katrina Was Caused by Global Warming'. *New Scientist*, 16 May. Available at: www. newscientist.com/article/dn11661-climate-myths-hurricane-katrina-was-caused-by-global-warming.html.

Žižek, S. (2007), 'Censorship Today: Violence, or Ecology as a New Opium for the Masses'. Available at: www.lacan.com/zizecology1.htm.

WEBSITES

www.cdm.unfccc.int
www.climatecamp.org.uk
www.greennewdealgroup.org
www.optimumpopulation.org
www.oyalbankofscotland.com
www.planestupid.com

VIDEO CLIPS

'Plane Stupid's Joss Garman on Newsnight' www.youtube.com/watch?v=PzFqjfgbKBg
'Climate Camp: Leila vs the Voice of Evil' www.youtube.com/watch?v=0c99sq7QFcg&feature=related
'Plane Stupid's Leo Murray on CNN' www.youtube.com/watch?v=5JBaI34YJXw

CHAPTER NINE

THE ULTIMATE PARADIGM SHIFT

ENVIRONMENTALISM AS ANTITHESIS TO THE MODERN PARADIGM OF PROGRESS

RICHARD MCNEILL DOUGLAS

When the child is to be weaned the mother has more solid food at hand, so that the child will not perish. Lucky the one that has more solid food at hand!

Søren Kierkegaard (1985: 48)

INTRODUCTION

In 1992 the Rio Summit established the UN Framework Convention on Climate Change. In the years since, growing awareness of the catastrophic potential of climate change has propelled environmentalism towards the centre stage of mainstream politics. From Tony Blair, in 2006, describing climate change as 'probably the greatest long-term challenge facing the human race' (Defra, 2006: iii), to Barack Obama, in 2009, warning that it could, if left unchecked, 'result in violent conflict [. . .] and irreversible catastrophe' (Romm, 2009), the rhetoric of many of the world's most powerful politicians has in recent years taken environmentalism more seriously than ever before.

And yet: despite all the soundbites, the targets, and the conferences, industrial carbon emissions continue to rise. In fact, from around 2000 they began to accelerate, their annual rate of increase rising from 0.9 to 3.5 per cent (Global Carbon Project, 2008). In other words, during precisely the time in which climate change had broken through to become possibly the pre-eminent global issue, our collective emissions began going up faster than ever.

This disjunction between rhetoric and action has much to do with the way in which, where it is admitted to mainstream political debate, climate change is generally presented as a problem with practical, mainly technological, solutions we can already map out. In this way, carbon mitigation blueprints – exemplified by the *Stern Review* (Stern, 2007) – seek not just to set out practical ways of tackling the problem, but, by emphasizing the reasons for hope, to inspire people to act. The problem with this is that the emphasis on climate change as a practical problem we know how to solve also helps to foster a certain atmosphere of complacency and wishful thinking, a sense that we are almost bound in time to solve it. This, in turn, discourages the perception of climate change as representing a crisis, the kind of existential threat to society that might give rise to a widespread and fundamental questioning of dominant social structures and ideologies – not least to ask whether they are compatible with an unprecedented, rapid and absolute decarbonization of our economies. Thus, where climate change has won the attention of mainstream politicians, they have tended to treat its successful mitigation as something that can be fitted into contemporary economic orthodoxy. More radical proposals to cut emissions which lie outside such convention – those, in particular, based on the principle of cutting back on consumption – remain firmly marginalized.

This chapter seeks to put this dichotomy in climate change policy – between the acknowledged seriousness of the problem and the less acknowledged modesty of the response – into the wider context of the faults and complexities of environmentalism, and its (inadequate) influence on mainstream politics.

It starts from the premise that one of the key contributions of environmentalism is to show how the physics of entropy applies to economics; it is this which underpins environmentalism's central message, that there are limits to material production and consumption. But, this essay argues, environmentalists characteristically stop short of attending to the most profound implication of this set of ideas – and that it is this which is largely responsible for their failing to decisively alter the direction of politics and economics in the past four decades.

It is an acknowledged implication from the laws of thermodynamics (referred to here as the physics of entropy) that all physical systems, from microscopic organisms to stars, continually consume a necessarily finite supply of available energy from their environment; thus that all life, all activities, all structures have a necessarily limited lifespan. The related implication ought to follow from environmentalism's application of this understanding to human society: that humanity itself is necessarily mortal (since the resource base it depends on is necessarily finite, and its available energy continually becoming more exhausted). Furthermore, since this is dictated by the laws of physics themselves, there is no possibility of a future technological fix that would enable us to perpetually postpone this fate. This implication is generally overlooked by environmentalists, this essay argues, because perception of this message, even if unconscious, triggers the psychological defence of denial.

Environmentalism fails ultimately to win over society as a whole to the idea of a radical change in the use of resources because it fails to address the philosophical questions and psychological needs that are tangled up in its explicit arguments. What environmentalists need to do is to realize that their movement uncovers not just an environmental but a philosophical crisis – the inadequacy of modern belief systems in offering a sense of understanding of, and consolation for, death. By explicitly focusing on this conclusion, environmentalists could encourage the kind of philosophical engagement that might result in a new paradigm, one that could successfully provide a sense of meaning for life in a society conscious of its own mortality. This at last might unlock, as a decisive practical influence, environmentalism's positive ethical message: that by changing the intensity with which we consume resources we have the power to prolong our collective future – thus our every use of resources is important, how we choose to spend them at every moment pregnant with meaning.

IMPLICATIONS OF THE 'LIMITS TO GROWTH'

Environmentalism comes in a variety of forms. Arne Naess famously drew a contrast between a 'deep ecology', which was concerned for non-human nature in its own right, and by implication a 'shallow ecology' whose interest in nature was primarily motivated by concern for its impacts on human health and welfare. Another influential classification was made by Timothy

O'Riordan, who contrasted 'technocentricism', a form of environmentalism pre-occupied with technological and policy solutions to environmental problems, with 'ecocentricism', which was more focused on adapting human activity to the natural world (Smith, 1999: 32–40, 196–9).

But while environmentalism means different things to different people, almost all its forms are united by a central core premise: that nature imposes physical limits to human consumption, what is commonly known as the 'limits to growth' thesis. In their *Politics and the Environment*, Connelly and Smith identify 'acceptance of the limits to growth' as being one of 'the two core principles of green political thought' (the other being 'the ethical basis of our obligations to the non-human world') (Connelly and Smith, 2002: 52). They are clear that this essential principle spans both technocentric and ecocentric forms of environmentalism: 'Whichever trajectory we follow, the limits to growth thesis remains central to the green standpoint' (Connelly and Smith, 2002: 52). In his *Green Political Thought* Andrew Dobson writes 'the belief that our finite Earth places limits on industrial growth' is 'a foundation-stone of radical green politics', and that: 'This finitude, and the scarcity it implies, is an article of faith of green ideologues, and it provides the fundamental framework within which any putative picture of a green society must be drawn' (Dobson, 2007: 52).

The 'limits to growth' thesis is most closely associated with the report of that name published by the Club of Rome in 1972. But this did not emerge in a vacuum; it was produced in a time of growing consciousness about the impossibility of endless growth in human consumption. The intellectual kernel of this school of thought was provided by the likes of Nicholas Georgescu-Roegen and Herman Daly, economists who in the late 1960s and early 1970s took the revolutionary step of applying the physics of entropy to economics; in doing so they founded the discipline of ecological economics. As Douglas Booth puts it in his entry on the 'Limits to Growth' in the Routledge *Encyclopedia of Political Economy*: 'Those who believe that there are limits to growth suggest that conventional economic thought ignores the reality of the law of entropy and the limited ability of the global ecosystem to supply environmental services' (O'Hara, 2001: 668).

In works such as *The Entropy Law and the Economic Process* (1971) Georgescu-Roegen wrote about the implications of his observation that all economic production is subject to the second law of thermodynamics (sometimes known as 'the entropy law'). This states that the entropy of a closed system must continually increase; which is another way of saying that all physical processes irrevocably consume available energy, turning it into other less usable forms. In a context familiar to us, this means that burning a lump of coal turns the energy that was available in it into dissipated heat and ashes, which cannot be burnt again. On a global scale this means our industrial activities are continually decreasing the total stock of raw materials available to us, while continually increasing waste products in their place. As Georgescu-Roegen puts it:

> We must continuously bear in mind that [. . .] our accessible environment is like an hourglass which cannot, however, be turned upside down and in which the useful matter-energy from the upper half turns irrevocably into waste as it continuously pours down into the lower half. (Georgescu-Roegen, 1976: xvi)

The main radical lesson this school of economists is known for is that the laws of physics themselves preclude the possibility that some as yet unobtained technological advance will reconcile continued economic growth with finite environmental limits. (This argument has been challenged by technological optimists such as Julian Simon and, more recently, Bjørn Lomborg; but their arguments have been shown to be severely flawed.) (Douglas, 2008: 176–89) As Jeremy Rifkin has written, the entropy law means that pollution is not a contingent by-product of industrial production that might be eliminated through improved technology; it is an essential product of the using up of the available energy in a material (Rifkin, 1980: 35). As he comments, there is no possibility of 'magic bullet' solutions for the 'problem' of environmental limits; even if we were to fully replace fossil fuels with solar power

> we would continue to witness the exponential increase of entropy here on earth as solar energy is used to convert more

and more of our limited terrestrial energy resources (matter) into the production process, transforming them from a usable to an unusable state. (Rifkin, 1980: 199)

The most influential articulation of the political vision such arguments point towards was outlined by Daly in the early 1970s under the name 'the steady state economy': a prescription for a society that would reduce its resource consumption to a level that would remain sustainable over the very long term.

What is hardly acknowledged is that the implications of ecological economics do not stop here, but are yet more radical. They are that globalized civilization – and ultimately humanity itself – is mortal. In a sense this is a truism; and that it is such is one reason it is overlooked. The physics of entropy have long been understood to dictate that mortality is the necessary condition of everything in the universe; that all the stars and galaxies will eventually run out of available energy and burn out, resulting in what became popularly known in the mid-nineteenth century as 'the heat death of the universe'. This same exhaustion of available energy must extend to all physical systems, including our own sun and planet. As far ago as 1852, William Thompson, later Lord Kelvin, wrote that within a finite period of time the earth must become 'unfit for the habitation of man' according to 'the laws to which the known operations going on at present in the material world are subject' (Freese, 1997: 92). But despite this being known about for over a century and a half, it has made little impact on politics, philosophy or culture, or popular ideas about the future. For all intents and purposes, such eventualities, if they are ever considered at all, are treated effectively as works of science fiction, projected to occur so far in the future as to have no relevance or reality for us at all.

Ecological economics challenges this. It says more than that humanity is mortal on a geological timescale, as a result of the expansion in its death-throes of the sun. What the application of the physics of entropy to economics does is connect the ultimate fate of the earth with our every action at every moment. To understand it is to appreciate how, following the industrial revolution, humanity itself has 'become a geological agent who continuously speeds up the entropic degradation of the finite stock of mineral resources' (Georgescu-Roegen, 1976: xiv). Thus we are as a global society connecting the present with an ending that until now has been viewed as inhumanly distant. The crucial point to realize is that it is the same force – entropy – that dictates both that the sun will run out of energy, and that human access to matter-energy on earth is limited. As Beard and Lozada put it in their study on the thought of Georgescu-Roegen: '[His] core insight is that all economic transformations, regardless of their type, must result in the entropy of the universe rising – otherwise the transformation could not occur. The passing of each moment leaves us in a universe of ever-greater entropy' (Beard and Lozada, 1999: 101). Given the finitude of the resources we are drawing on, and the scale on which our globalized economy is operating, how we choose to use these resources matters greatly. Civilization itself is hastening its own end, by its very advanced development; the more technologies we master, the more powerful and comfortable we become, the quicker we burn through non-renewable resources. Though we *can* change the intensity with which we consume resources, and with it the amount of time we have left, this fundamental condition of mortality is not just contingent, something we could overcome through our invention; it is rooted in one of the central laws of physics.

Even those most familiar with ecological economics tend not to talk about these, its fullest implications. Ultimately there is no such thing as a sustainable society; even to persist in a steady state is to continue to expand in time, hence in entropy. The lack of interest in – or simple awareness of – this, even on the more radical wings of the environmentalist movement, is illustrated by the complete lack of any reference to it in Andrew Dobson's extensive survey of the concept of the 'sustainable society' within radical green thought (Dobson, 2007).

This most radical implication of the core limits to growth thesis, and the way in which it is almost entirely passed over by environmentalists themselves, helps to put environmentalism's lack of success in decisively altering the economic direction of society in context. To understand it further we need to dwell on the mechanics by which potentially dominant ideas are embraced or denied.

ON PARADIGM SHIFTS AND ENVIRONMENTALISTS

It is common for environmentalists to call for a 'paradigm shift' in the Western – now globalized – political and economic world-view. Ophuls and Boyan, for instance, tell us: 'In brief, liberal democracy as we know it – that is, our theory or 'paradigm' of politics – is doomed by ecological scarcity; we need a completely new political philosophy and set of political institutions' (Bryner, 2001: xxiii). Herman Daly writes that the 'steady-state paradigm . . . represents a radical shift from the standard growth paradigm' (Daly, 1992: 140). Lester Brown tells us: 'The time has come for what science historian Thomas Kuhn describes as a paradigm shift' (Brown, 2000: 9).

Brown is of course correct in tracing this use of language to Thomas Kuhn, whose *The Structure of Scientific Revolutions* (1962) did much to make 'paradigm' and 'paradigm shift' features of the everyday speech of intellectuals. Kuhn famously argued that the advancement of scientific knowledge did not conform to its classic picture as a smooth continuum of progress, each scientist adding a little more research to the collective understanding. Rather, scientific theory advanced in fits and starts – in revolutions, in which major theories, or paradigms, once their particular inadequacies as descriptions of natural phenomena had become exposed and grown intolerable, were overthrown, and new ones adopted in their place.

One of the key elements of Kuhn's argument states that ruling paradigms are not given up by the scientific community as a whole just because such theories are shown to have holes in them. This is merely the initial requirement. Not only do such theories need to be shown to have holes in them, but a whole new theory has to be available to take their place; only when it can be instantly replaced will a major theory be rejected. In order for this to happen, the new theory must possess at least as much explanatory power as the old – plus the power to explain those further phenomena which the last was notably unable to explain. As Kuhn puts it:

'[O]nce it has achieved the status of paradigm, a scientific theory is declared invalid only if an alternate candidate is available to take its place [. . .] The decision to reject one paradigm is always simultaneously the decision to accept another. (Kuhn, 1962: 77)

Why is there this reluctance to reject a theory, even when it has become notoriously unable to explain known phenomena? One reason is that what turns a theory into a Kuhnian paradigm is its very explanatory power, the way it fits together with and implies many other testable theories; in other words, one cannot just reject it in isolation, since it acts as a keystone in a much wider organization of ideas. Another reason is that scientists are supposed to regard all scientific theories not as the literal truth but merely as working hypotheses; in this sense, so long as a paradigm still works in many areas there is no reason to abandon it, simply because it becomes clear that it fails to work in some others. But another, deeper reason, is that, while scient-ific *theories* are meant to be merely working hypotheses, the *subject* of scientific theories is effectively regarded as objective reality. This means that, without an adequate replacement, to abandon a ruling paradigm is in a very important sense to loosen one's grasp on reality; to abandon oneself to a greater degree of ontological insecurity.

As Kuhn describes it, only scientists of a younger generation, or newcomers to a particular field, less attached to the old para-digms and more preoccupied with their failings, are able to contemplate tearing paradigms down and searching for others; it is among these creative novices that new paradigms are incu-bated. In this process, we might reflect, these young revolution-aries are still, as scientists, believers in the principles both that objective reality conforms to intelligible laws, and that scientific method is our means of discovering such laws. Thus they still retain a faith that there must be another theory out there, waiting to be discovered, one that will actually be closer to reality than that which is currently held. Indeed, it will be this faith that will prompt them to turn against the current paradigm: its glaring faults will have betrayed it; there *must* be another law or principle which it is failing to describe. This faith will itself, in the interim before a replacement can be discovered, act as a substitute, and allow the revolutionary to put the ruling paradigm into suspension; to disconnect it from their understanding of ultimate reality, and yet still retain a sense of ontological security, a firm sense of solid ground beneath the feet. Or, we might say, this faith acts as the metaphysical clutch which allows scientists to shift the gears of belief.

There are obvious differences between Kuhn's theory and the more general use of 'paradigm shift' made by environmentalists. But while the latter use is more of a figure of speech than a worked out theory, there are still pronounced similarities.

In the case of environmentalism the need for a readymade replacement paradigm to be available before the existing dominant paradigm is abandoned would seem to be especially important. This is because the core principle of environmentalism, that there are limits to growth, implies certain lessons, regarding the limitations of technological power and ultimately human mortality, such that it naturally provokes a strong response of denial and wishful thinking. Without an adequate replacement world-view which is able to successfully address such concerns, to make sense of and offer consolation for them, it is simply inconceivable that society as a whole will reject the paradigm of unending economic growth which environmentalism attacks. So it is that, while in the last four decades environmentalism has won a significant popular acceptance for the idea that there are severe problems with this paradigm, it has made relatively slow progress in transforming political and economic organization: the replacement ideas it offers are not adequate for the job they have to do.

THE PARADIGM OF PROGRESS

The implications of the environmentalist world-view contradict something larger than the paradigm of unending economic growth; beyond this, they undermine what has been described as 'the working faith of our civilization' (Lasch, 1991: 43) – the paradigm of progress. Environmentalism strikes at the common assumption of the modern world, that history only runs in one direction, and that the future must inevitably be better than the past; that humankind has discovered the key to taking control of its fate, and that we will inevitably enjoy an ever-increasing sense of material wealth and power. As part of this it strikes in particular at what the political philosopher Eric Voegelin described as 'the power fantasy of science', the faith that science would bestow on us an ever-expanding range of material powers. Accompanying this, it strikes at the vision, if only subconscious for many today, of the future as a utopia of technological advance and social justice; the great human project to which each might contribute while they were alive, and thereby share virtually in its fruits.

Perhaps, we might think, progress seems like a bit of a chimera these days; who actively believes in it, who actually uses the word anymore? But this would be a misapprehension; progress is still there as our working faith. Certainly, the more fanciful aspects of the faith in progress – belief in an inevitable perfectibility in international peace, individual leisure time and the rational organization of social life – may have been shorn away by the atavistic shocks of the twentieth century; an *explicit* faith in progress was just one of those aspects to be lost. But still we retain our unconscious belief, if for no other reason than the most powerful: as the historian Sidney Pollard observes, because the alternative would be total despair (Pollard, 1971: 205).

One of the most profound implications of environmentalism is that it sounds the death knell for the modern. This is not to say that it promises a literal return to the dark ages, an undoing of the intellectual and technological advances made since the Renaissance. For this is not to speak of the modern as the chronological span that has elapsed, with all the real, individual events that have taken place within it, since the fifteenth or sixteenth centuries. This is, rather, to speak of the modern as a paradigm, as the *idea* of an epoch in which humankind has made a revolutionary break with its past, entering an unprecedented age in which new rules apply, and where we have the possibility to realize what in past ages we merely dreamt about.

This is to discuss the modern in terms similar to those explored by Eric Voegelin, notably in *The New Science of Politics* (1952/1987); and more recently by John Gray in his *Black Mass* (Gray, 2007: 9). As Voegelin saw it, the essence of the modern is the concept of history's reaching a final but unending epoch, based on the belief that scientific inquiry would lay bare all the secrets of nature and hand humankind unlimited power. He argued that this 'destroys the oldest wisdom of mankind concerning the rhythm of growth and decay which is the fate of all things under the sun'. Quoting from the Kohelet ('To every thing there is a season, And a time to every purpose under heaven: A time to be born and a time to die'), he sums up this teaching as: 'What comes into being will have an end, and the mystery of this stream of being is impenetrable. These are the two great principles governing existence.' His argument is that the modern embraces the very opposite of these principles: 'The idea of the [modern age] assumes a society that will come into being but have no end, and the mystery of the stream is solved through speculative knowledge of its goal' (Voegelin, 1952/1987: 167).

Environmentalism reasserts the validity of ancient wisdom about these essential principles of existence – that all things have natural limits, and that nothing will last forever. As William Ophuls put it, in this respect environmentalism comprises 'a sharp break with the principles of the modern era' (Dobson, 2007: 72). The idea of the modern tells us that we live in a completely new reality, and in doing so gives us a sense of already dwelling in a kind of afterlife. Little wonder the emphatic rejection of the notion that our contemporary, globalized civilization might decline or collapse like civilizations in the past. As Lasch writes:

> [W]e cannot imagine that [our civilization] might die a natural death, like the great civilizations of the past. That civilizations pass through a life cycle analogous to the biological rhythm of birth, maturity, old age, and death now strikes us as another discredited superstition, like the immortality of the soul. Only science, we suppose, is immortal; and [. . .] the apparently irreversible character of its historical development defines the modern sense of time and makes it unnecessary to raise the question that haunted our predecessors: how should nations conduct themselves under sentence of death? (Lasch, 1991: 48)

Most importantly, environmentalism attacks the modern idea of immortality. This consists both in the idea of living on in the memory of others, and in identifying oneself with humanity as a whole (and believing it will survive and grow ever more perfected into the indefinite future) (Jalland, 1999: 359). No matter that such explicit treatment of this attitude belongs to a time past, when religious faith was being actively undermined by the advance of science; such thinking is still influential, informing a background belief. An assumption, even if unconscious, in the indefinite and progressing future of humanity is what has provided a social sense of meaning in life and consolation for death in a scientific age. The difficulty with environmentalism is that, in its focus on the implications of the physics of entropy to society, it teaches that science itself contradicts this idea.

ON DENIAL

Nothing should be less surprising than that the greater implications of environmentalism are not consciously acknowledged; nor that subconscious awareness of them accounts for the very stubborn resistance so often encountered towards environmentalism as a whole. It is inevitable that these ideas will trigger the basic psychological impulse to deny the existence of bad news. The very way in which Bjørn Lomborg describes accounts of environmental degradation as 'the Litany', for instance, suggests that his criticism of such evidence is to an extent simply that its tone is too negative.

It is a well-known phenomenon, this denial in the face of knowledge of the likelihood of future death or bad fortune. Jared Diamond writes perceptively about it in *Collapse* (2005), his book about the factors that throughout history have led to the decline and fall of entire societies. He draws attention, for example, to the well-documented effects of denial on people who live in the valleys immediately beneath large dams, thus almost literally in the shadow of death: 'the only way of preserving one's sanity while looking up every day at the dam is to deny the possibility that it could burst' (Diamond, 2005: 436).

Notably, Diamond finds much this same phenomenon of denial at work in one of the most prominent predecessors to his own book – *The Collapse of Complex Societies* by Joseph Tainter. While Diamond places over-expansion of populations and over-consumption of resources high on his list of key factors responsible for the decline of many historical peoples, Tainter cannot bring himself to make the same conclusion, preferring to hypothesize that such declines must have been the result of more sudden, extraneous disasters. His reasoning is simply that it would have been irrational for societies to continue over-exploiting their resources, when this was obviously suicidal behaviour. Diamond rejoins, reviewing the many examples in his own book, that Tainter is certainly wrong; idleness in the face of disaster is precisely what such societies have exhibited.

Two decades ago Richard Falk wrote that one of the reasons environmentalism had struggled to transform politics is that, in the catastrophic nature of its arguments, it immobilizes as it persuades (Lasch, 1985: 17). Another version of this point, with specific reference to climate change, has gained a certain prominence more recently. Mike Hulme, founding director of the Tyndall Centre for Climate Change Research, has written that environmentalists' presentation of climate change as a conditional catastrophe (i.e. the future will be catastrophic unless we take radical action today) is actually counter-productive. As he puts it: 'Framing climate change as an issue which evokes fear and personal stress becomes a self-fulfilling prophecy' (Hulme, 2006). Hulme sometimes appears to be arguing against any discussion of potentially catastrophic developments, as being scientifically unjustifiable; this would be a curious position, since there are many entirely plausible scenarios in which climate change would have disastrous effects on biodiversity and human societies. His argument is strongest in making the case that a focus on the potential catastrophes that climate change may lead to might in fact retard the practical efforts that could help us avoid them, by actually increasing denial and inaction.

One way to head off such a response, while still accepting the seriousness of our environmental situation, is to find a positive and inspiring aspect to an apocalyptic vision. As Stefan Skrimshire has stressed:

> 'apocalypse' is derived from the Greek word for revelation, or the unveiling of divine truth to mortal man. To many people apocalyptic literature [. . .] represented the imaginative attempt to portray the corruption of the present in order to inspire radical social transformation. [. . .] Perhaps what is needed, therefore, is more, not less, of the imaginative apocalyptic. (Skrimshire, 2008)

Within the environmentalist movement one of the most prominent attempts to sketch out an inspiring alternative vision of the future in recent times has come from Jonathan Porritt, in his *Capitalism As If the World Matters* (2006). While on the one hand aiming to educate environmentalists to work within the prevailing economic paradigm, it portrays on the other a quite utopian vision of a new 'sustainable society' which environmental policies could bring into being. In a memorable passage Porritt discusses the proposal for an equal per capita limit on global carbon emissions:

> When all the calculations are done in terms of concentrations of CO_2 [. . .] each and every one of us will be able to emit the equivalent of approximately 1 tonne of carbon per annum. Welcome to the One Tonne World! [. . .] At this point, environmentalists usually proffer the sackcloth and ashes [. . .] and are a little taken aback when people rapidly decline the invitation. But what if that 'offer' was reworked – promising entry into the One Tonne World on the basis of better value for money, lower electricity and gas bills, better food, less hassle in terms of getting to and from work, improved health, more jobs in the cutting-edge industries of the future, cleaner air, more convivial communities, more time at home or reconnecting with the natural world? One Tonne – real fun! (Porritt, 2006: 206)

There is much to admire in this book. Yet ultimately its arguments are insufficient – for the reasons common to other such attempts, as highlighted by Dobson:

> Reducing the material consumption of those who consume too much is an integral part of ecologism's project, and so the green movement has a profound political and intellectual problem on its hands. It is faced, in the first place, with persuading potential supporters that this is a desireable aspiration, and it is saddled with a series of intellectual arguments for its position that currently appear too weak to do the job required. The assertion [. . .] that a society organized around reduced consumption just *would* be more pleasurable to live in seems unlikely to cut the necessary ice. (Dobson, 2007: 73–4)

The problem with Porritt's vision is that it is not nearly apocalyptic enough. It portrays a vision of a future that is on the surface radically different, in terms of politics, economy and society; but presents it in terms of ethical values that are largely of our current, consumerist society. There is little sense of a transformation in social values; most of the radical changes he outlines are presented in terms of appeals to fun, pleasure and convenience. Yet this is to overlook the enormous upheavals and sacrifices (not to mention the commitment to radical, world-wide egalitarianism) his vision of a 'One Tonne World' would require. It is one thing to argue that a 'sustainable society' could be better in many ways than our current arrangements; but quite another to suggest it would *simply* be better, or even more that it would be simply more fun.

Environmentalists have found themselves in this catch-22: by denying the full conclusions of their arguments, they are attempting to avoid immobilizing themselves as well as the public; but so long as the public are able to believe that it is possible to solve environmental problems in such a way that we can go on just as before, they are unlikely to believe in the conditional catastrophes which environmentalists *do* hold out as warnings, nor make the kind of sacrifices they are told are needed to avoid them.

CONCLUSION: THE NEED FOR MORE APOCALYPTIC ARGUMENTS

There is one path out of this impasse – to be *more* apocalyptic, not less. Environmentalism needs to focus on the full implications of the limits to growth thesis at its core – principally the lesson that the inescapability of entropy means that all things, including our global civilization, are mortal. This is vital to undermining the modern myth of progress, the secular faith in the infinite potential of humanity to acquire more knowledge and power. It is this which underlies the orthodox response to climate change and other environmental problems, the reliance on technological fixes that would allow economic growth to continue indefinitely.

To say civilization is mortal is also to say it is killable, that too many abuses, shocks and misfortunes will finally take their toll.

Simply to make this argument is not to bring the end any closer. In fact, a widespread acceptance of this idea might be the key to prolonging civilization's lifespan in practice. We still have it in our power, by changing our uses of resources, to soften the environmental crises we are currently headed towards, and to postpone a fatal collapse of global civilization for who knows how long beyond that.

In making such an argument, environmentalists would need to face up to the following objection: why bother taking radical action and making economic sacrifices today in the pursuit of creating a 'sustainable society', when even this will not be sustainable forever? In turn this would mean dealing with the profoundly difficult ethical questions relating to how far into the future to plan and budget for, how far to moderate present consumption. A suggested answer would be not to plan too far into the future, but to focus on the intermediate steps, the transition from our current economic patterns to a steady state society that could continue for an undefined very long term. More to the point, the focus should be on avoiding the possibility of a rapid and bloody collapse of global civilization, through the breaching of environmental limits and the warfare that could be brought on by competition for resources, in a similar way to the collapse of historical societies described in Diamond's book.

But this still would not be enough. There has to be something more to hold out to people than simply the eking out of natural resources for as long as it takes to finally run through them. If this cannot be a vision of a more perfect version of the consumerist society we live in today (because such a society is unsustainable), then it must be one based on non-material aspects of the good life which philosophers and political movements have striven for and dreamed of for centuries – those which are often thwarted by our current obsession with economic growth. That is, a world of greater democracy, equality and truly private personal time; a world so organized as to be free from absolute want, and yet equally free from the twin pressures of long hours and 'competitive consumption' (Schor, 1998).

Yet even this would be not be enough, not to decisively shift the dominant economic paradigm of global society. If the practical content of this vision would teach us to become less materialistic, and that materialism were in any case doomed, then the overarching philosophy of the movement has to provide some answers to the ancient, fundamental questions this necessarily raises. That is, questions about the purpose and meaning of mortal lives in a world that is itself finite. This would be essential to give this sense of an apocalyptic vision its meaning as an 'unveiling', something which could inform our understanding of ourselves and shape our sense of, as Christopher Lasch puts it, how we as a society should live under sentence of death.

What environmentalists need to realize is that their ideas are highlighting not just an environmental crisis but a philosophical crisis. The limits to growth thesis exposes fatal contradictions in the modern paradigm of progress; and in so doing undermines the modern sense of human identity and collective immortality, without offering any effective replacements for them. Until environmentalists realize that they need ultimately to be confronting such questions, questions which go far beyond the essential scope of environmentalism itself, their arguments are essentially doomed to failure. Society will not decisively change its economic course until its governing paradigm is rejected; this will not happen until there is a replacement paradigm ready, one which points out the flaws in the current paradigm and solves them; and such a replacement paradigm will not be developed until more people realize just what it needs to do, philosophically. Environmentalism itself is not the paradigm, rather the antithesis, erupting from the growing contradiction between progress and reality, which tells us that a new paradigm is needed.

REFERENCES

Booth, D., in O'Hara, P. A. (ed.) (2001), *Encyclopedia of Political Economy L–Z*. London: Routledge.
Brown, L. R. (2000), 'Challenges of the New Century', in L. R. Brown (ed.) *State of the World 2000*. London: W. W. Norton.
Bryner, G. C. (2001), *Gaia's Wager*. Oxford: Rowman & Littlefield.
Connelly, J. and Smith, G. (2002), *Politics and the Environment: From Theory to Practice*. 2nd edn. London: Routledge.
Daly, H. (1992), *Steady-State Economics*. 2nd edn. London: Earthscan.
Department for the Environment, Food and Rural Affairs (Defra) (2006), *Climate Change: The UK Programme 2006*. p. iii.
Diamond, J. (2005), *Collapse*. London: Allen Lane.
Dobson, A. (2007), *Green Political Thought*. 4th edn. London: Routledge.

Douglas, R. M. (2008), 'Historicism and the Green Backlash: A study of Julian Simon and Bjorn Lomborg'. *International Journal of Green Economics* 2 (2), 176–89.

Freese, P. (1997), *From Apocalypse to Entropy and Beyond: The Second Law of Thermodynamics in Post-War American Fiction*. Essen: Die Blaue Eule.

Georgescu-Roegen, N. (1976), *Energy and Economic Myths*. Oxford: Pergamon.

Global Carbon Project (2008), 'Carbon Budget and Trends 2007'. Available at: www.globalcarbonproject.org.

Gray, J. (2007), *Black Mass: Apocalyptic Religion and the Death of Utopia*. London: Allen Lane.

Hulme, M. (2006), 'Chaotic World of Climate Truth'. *BBC News*, 4 November. Available at: www.news.bbc.co.uk.

Jalland, P. (1999), *Death in the Victorian Family*. New edn. Oxford: Oxford University Press.

Kierkegaard, S. (1985), *Fear and Trembling*. London: Penguin.

Kuhn, T. S. (1962), *The Structure of Scientific Revolutions*. London: University of Chicago Press.

Lasch, C. (1985), *The Minimal Self*. London: Picador.

—(1991), *The True and Only Heaven*. London: Norton.

Pollard, S. (1971), *The Idea of Progress*. Harmondsworth: Penguin.

Porritt, J. (2006), *Capitalism as if the World Matters*. London: Earthscan.

Randolph Beard, T. and Lozada, G. A. (1999), *Economics, Entropy and the Environment: The Extraordinary Economics of Nicholas Georgescu-Roegen*. Cheltenham: Edward Elgar.

Rifkin, J. (1980), *Entropy: A New World View*. New York: Viking Press.

Romm, J. (2009), 'Must-read Obama Speech Warns of "Irreversible Catastrophe" from Climate Change'. Available at: www.alternet.org

Schor, J. (1998), *The Overspent American: Upscaling, Downshifting and the New Consumer*. New York: Basic Books.

Skrimshire, S. (2008), 'Curb Your Catastrophism'. *Red Pepper*, 5 July. Available at: www.redpepper.org.uk.

Smith, M. J. (1999), *Thinking Through the Environment*. London: Routledge.

Stern, N. (2007), *The Economics of Climate Change: The Stern Review*. Cambridge: Cambridge University Press.

Voegelin, E. (1952/1987), *The New Science of Politics*. London: University of Chicago Press.

PART IV

RELIGION

CHAPTER TEN

ETERNAL RETURN OF APOCALYPSE

STEFAN SKRIMSHIRE[1]

*This topicality (of the Apocalypse of John) does not consist
. . . in the suprahistorical sentiment of the end of the world, nor
in the atomic, economic, ecologic, and science fiction panic
of the millenarians. If we are steeped in the Apocalypse, it is
rather because it inspires ways of living, surviving and judging
in each of us. It is a book for all those who think of themselves
as survivors. It is the book of Zombies.*

Gilles Deleuze (1998: 37)

INTRODUCTION

Western culture's recourse to the trope of biblical apocalypse
to describe planetary crises is well known, and, at least in media
circles, clichéd (Edelstein, 2009). What more can be said about
this relationship? Is the concept of apocalyptic appropriate?
Revealing? Instructive? Or is it simply grist to the mill of
Hollywood's delight in macro-scale disaster? In contemporary
English, the noun *apocalyptic*[2] can refer to 'disaster resulting
in drastic, irreversible damage to human society or the environment, esp. on a global scale' (OED, 2008). Its connection to
apocalyptic literature is therefore the vision of a world that
is, often violently, passing away. But the meaning of the Greek
apokalupsis is revelation or disclosure. In their original context,
literary apocalypses written in the intertestamental period, such
as the books of Enoch, Daniel or Revelation, unveil divine
secrets to a mortal humanity, often focusing on the theme of
future salvation. Through an angel intermediary, such secrets
are given via vision, dreams or otherworldly journeys.

By correlating apocalyp*tic* to characteristics of late Jewish
and early Christian literary apocalyp*ses*, then, we can find an
even more intriguing connection than that of mere catastrophe.

We can associate the principle of revelation itself with the narration of ultimate meaning, consummation and culmination *in* world history. This element of apocalyptic has arguably constituted one of the most influential themes in the development of a western philosophy of history. For, what is revealed, in apocalyptic vision? A transformed world, temporally and spatially, given *in time* and experienced in the historical process itself (Collins, 1984: 4).

It is also this notion of an underlying truth about world history that is dramatically revealed, I want to argue, as opposed to the fixation with its final, violent termination in the future, that most resonates with our 'apocalyptic' experience of climate change, and which sheds light on the way we understand the future. This is not to downplay the significance of the imagination of violence in this context.[3] Religious responses to events such as hurricane Katrina in 2006 or the Asian Tsunami in 2004 as divine retribution for sins or as the sign of approaching end-times have already demonstrated the imaginative power of religious apocalypse (Arroyo, 2008). The four horsemen of the book of Revelation were a prominent theatrical image at the G-20 London summit protests in April 2009, against the effects of economic and ecological crisis, and also as a Greenpeace stunt at the UN Climate talks in Copenhagen in December 2009. And a powerful rhetoric of *finality* with reference to climate tipping points and points of no return – beyond which 'there is no salvation' as NASA scientist Jim Hansen intones – is also seductively allied to the term 'apocalypse', as the *Independent on Sunday*'s climate change headline, 'Apocalypse Now' in 2005 made obvious (Lean, 2005).

Nevertheless, I would like to argue in the following that the concept or image of future apocalyptic finality – its eschatological component[4] – functions as something of a smokescreen. Indeed, inasmuch as it encourages the calculation and prediction of prescribed timeframes for viable action, it might also be an illusory consolation, by suggesting that (if a particular timeframe is exceeded) the fight is over. Far more problematic for us, ethically and politically, is the framing of climate change in terms of the transformation of the present; of the revelation of crisis in our midst with no *predictable* end. Like Deleuze's sentiment about Zombies, what should interest us about an apocalyptic sensibility are the ethical questions that it generates about ways of living in this indefinite period of waiting and surviving.

I hope to demonstrate that an originally religious notion of the revelation of divine purpose in history persists in the way we experience life *in* crisis, this living 'in the middest' (Kermode 1966/2000: 8). It is also my conviction that knowing about the sources of such attitudes is important to understanding contemporary responses to climate change. Because it is largely ignored, I find the most problematic form of this persistence not in the visible revival of fundamentalist religion, but, rather, in key trends of 'secular' European philosophical thought. The roots of a modern idea of world *progress* in particular can be seen as the carrier of an 'immanent' apocalyptic belief.

FUTURE TENSE: THE AMBIGUITIES OF APOCALYPSE

Crucial to my argument is the notion that 'an apocalypse', on top of being a revelation of the divine *spatial* order of reality, is, at its heart, an experiment in thinking about time. More specifically, about the concept of time that is 'allotted' to humans. It is this aspect that will bear directly upon how we think and speak about climate change through a language of time running out. Time is conjured up in various ways in biblical apocalypses, including revelations of the distant future, near future, ultimate future, penultimate future, earthly or otherworldly futures, or indeed that of an unfolding present (Gilbertson, 2003: 110). For instance, a common perception of the New Testament book of Revelation focuses typically on the events that come either side of the millennium (the period in which Satan is bound) as bearing ultimate historical significance.

Signalling the closeness of the ultimate 'end' presumably allows Christians to better recognize and prepare for it: the inauguration of a New Jerusalem, or the restoration of a cosmic balance. But the temporal construction of the book of Revelation is also problematic in this respect. Its numerical construction of time speaks not primarily of the end itself but of the time preceding this end. Graphic, violent images (frequently of an ecological nature) in which the old world is destroyed are thus laden with symbolic tension surrounding the character of the *passing* of this time. In addition to the one thousand year 'break' from evil's dominion – the millennium – (20: 4–5), there is the period of 'half an hour' in which 'there was silence in heaven' (8: 1) at the opening of the seventh seal, the unsettling period in which catastrophe is awaited.

An idea of this 'time that remains' for survivors is also produced through the juxtaposition of the number seven, symbolizing completeness to a Jewish audience (hence completeness/ fulfilment on the side of God and God's vengeance: seven churches, seven trumpets, seven seals, seven bowls), to three and a half (or 'time, times and half a time' – *Daniel* 7:25; Rev 12:14). Half of seven symbolizes incompleteness, an indefinite duration, and by some interpretations a period of crisis and transition (Gilbertson, 2003: 113). Thus, there are three and a half years, 42 months or 1260 days in which the holy city will be trampled (11:2), and in which the bodies of the dead will lay in its streets (11:11). Why might this be significant? Exegetical theories abound (e.g. Kovacs and Rowland, 2004: 125), but I wish simply to suggest that with numerical symbolism the author of Revelation is perhaps consciously mixing temporal qualities of waiting within the drama of the last times. Desires for completeness and finality are juxtaposed with those of uncertainty and calamity for those remaining.

When we consider the long and bloody history of the precise calculations of time periods in Revelation, my suggestion of a quality of indefinite, ambiguous time of waiting would appear to be at best ironic, at worst fatefully unpersuasive. It was, after all, the *one thousand* year period that won the European imagination in the end: from the end-time hysteria at the close of the first millennium and the start of the crusades, through to our own technological anxiety at the end of the second. And in our own context, it appears that the language of catastrophe again defaults to the sense of decadal completeness. Jim Hansen's '10 years to avert climate catastrophe' was as irresistible for journalists as it was for campaigners. Hot on its heels came the '100 months' campaign, complete with ticking countdown clock on its website, and later the '10:10' campaign, calling for 10 per cent emissions cuts by 2010.[5] Perhaps those campaigners would argue that working with the number 10 represents a clear target, however difficult it might be to actually attain. It is also

true that, inasmuch as it is mediated through the scientific understanding of (for instance) 'counting the carbon', climate change
is literally understood numerically.[6] And yet the case I want to
make is that, in reality, climate change isn't like the number ten.
That is, climate change also describes a complex cultural dynamic
that quite eludes the desire for decadal neatness and predictability. Rather, climate change is experienced as *both* immediate
and long-term upheaval. Furthermore, climate change is framed
in terms of 'points' (of global warming) that we should wish to
avoid, and those that have already passed. This creates a sense
of confusion over what exactly is required, and achievable, of
political action in the 'time that remains'.

To repeat, this perspective on apocalyptic interpretation
suggests that appealing to definite timescales, announcing the
imminence of catastrophe, really masks an additional, deeper
anxiety that is closer to the *immanent* apocalyptic instability
introduced above. This distinction might be described, in the
manner of Frank Kermode's celebrated study (1966/2000), as a
twentieth century transition from thinking of the end as always
on the horizon (imminent, about to arrive) to thinking of the
end occurring 'at every moment' (ibid.: 25) – a philosophy of
permanent crisis. With this in mind, it is now possible to look
at the influence of this apocalyptic tension not only on a fervent
religious mindset but on developments much closer to home:
those of modern secular thought, and the concept of *progress*
in history in particular.

PROGRESS: CRISIS OF THE FUTURE

The confluence of economic, climate and energy crises are today
perceived no longer as acts of God, but internal and inevitable
failures of a system. Climate change, for example, is portrayed
as the contradiction, or collision-course (Speth, 2008: 1), of a
modern ideology of limitless growth. This description is significant, since it establishes the bias of *linear* history with which an
apocalyptic end is considered appropriate. Hear, for example,
the polemical environmental writer, Derrick Jensen:

> There can be only one end to this, of course. Apocalypse.
> Gotterdammerung . . . The end of all life, if the dominant
> culture has its way. It's where we've been headed from the

beginning of this several-thousand year journey. It is the only possible end for a culture of linear – as opposed to cyclical – progress. Beginning, middle, end. Self-extinguishment. The only solace and escape from separation: from ourselves, from each other, from the rest of the planet. Plutonium. DDT. Dioxin. Why else would we poison ourselves? No other explanation makes comprehensive sense. Apocalypse. (2000: 278)

In the following pages Jensen invokes the hackneyed trope of the seventh seal from the book of Revelation, chapter 8 (in which the sea turns to blood, the earth burns up, etc. Though the unleashing of the seven plagues of the earth in 15 and 16 would have been even better: 'The fourth angel poured his bowl on the sun, and it was allowed to scorch people with fire; they were scorched by the fierce heat . . . [16: 8–9]). But even more illuminating is his appeal to the apparent self-perception of modernity itself. As children of a linear temporal mentality, or the 'Time's Arrow' paradigm (Gould, 1991), the argument goes, we are *bound* to see our own 'end' in one way or another.

But in what sense are we predisposed to regard history as progressing towards any sort of *telos*, or end, let alone marching inevitably towards self-destruction? And in what sense is this connected to apocalypse? Philosophers (Kant, in particular) have long attempted to answer that question on the basis of a *rational* pursuit of infinite progress in addition to revealed religion: humans, the argument goes, naturally work towards individual and collective improvement, even when such improvement *appears* to involve a regression, and the involvement of periodic crises (such as the bloodshed of revolution, in Kant's case). Even so, a fascination with ends has refused to give up its basic foundation in pre-modern, religious apocalypse. The German philosopher Karl Löwith went as far as to propose that a modern philosophy of history was always 'entirely dependent on theology of history, in particular on the theological concept of history as a history of fulfilment and salvation' (1949: 1).

The advance of progress relies upon a principle in Western thought – linking figures as disparate as Augustine, Condorcet and Marx – of the ultimate 'meaning in history' (ibid.). But what makes this notion apocalyptic is, to repeat my emphasis from the introduction, the *revealed* aspect of this history: the received vision of a world narrative. As Mircea Eliade discovered, what marked the pivotal break of Hebrew religion[7] from Hellenistic and Near Eastern cosmology, was its rejection of cyclical narratives of eternal recurrence to an archetypal existence (Eliade, 1954). Prior to that break, social life could be framed around the promise of the 'return' (dramatized in the Egyptian solar year, or the Babylonian creation myth, for example). *Subsequent* to that break, violence, suffering and ecological disorder could be seen no longer as arbitrary, or endlessly repeated (Eliade, 1954: 104). Oppression by colonial overlords, or the vicissitudes of dangerous climatic change would henceforth appear as morally significant, whether as wake-up calls or signals of divine punishment. History was decoupled from its primitive dependence on repetitive natural cycles. More precisely, history was endowed with meaning inasmuch as events in it (including bloody, unjust and catastrophic events) were couched within the actions of a divine agent. History, therefore, was no longer arbitrary: it became a story, or a narrative, whose beginning, Genesis, also pointed to, or revealed, its end(s): Apocalypse.

From the historical emergence of apocalypse, to a salvation history, to a secularized philosophy of history. What does this intellectual development tell us? To see progress as fulfilment in time invites simultaneously notions of achievement and termination. And this goes some way to explaining how a cultural fascination with the 'end of the world' can involve a tension between naturalistic progress (achievement) and a desire for the hastening of its conclusion. In religious terms, what is eagerly anticipated is the final disclosure of God in history. The latter concept is commonly (and perhaps prejudicially) associated with the attraction of ecological destruction to 'premillennialist' evangelical Christianity.[8] Many assume that fundamentalist Christians welcome the catastrophic prelude to ultimate salvation. There may even be a common presumption that it is *this* that makes an apocalyptic attitude so relevant to contemporary approaches to climate change. In other words, its ability to generate millennial expectation in the face of imminent disaster, leading to a total disengagement from political responses to the crisis.

However, we needn't stray this far from 'secular' thought to explain the tension between fulfilment and destruction that lies at the roots of modern thought on progress. Early modern developments of science, for example, explain much about the formation of attitudes towards *both* the degradation of the earth *and* an optimistic faith in its glorious renewal. It is believed that central to Isaac Newton's new mechanical philosophy, in particular, was a belief in the gradual decay of the 'powers' of the cosmos, due to observations of increasing irregularities of planetary orbits, etc. (Kubrin, 1967: 344). The view of a decaying earth inferred from symptoms of fatigue in the natural world was an old one: we see it, for instance, in the treatises of St. Cyprian, bishop of Carthage in the middle of the third century. Indeed the analogy was made that the world, given its perceived geological and atmospheric instability, resembled a person in the last years of his life. It was an idea adopted later by Immanuel Kant (1754), and used rhetorically in more recent times by James Lovelock (2009: 62).

Now, a simplistic, imminentist apocalyptic anticipation of 'the end is near' is certainly operative here. Just as the battle cry of political upheaval did for religious conflicts around the Reformation period, evidence of the degradation of the earth became one more signal that the end of all things was just around the corner. But there is clearly *more* than simply millennial hysteria for a hastened end within such views. What is relevant about mentioning Newtonian science, for instance, is that it attempted to square the belief that the decaying of the earth was also accompanied by powers to restore it, in successive cycles, thus renewing belief in both the physical, and divine, powers, of world progress. Thus Newton, it is argued, was convinced that the creator provided mechanical means – via comets – to prevent the pessimistic, and unbiblical scenario, that the world would simply end in a winding down, an 'ignoble dissolution' of creation's powers (Kubrin, 1967: 345). On the contrary, planetary decay in seventeenth century England 'was associated with a joyous expectation of the dissolution and subsequent reconstitution of the world' (ibid.). Newton's predictions of the end of the world based upon the book of Daniel and Revelation (Niewiadomski, 2007: 54) sat alongside an optimistic and millennial promise of achieving the 'new Earth' (Kubrin, 1967: 332).

This may go some way to explaining the roots, in early theories of progress, of an immanentist apocalyptic in the sense

I have introduced. For, in the confident developments of natural philosophy, one is not permitted simply to see natural catastrophe as the sign of an impending end time that 'relieves' the pressure of the traumas of the present. Rather, crises in the cosmos are to be viewed as natural cycles in the succession of decay and rebirth. Progress, both in the physical sense and in the common belief at the time of the near perfection of human (scientific) knowledge (Kubrin, 1967: 346) was the sign of apocalypse itself; the sign that the 'ends' of the earth were being revealed in the progress of humanity towards its perfection.

There is, of course, a further, and perhaps clearer connection to be made between a modern, scientific progress as 'enlightenment' and apocalypse as revelation. For science introduced *knowledge* of nature's powers and reasons, and hence, the idea that humans participated in the unfolding *revelation* of the secrets of the universe towards its perfection. The association between revealed knowledge, or *scientia*, and apocalypse, is more than a semantic one. It is well known, for example, that Francis Bacon's total confidence in the future discoveries of science was couched, in parts, by his adherence to an idiosyncratic interpretation of the apocalypse of Daniel 12:4 which presaged great advances in human knowledge: 'For many shall pass to and fro, and science[9] shall be increased'. The future achievement of the new Kingdom of Heaven on Earth, and the scientific bases for his utopian vision in *Atlantis*, were viewed as a return to, or restoration of, Edenic bliss after the fall (Matthews, 2006: 98). It would only be truly fulfilled at the end of the world / end of time, 'the manner whereof is not yet revealed' (*Works* quoted in Stewart, 2001: 77).

What all of this affirms for my argument is an understanding that the concept of progress which we inherit from modernity is not one that simply replaces an imminentist, 'end is near' apocalyptic vision in the interests of promising a vision of steadily increasing perfection on earth. Rather, the two ideas become fused. Faith in the eventual perfection of creation is coupled with an acceptance of periodic crises in the world. Those crises are seen as an aspect of its unfolding 'reason' or story. As increased knowledge unfolds, crises are accepted as necessary within a bigger picture whose narrative 'truth' is evident to the wise, or those reading the signs of the times.

From its outset, then, the apocalyptic resourcing of progress contains an internal tension, or a pulling in opposite directions, with regard to the very future of the earth. On the one hand there is a linear fantasy of its termination. And on the other, an assurance of the fulfilment or revelation of human potential through ingenuity and increased knowledge. And in many ways today, climate change is portrayed as a discourse of the future that is at once the revelation of ends, or limits, as well as the symbol of necessary transformation itself. This is true even where, in modern terms, we might associate such transformation as the proliferation of *risk* in everyday life (see Chris Groves, in this volume). We might even understand the rediscovery of a scientific faith through the turn to Geo-engineering (Webb, 2008) in precisely these terms. Namely, the apocalyptic anticipation of worsening crisis (particularly in the sense that many future catastrophes will be in part the result of emissions already committed, and thus irreversible), alongside the certain culmination of human ingenuity and knowledge, the unfolding of its own brave new world.

DIALECTIC: CRISIS OF THE PRESENT

Through the developments of modern philosophy, then, apocalyptic belief was not destined to be understood simply as the culmination of history in a literal 'end of time' that was just around the corner. Kant, for one, argued that this very idea 'outrages the imagination' (1794/1994: 201) and could not be the basis for rational deliberation. And against Löwith's theory on the theological basis of modern progress, Hans Blumenberg famously argued that the innovation of the idea of progress was, in *distinction* to religious apocalyptic belief, to describe the transformation of the world within the historic process itself. According to Blumenberg, progress was an idea that broke decisively from the Jewish appeal to a transcendent God who would rescue history (1983: 29).

The implications for the problem I have set out can be noticed immediately. For a language of climate crisis that looks only to the definitive 'event' in the future, that seals either salvation or damnation for humanity or the earth, would seem to borrow more from Christian eschatology. Eschatology traditionally means discourse on the end times (from the Greek *eschatos*, meaning 'the last'): what happens at the end of one's life, of history, or that of the life of the world. Blumenberg defined it ultimately as a politics of fear, 'an aggregate of terror and dread' (1983: 30). The appeal to 'immediate expectation' constituted, for Blumenberg, the most effective political propaganda for taking emergency action (1983: 42). In much the same way do critics of environmental propaganda view the use of emergency timescales to convey an urgency to climate change (Hansen's choice of the word 'salvation' in the context of tipping points would appear to confirm this). But I am attempting to prove that what makes climate discourse apocalyptic is precisely beyond a politics of fear (in the future) and closer to Blumenberg's concept of optimistic, modern progress. Namely, by virtue of its ability to reveal the current ecological crisis as a necessary part in some higher destiny or culmination of world history. I am therefore suggesting that Blumenberg was mistaken to separate progress from apocalyptic belief.[10]

Once we accept this element of apocalyptic I have been developing as immanent, that is, revealed crisis in the present, then it begins to resemble very much a secular philosophy of progress. For progress represents the irrepressible and inevitable march or advance of history; its 'truth' ever unfolding. And history's unfolding has for centuries been assumed to take place with successive military and imperial conquests, giving rise to an association of history with *necessary* crisis. A reading of climate change (as many campaign groups attempt) as the momentous new threshold of opportunity for universal transformation (e.g. Homer-Dixon, 2006) can, I think, also be understood within this wider historic association of periodic crises as the inevitable birth pangs of the awaited new world, forever revealing itself. A contemporary temptation to view climate crisis as the historic, or even *cosmic* opportunity for a paradigm shift or global transformation for the better, can, in this sense, also be seen as apocalyptic.

To understand this idea that global crisis somehow reveals a hidden truth of the world, we cannot avoid mentioning the legacy of Hegelian dialectical philosophy. Hegel is pivotal in framing the concept of progress as the unfolding of reason in time. As Löwith claimed, '[e]ven those who know nothing of Hegel continue to think today in the Hegelian spirit, to the extent that they share his admiration for the power of history' (1964: 217). If this is true, it is all the more so for Hegel's achievement of synthesizing the two dimensions of apocalyptic I have tried to link to climate change. Namely, the imminent apocalyptic of the event that is 'to come' on the one hand, and material history as the unfolding of reason, or God, in time, on the other. In Hegel's philosophy of history, the two become one and the same: the progress of reason simply *is* the self-emptying of God in history, in time. The premise of a Hegelian philosophy of history is the 'unconquerable belief that there is Reason in history, together with the belief that the world of intelligence and self-conscious will is not subject to chance . . . ' (Hegel 1837/1988: 13). Hegel, for this reason, represents a key point in Western thought in which apocalyptic as fearful, 'imminent expectation' is replaced by an apocalyptic immanence: a notion of history and historic crises as an unfolding of the 'end (purpose) of the world' in time.

A contemporary attitude with regard to climatic catastrophe owes much to this concept of dialectic. For Hegel saw progress in terms of the liberation of *human* history from the vicissitudes of nature, and the repetition of arbitrary natural cycles: 'the world of spirit and the world of nature continue to have this distinction, that the latter moves only in a recurring cycle, while the former certainly also makes progress' (1817: 234). He is also thought to have been influenced by the medieval apocalypticism of Joachim of Fiore, the twelfth century abbot whose division of world history into three *status*, or ages, became a staple apocalyptic foundation for the idea of world progress (O'Regan, 1994). Such a concept has arguably influenced subsequent models of historic progress, including movements as disparate as Marx's stages of historic crisis, and Hitler's idea of the millennial Reich. Both examples go some way to understanding modern, immanentist apocalyptic as a mesmerizing attraction to unfolding catastrophe. Rather than seeing the catastrophe to come as an anticipated, millennial 'event', we are capitulated to the sort of 'knowing' realization that perhaps Jensen's cynicism was close to after all: disaster is written into the very unfolding of progress, no longer feared, but expected within the course of history.

LOOKING TO THE HEAVENS (AGAIN): THE ETERNAL RETURN OF CLIMATE CRISIS

The dialectic approach just described demonstrates a certain resistance to the idea that apocalyptic represents a 'get out clause' from the struggle of history, by anticipating its final days. The 'death of God' theologian Thomas Altizer described the birth of secular modernity precisely as this shift in thinking about history without the transcendence of God. It was, he said, the unleashing of a new apocalypticism (1993: 170), whose revelation of divine truth had, without reference to the external wrath of God, simply become *pure history*, or historic process itself. But we can now begin to square this concept with the persistence, in Western culture, of the *recurrence*, or cycles, of global crisis. For if history is apocalyptic without the anticipation of an imminent, divine apocalyptic event that will put all to rights (or simply put us out of our misery) then it becomes easy to see how history represents, with one crisis after another, an apocalyptic repetition of cycles within this constantly evolving history.

The roots of thinking of cyclical crisis go back to the ability to perceive historic change on a cosmic, macroscopic scale. It goes back to the discovery of 'deep time' as the cyclical, geological traumas of the earth's history (Gould, 1991: 2). Such was arguably Blumenberg's observation in the search for the origins of the idea of progress. The idea of progress, thought Blumenberg, owed more to the discoveries of astronomy and meteorology than to theology (1974: 7). Astronomy played a crucial role in the secularization of apocalyptic belief, since it generated perspectives of a *cosmic* sort of progress of vast, planetary timescales denied a medieval consciousness (Bull, 1999: 117–18; Iliffe, 2000). As I have already claimed, the early moderns' discovery of natural laws regulating the cosmos were 'progressively' apocalyptic precisely in their functioning as the revelation of the hitherto *hidden* secrets of the universe. They supplemented biblical predictions of an encroaching millennium through a newfound revelation of nature herself. Such discoveries remained faithful to an apocalyptic sensibility, however. For nature still unveiled divine purpose in the process of history through time; only now they could be viewed on a macroscopic, geological scale. From this perspective, perhaps we can say that climate science has always been, by definition, an apocalyptic art: an epistemological balancing act between necessary, avoidable, predictable and recurring crises. For an association can also be traced between the philosophy of progress in the movements of the cosmos, with the belief in the endlessness, or recurrence, of world crises. Apparently, this is old news. According to Eliade, despite the triumph of linear Abrahamic religion, news of the death of a pagan myth of the archetypal return had always been premature. The concept of time's cyclical recurrence persisted in other ways, and not only in the history of geology. Indeed, Ned Lukacher (1998) has argued that the idea of eternal recurrence (the belief that all things experienced in the present repeat eternally) has persisted as a heretical 'secret history' throughout Western thought, from the persistent influence of Stoic philosophy, to explorations of time in Shakespeare, through to thinkers such as Hegel, Heidegger and, most obviously, Nietzsche.

The purpose of this brief description of the historical struggles between linear and cyclical time views is actually to make 'modern' sense of my previous suggestion that apocalypse represents an experiment with the experience of time. For we should now be able to appreciate the persistence of cyclical time as a pivotal underside to Western apocalyptic. The persistence of cyclical time *within an overall philosophy of progress* enables ecological change to appear as simultaneously threatening, unchanging, *and* revelatory and necessary: the source of our stories that make our lives meaningful. Once this is understood, we can understand better how climate crisis might both present an ultimatum on the future of the human, and yet refuse to inspire action to combat it. 'Apocalyptic' now means something quite different to the fear of future, final calamity. What we are confronted with instead is the frightening possibility of the endlessness of the present catastrophe, an *immanent* apocalypse in the sense that it does *not* promise a fast, decisive rupture in the future.

What marks the challenge of contemporary apocalyptic is therefore the transformation of a future expectation into the perpetuation, and normalization, of the present (a point also made by Buell in this volume). This includes its periodic cycles of catastrophe, *not* the promise of escape from the vicissitudes of nature. This is an ironic twist on Hegel's own antipathy to natural cycles. In Hegel's terms progress means 'the *comprehension of the present and the actual,* not the setting up of a *world beyond* which God knows where' (Hegel, 1821/1991: 20). But this is the very antithesis of utopian hubris, or messianic hope in the face of crisis. Implicit to such a view is an absence of striving or the *overcoming* of crisis, or indeed, perhaps, the need for striving at all.

There are clear historical precedents of this notion: Fukuyama's 'end of history' apologetic is an example. For who now would characterize the triumphal victory of neo-liberal capitalism and its destruction of opponent ideologies as anything but a recurring nightmare for the majority world? The example is appropriate also to the techno-fix and authoritarian proposals in the face of catastrophic climate change. In the alleged triumph of liberal capitalism is vindicated the worst of both worlds: both the linear march of progress, and the static acceptance of cycles.

But what exactly is meant by a 'static acceptance of cycles' in our own context? The popular responses to the recent economic crisis revealed a desire to see periodic collapse – boom and bust – as part of unavoidable sequences in which all were caught. A revolutionary apocalyptic imagination – one that could imagine that 'another world is possible', that could imagine the end of imperial power, was rejected in favour of the apocalyptic cycle of expected crises. And in reference to climate change, we may have reached a point at which the idea of human agency – the ability to act – has also become swallowed up in some larger meta-narrative in which the end of the story is beyond people's control. We are, for example, witnessing what Mark Lynas calls 'geological fatalism': 'the oft-heard refrain that life will go on, with us or without us, and that at the end of the day it doesn't really matter' (Lynas, 2007: 257–8). Such a fatalism might also be thought to manifest in the recent explosion of thought experiments on the survival of life on earth after humans have (by entirely arbitrary causes) disappeared: thought experiments such as Alan Weisman's *The World Without Us* (2008); Jan

Zalasiewicz' *The Earth After Us* (2008); the National Geographic's *Aftermath: Population Zero* (2008) and the History Channel's *Life After People* (2008).

One can see the inheritance of that 'astronomical' value of progress introduced earlier, or the shift in perspective that occurred with the discovery of deep time. But could there be a morally binding sentiment that underlies this trend, that places the value of humanity within the wider interests of the biosphere, and beyond, from which our life is generated? Some ethical perspectives (among them, deep ecology and contemporary environmental action groups, eco-feminism and indigenous environmental movements) argue precisely for this greater awareness of the scope of evolution of life on earth, including its cycles of mass extinctions, in order to move from anthropocentrism to 'geocentrism'. But in the light of climate change, it could also be seen as the normalization of the environmental consequences of 'business as usual' – the very processes deemed *unnatural* by their labelling as 'anthropogenic'. Read, for example, John Gray:

> It is only in human terms that climate change can be viewed as apocalyptic, however. In the life of the planet, it is normal . . . Much biodiversity will be lost, but the earth will renew itself. Life will continue and will thrive – whether or not humans are around to see it. (2006)

The idea of recurring cycles is clearly not without its appeal. It is also significant to recall that a reference to natural cycles was also the first rhetorical port of call among climate sceptics' attempts to head off the allegedly catastrophist agenda of the environmental lobby. A good example was the controversial Channel 4 documentary *The Great Global Warming Swindle* (2007). The main premise of that documentary was that climate change could be understood within natural warming cycles on a much larger geological timescale than is normally perceived.

Irrespective of the film's discredited uses of 'science', it does raise the question of what political and psychological concerns might underlie such recourse to natural cyclical movement. Far from the rationalist pursuit of 'the truth' against an oppressive apocalyptic hysteria (as the director, Michael Durkin has portrayed the environmental lobby), might it represent the consolation of resignation: a realization, to our relief, that there might be 'nothing we can do'? An article in *Orion* magazine on the 'consolations of extinction' would typify this switch:

> The consolations of extinction are an acceptance of death, of *all* deaths, *always*, in *all* places . . . Families die. Genera die. Whole ecosystems die. The solar system's planets – nine, no, eight, or, okay, maybe twelve, count 'em how you will – they're goners too. Stars, including all 400 billion in the Milky Way: doomed. Galaxies, all of them, all 100-plus billion of them: doomed. Even protons will decay someday, the ages of the atom finally closed. This universe – one, perhaps, in an infinite multiverse – will die in a darkness and cold beyond our imaginings. (Cokinos, 2007)

Fans of the science fiction novels of Olaf Stapledon will be familiar with the potential for this galactic time perspective to take on the form of an ethical conundrum. It is a sort of inverted question to the one I posed in the introduction: Does the *relinquishing* of an imminent, human centred apocalyptic vision, galvanize action, or not? As if pre-empting this question, Cokinos goes on to clarify:

> I'm not counselling a life of civic inaction or, worse, a life of civic inaction coupled with consumerist bliss. I don't muse on stellar eschatology in order to cultivate a sophisticated nihilism or to justify purchasing a 900-inch-wide plasma-screen television. I'm counseling (sic) diligence, but also calm: hands that work in the present and eyes that see through it . . . I'm saying that too much grief for the world means less energy to help it along. (ibid.)

So recurrence is Janus-faced: it allows us to keep faith in progress, the unfolding, revealed, story of the universe, beyond the failures and death of the human. But it also allows us to give up on the human, to laugh 'knowingly' in the face of activism. For people like John Gray, for example, the very principle of climate activism would presumably confirm the illusory and consolatory pursuit of meaning and purpose in life that typified the traditional apocalyptic approach. A more authentic life of reflection embraces, according to him, a 'willing surrender to never-returning moments' (Gray, 2002: 199).

Though diametrically opposed to the notion of moments returning *eternally,* Gray's sentiment on activism could have come as easily from Nietzsche. For Nietzsche heaped praise upon those who, like Hamlet, lovingly accept their own fate: 'they have *understood,* and action repels them; for their action can change nothing in the essence of things' (1872/1973: 39). Perhaps, then, it is this Nietzschean revelation of tragedy in its dizzyingly cyclical form that best represents an apocalyptic ethos for climate change today. Nietzsche's own brand of apocalyptic revelation, 'insight into the terrible truth', is a rejection of the consolation of approaching, imminent *ends* and fear of the future: 'We have invented the concept of 'end': In reality, there is no end. One is necessary, one is a piece of fatefulness, one belongs to the whole, one is in the whole . . . ' (1888/1976: 500).

CONCLUSION

The populist media concept of apocalyptic faith – the terrifying promise that we shall soon be removed from the present history by a tidal wave, storm or conflagration – has not gone away. On the contrary, I hope to have shown how it is in fact stitched into a larger and more universal faith in world history that we have called modern progress. A Baconian faith in the increase of human knowledge up to its perfection in a utopian society has far from disappeared in our postmodern distaste for grand ideologies. Rather, we have incorporated a faith in revealed progress as the acceptance of a darker, catastrophist side to the universe. We have also acknowledged that perhaps its revelation to us humans is that the universe no longer needs us. Within the picture of a far future, our present crises pale into insignificance within the larger life of the cosmos. The continuation of the cosmos, indeed, is celebrated as the recurrence of cycles. If this represents something of a consolation, it does not for that relinquish the ethical task ahead. For exactly *how* we perceive climate change as shaping the character of life that 'persists' is always an open question, and generates a host of diverse social and political responses.

The appearance, in media and Hollywood portrayals, that climate change is feared as impending, total disaster, is, to repeat, a smokescreen to its more challenging apocalyptic framing. Namely, the prospect of a continuing, unfolding and transformed reality of which our current actions are unavoidably a part. The cultural obsession with the '2012' phenomenon crudely (and incorrectly, according to most Mayanist scholars) derived from classical Mayan prophecy reflects this contradiction well. Far from exploring the meanings of the calendrical completion of the Mesoamerican 'long count' *cycle*, a period of transition (Webster, 2007; León-Portilla, 1988), Emmerich's blockbuster portrayal of *2012* faithfully represents the purest of endist fantasies: the type of 'apocalypse porn' (Harris, 2009) to which we have become accustomed and thoroughly entertained.

Questions such as whether apocalyptic rhetoric galvanizes political engagement or simply disempowers, is therefore perhaps the wrong question. Or, if we want to ask that question, then we need to disentangle the meaning of apocalyptic further than we have wanted to. For if the obsession with a violent apocalyptic future is caught up in the inertia of cyclical recurrence, the danger is that political action might simply mean adapting to the recurrence of both unavoidable and avoidable crises: an inability to imagine (or reveal) the future differently. But today, it is not the Hollywood fantasy of our end, but the hard, ethical question of what human life means – indeed, what *hope* might mean – in the time that remains, that represents our apocalyptic challenge.

NOTES

1 Many thanks to Peter Scott, Andrew Bowman, Alastair McIntosh and Christopher Rowland for their comments on this chapter.
2 *The Oxford English Dictionary* cites the uses of 'apocalyptic' as noun as far back as 1898, and defines it as 'apocalyptic teaching, philosophy or literature'.
3 For a study of the political and cultural uses of apocalyptic violence, see Amanat and Collins, 2004.
4 I follow Brian Schroeder's distinction between eschatology and apocalypse along the lines of epistemology, or ways of *knowing*. If eschatology means discourse about faith in the 'end times', apocalyptic emphasizes the principle of knowing, apprehending, seeing or having revealed, the 'end' in question (Schroeder, 2009: 236) and need not emphasize an imminent eschaton at all. Biblical scholars confirm this, pointing out that more crucial to the apocalypse genre is its

claim that the truth of the world is not all that is visible or conceivable by human means (Collins, 1997: 92).

5 For a fascinating study of the relationship between decadal timescales, climate change and the automobile industry, see Karen Pinkus, 'On Climate, Cars, and Literary Theory'. *Technology and Culture* 49 (4), 1002–9.

6 I am grateful to Andrew Bowman for this insight.

7 For a discussion of the contested relationship between Persian and Hebrew apocalyptic belief, however, see Cohn (2001).

8 A more nuanced study of ecological attitudes among (US) evangelical premillennialists is given by Annette Ahern (2009).

9 Bacon's own translation of the Vulgate version is extremely significant: in other translations, including the *NRSV*, the word 'evil' is used instead of 'knowledge'.

10 But see Note 4, for my distinction between eschatology and apocalypse, which I think lies at odds with Blumenberg's conflation of the two.

REFERENCES

Ahern, A. (2009), 'Broken Churches – Devastated Planet: Looking for Common Ground between Evangelicals and Feminists in the War on Climate Change', in *Ecothee: Ecological Theology and Environmental Ethics* (ed. Andrianos, L. et al.) Chania: Orthodox Academy of Crete.

Altizer, T. (1993), *The Genesis of God: A Theological Genealogy*. Louisville, KY: Westminster/John Knox Press.

Amanat, A. and Collins, J. J. (eds) (2004), *Apocalypse and Violence*. New Haven, CT: Yale Centre for International and Area Studies.

Arroyo, E. B. (1994), *The Illusion of the End*. London: Stanford University Press.

—(2008), 'Contemplating the Katrina Whirlwind: From "Apocalypse Now" to Solidarity for the Common Good'. *Seattle Journal for Social Justice* 7 (1).

Blumenberg, H. (1974), 'On a Lineage of the Idea of Progress'. *Social Research* 41 (1), 5–27.

—(1983), *The Legitimacy of the Modern Age*. Trans. Robert M. Wallace. Cambridge: MIT Press.

Bull, M. (1999), *Seeing Things Hidden: Apocalypse, Vision and Totality*. London: Verso.

Cohn, N. (2001), *Cosmos, Chaos and the World to Come*. London: Yale.

Cokinos, C. (2007), 'The Consolations of Extinction'. *Orion Magazine* May/June. Available at: www.orionmagazine.org/index.php/articles/article/268/ (accessed September 2008).

Collins, J. J. (1984), *The Apocalyptic Imagination: An Introduction to the Jewish Matrix of Christianity*. New York: Crossroad.

—(1997), *Seers, Sybils and Sages in Hellenistic-Roman Judaism*. Leiden: Brill.

Deleuze, G. (1998), *Essays Clinical and Critical*. Trans. Daniel W. Smith and Michael A. Greco. London: Verso.

Edelstein, K. (2009), 'Media Mayhem: My Last "Apocalypse Now" Headline', *Mother Nature Network* 15 June. Available at: www.mnn.com/earth-matters/climate-change/stories/media-mayhem-my-last-apocalypse-now-headline (accessed 7 August 2009).

Eliade, M. (1954), *The Myth of the Eternal Return*. London: Routledge and Keegan Paul.

Gilbertson, M. (2003), *God and History in the Book of Revelation: New Testament Studies in Dialogue with Pannenberg and Moltmann*. Cambridge: Cambridge University Press.

Gould, S. J. (1991), *Time's Arrow, Time's Cycle: Myth and Metaphor in the Discovery of Geological Time*. London: Penguin.

—(2002), *Straw Dogs: Thoughts on Humans and Other Animals*. London: Granta.

—(2006), 'Letting Climate Change Happen', *New Statesman* 29 May. Available at: www.newstatesman.com/200605290019 (accessed 4 February 2009).

Harris, P. (2009), 'Hollywood's New "zeitgeist of doom" Is Sparked by Anxious Times'. *The Observer*, 9 August, p. 22.

Hegel, G. W. F. (1817), *Encyclopedia of Philosophical Sciences: The Logic* Available at: www.marxists.org/reference/archive/hegel/works/sl/slidea.htm#SL234 (accessed 12 June 2009).

—(1821/1991), *Elements of the Philosophy of Right*. Ed. Allen Wood; trans. H. B. Nisbet. Cambridge: Cambridge University Press.

—(1837/1988), *Introduction to the Philosophy of History*. Trans. Leo Rauch. Indianapolis, IN: Hackett.

Homer-Dixon, H. (2006), *The Upside of Down: Catastrophe, Creativity and the Renewal of Civilisation*. London: Souvenir Press.

Iliffe, R. (2000), 'The Masculine Birth of Time: Temporal Frameworks of Early Modern Natural Philosophy'. *British Journal of the History of Science* 33, 427–53.

Jensen, D. (2000), *A Language Older Than Words*. New York: Context Books.

Kant, I. (1754/1982), 'The Question, Whether the Earth Is Ageing, Considered Physically', in Reinhardt, O. and D. R. Oldroyd, 'Kant's Thoughts on the Ageing of the Earth'. *Annals of Science* 39 (4), 349–69.

—(1794/1994), 'The End of All Things', in *Religion within the Boundaries of Mere Reason and Other Writings* (Allen Wood and George Di Giovanni, eds). Cambridge: Cambridge University Press.

Kermode, F. (1966/2000), *The Sense of an Ending: Studies in the Theory of Fiction*. Oxford: Oxford University Press.

Kovacs, J. and Rowland, C. (2004), *Revelation*. Oxford: Blackwell.

Kubrin, D. (1967), 'Newton and the Cyclical Cosmos: Providence and the Mechanical Philosophy'. *Journal of the History of Ideas* 28 (3) (July–September), 325–46.

Lean, G. (2005), 'Apocalypse Now: How Humanity Is Sleepwalking to the Ends of the Earth'. *The Independent on Sunday,* 6 February. Available at: www.independent.co.uk/environment/apocalypse-now-how-mankind-is-sleepwalking-to-the-end-of-the-earth-485640.html (accessed 26 June 2009).

León-Portilla, M. (1988), *Time and Reality in the Thought of the Maya.* London: University of Oklahoma Press.

Lovelock, J. (2009), *The Vanishing Face of Gaia: A Final Warning.* London: Allen Lane.

Löwith, K. (1949), *Meaning in History.* London: University of Chicago Press.

—(1964), *From Hegel to Nietzsche: The Revolution in Nineteenth Century Thought.* Trans. David E. Green. London: Constable.

Lukacher, N. (1998), *Time-Fetishes: The Secret History of Eternal Recurrence.* London: Duke University Press.

Lynas, M. (2007), *Six Degrees: Our Future on a Hotter Planet.* London: Fourth Estate.

Matthews, S. (2006), 'Francis Bacon's Scientific Apocalypse', in *The End that Does: Art, Science, and Millennial Accomplishment* (Cathy Guttierez and Hillel Schwartz, eds). London: Equinox, pp. 97–115.

Nietzsche, F. (1872/1973), *The Birth of Tragedy.* Trans. Michael Tanner. London: Penguin Books.

—(1888/1976), 'Twilight of the Idols: Or, How One Philosophizes with a Hammer', in *The Portable Nietzsche* (ed. and trans. Walter Kaufmann). New York: Penguin Books, pp. 463–563.

Niewiadomski, J. (2007), ' "Denial of the apocalypse" versus "fascination with the final days": Current Theological Discussion of Apocalyptic Thinking in the Perspective of Mimetic Theory', in *Politics and Apocalypse* (ed. Robert Hamilton-Kelly) East Lansing, MI: University of Michigan Press.

OED (Oxford English Dictionary) (2008), 'apocalyptic' Draft Addition. Available at: http://dictionary.oed.com/cgi/entry/50010286?single=1&query_type=word&queryword=apocalyptic&first=1&max_to_show=10 (accessed 17 July 2009).

O'Regan, Cyril (1994), *The Heterodox Hegel* New York: State University of New York Press.

Persons, S. (1954), 'The Cyclical Theory of History in Eighteenth Century America'. *American Quarterly* 6 (2), 147–63, London: The Johns Hopkins University Press.

Pinkus, K. (2009), '*On Climate, Cars, and Literary Theory', Technology and Culture* 49 (4), 1002–9.

Schroeder, B. (2009), 'Apocalypse, Eschatology and the Death of God', in *Nietzsche and Levinas* (Jill Stauffer and Bettina Bergo, eds). New York: Columbia University Press, pp. 232–49.

Speth, J. G. (2008), *The Bridge at the Edge of the World: Capitalism, the Environment, and Crossing from Crisis to Sustainability.* London: Yale University Press.

Stewart, A. (2001), *Francis Bacon and the Transformation of Early-Modern Philosophy.* Cambridge: Cambridge University Press.

Webb, D. (2008), 'Geo-engineering and its Implications', paper delivered at *Climate Change and Violence, Workshop 1*, November 2008, Southampton University.

Webster, D. (2007), 'The uses and abuses of the ancient maya'. Talk delivered to *The Emergence of the Modern World* conference, Otzenhausen, Germany, 25 September.

CHAPTER ELEVEN

BEYOND HUMANITY'S END

AN EXPLORATION OF A DRAMATIC VERSUS NARRATIVE RHETORIC AND ITS ETHICAL IMPLICATIONS[1]

CELIA DEANE-DRUMMOND

INTRODUCTION

The spectre of the end of humanity through climate change has the capacity to generate a powerful narrative that can lead to very diverse ethical responses, from resignation through to revolutionary political action. These diverse ethical responses echo alternative narratives about the way humanity is connected with the natural world, either envisaging humanity as one species among many biota such as in Lovelock's Gaia hypothesis (1987), or humanity in a privileged position over and against the natural world, bolstered by the promise of new technologies. The recent reports by the Intergovernmental Panel on Climate Change (IPCC) reflect an epistemological starting point of humanity as superior to the natural world to some extent. The latter perspective shows up human agents as pitched to respond effectively to the challenges it faces either through mitigation or adaptation.[2] Buried in the text are also more gloomy predictions of the fate of the earth that are rather less optimistic, betraying nervousness about the possibility of a tipping point that bodes an uncertain future prospect for human life and life in all its diversity on earth, at least as we know and experience it in the twenty-first century. The purpose of this chapter is not so much to analyse the full variety of these secular responses to climate change, but, rather, to suggest that much academic analysis of apocalyptic rhetoric mapped onto climate change has so far put more emphasis on perceiving this in terms of narrative, rather

than drama. Media reporting, on the other hand, regularly pre-
fers drama as one of its primary ways of communicating ideas
connected with climate change. Maxwell and Jules Boykoff
(2007) argue that the media reporting of climate change uses
drama regularly but 'adherence to first-order journalistic norms –
personalization, dramatization and novelty – significantly influence the employment of second-order norms – authority-order
and balance – and that this has led to informationally deficient
mass-media coverage of this crucial issue'. In this they assume
that such dramatic reading in mass media necessarily distorts
the place that the media might play in the public realm. While
there may be some exaggerated examples of the use of drama
in the US media reporting of climate change, I will argue that
drama is significant in that it allows a greater attention to the
personal engagement with the issue compared with its portrayal
in narrative terms. Hence while I share Stefan Skrimshire's
fascination with the category of apocalyptic as a way of expressing the complexity of beliefs about the end, especially the end
as now envisaged through climate change, I consider that his
rendition of apocalypse as narrative is misleading.[3] The difference between narrative and drama is important, since a narrative
rhetoric will, arguably, have different outcomes, both ethically
and politically, compared with dramatic rhetoric. What is meant
by the term 'narrative' and its particular function in religious
terms is very diverse. It can mean, for example, simply the nature
of religious experience, so religion is about the way people tell
particular stories, or such stories give structure to the world
and try to make sense of it. Narrative can mean more than this,
however, in that it can mean not just the *form* in which an
encounter with the sacred takes place, but secondly the bearer
of the sacred itself, such as in narratives embedded in sacred
scripture. Thirdly, it can also refer to the life story (biography)
or experiences of a particular group or individual. Another
fourth form of narrative simply relates to the manner in which
biblical text is set forth. Finally, portraying theological issues
through narrative implies the use of narrative as a hermeneutic
tool.[4] I will argue here that a greater emphasis on *drama* is important from a secular as well as a theological perspective. I will
argue that it is particularly important in that the alternatives
of narrative or drama have considerable bearing on the ethical

and political outcomes of climate change discourse. While I cannot do justice to the full ramifications of this attention to drama in the present context, I seek to give sufficient indicators in order to generate debate and discussion on this issue.

Epic Narrative or Drama?

The most common way of reading history is through genealogies or through a systemization of the dynamics of historical change in various sorts of grand narratives (Quash, 2005: 6). This is also true of cosmic history, including that expressed through various grand proposals, such as the cosmic creation story of Thomas Berry and Brian Swimme, or the Gaia hypothesis of James Lovelock (Swimme and Berry, 1992; Lovelock, 1987, 2006). Lovelock's Gaia hypothesis, for example, puts great stress on stability or homeostasis of the planetary earth system around preset norms that have been operating on the earth for millennia. He could have called his idea the geophysiology hypothesis, but such a name would not have fired the imagination in the sense that Gaia evokes a story about the earth, a narrative in which the earth conveys a sense of agency. Lovelock traces the emergence of Gaia back to the dawn of the earth's appearing, and the different phases of anaerobic and aerobic conditions for life to develop on earth. It unfolds in a gripping and fascinating narrative about our past and the way such a past has unravelled so as to produce the living planet. For Lovelock the biota as a whole contribute in a vital way to the stability of that planet's life, such that gaseous composition of the atmosphere and temperature are kept within the boundaries that are suitable for life as we know it. Human players are intimately bound up with this narrative in as much as only humans are conscious of what is happening, and for Lovelock this consciousness is in some sense *representative* for the whole earth.[5] Yet, in spite of such an elevated awareness, as far as the earth is concerned, human beings do not seem to contribute to its flourishing. One might even view humanity, according to some readings of the Gaia hypothesis, as a cancerous growth on the planet, bent on its destruction. While some philosophers turn to the interconnectedness that is necessary for Gaia to function as an inspiration for a naturalistic basis for correct moral action, what is less well appreciated is that if humanity is more like a cancerous growth, then there is an inevitability to its destructive potential. A corollary is that the earth will inevitably respond in a negative way as a direct consequence of such human destructiveness. In practical terms this will lead to the collapse of the very systems that have underlain such stability of environmental conditions. Such a view is also expressed in Lovelock's more recent work where he engages with climate change (Primavesi, 2000). Lovelock did not intend his account to be religious, but its religious undertones were inescapable, given the resonance of Gaia imagery with goddess mythology, and the radical dethronement of the place of human beings in contrast with the anthropocentrism of most established religious traditions such as Judaism, Christianity and Islam. Most of the questions arising out of his earlier books were ones related to the religious (and often Christian) implications of his theory, rather than specifically scientific ones. More recently Anne Primavesi has deliberately sought to incorporate Lovelock's ideas into a theological position that identifies God with the earth, understood in Gaian terms (ibid.). Thomas Berry's cosmic creation story is similar in that it stresses the function of the earth as a whole, and its emergence from the beginning of time, though in this case evolutionary elements come more to the surface in his narration of the earth's history. Moreover, in this case theological elements are deliberately woven into an otherwise secular creation myth. We find, therefore, less pessimism about humanity as a destructive force compared with Lovelock's approach, but there is still a determinism here that when put on a cosmic scale seems almost impossible to resist. How, for example, can humanity possibly find a sense of self-worth and stand up before so many millennia of the earth's history, with its myriad upon myriad of both formation and natural destruction of species?

These epic accounts assume a standpoint from which one can observe or report impartially a given sequence of events, showing forth a measured progression, so that 'there is an element of necessity at the heart of the events and happenings that take place', leading, at its worse, to the 'genre of false objectification' so that epic 'reifies what is given to it to know. It substitutes monological narration for dialogue, without supposing that this is a loss for truth. And it tends towards determinism' (Quash, 2005: 42). In other words, narratives, when told in a certain way as grand narratives, create an aura of determinism, where what is anticipated seems an almost inevitable trajectory of the story as told so far. Once this is transposed into a way of perceiving religious truth, problems are accentuated. Where theology, for example, bases itself on Scripture as a single source, the more it tends towards an interpretation that sees itself as the written objective account of something that has taken place. In other words, it offers itself up as an epic-narrative theology, and 'will quite logically assume the role of judge over the events and their actualization' (Balthasar, 1990: 56). If we envisage narrative as a way of bringing structure and form to otherwise heterogeneous events it might seem relatively innocuous (Vanhoozer, 1990: 89).[6] Non-dramatic readings of history fail to give attention to individuals, exceptions to rules, resistances to explanation and densities of meaning.

The ethical and political implications of such epic readings are clear. If humanity is inevitably caught in a narrative that is not of its own making, guided by the force of millennia of the earth's history, then this will lead to a fatalistic attitude towards climate change, a resignation that nothing really can be done to stop it, and therefore that humanity just has to accept the inevitable. Politically, this will mean a shift in emphasis when confronted with the complexities of climate change, so that, where pessimism about any positive outcome of human inter-vention prevails, no action at all is taken. If such pessimism is weaker, but resignation about climate change is still a dominant rhetoric, then at best a discourse of adaptation replaces that of mitigation; what is the point of mitigation if there is very little we can do to influence the course of events?[7] I suggest that the shift towards adaptation is gaining greater momentum in the Western context, and one among many of the underlying rea-sons for this is likely to be a sense of inevitability of climate change brought about by strong secular creation myths. Gaia may, on the surface at least, appear to support a more ecologi-cally friendly ethic in its sensitivity to interrelationships. But, in as much as it generates a strong narrative, it counts against any such ethic. Furthermore, those interrelationships are not those most characterized by a positive view of the place of humanity.

In the Gaian scheme it is the mass effect of trillions of micro-organisms and other species lower in the evolutionary scale that has the greatest impact on climatic stability. A residual sense of guilt that humanity should not really be here, leads to a devaluation of humanity's place on the earth, an inversion of the kind of anthropocentrism that has been a dominant cultural motif in human history, especially in the centuries immediately following the Enlightenment. This underlying sense of guilt about humanity's place on the earth would also shift the focus away from policies that promote mitigation, since it would be expected that humanity is highly likely to interfere in negative ways, and therefore imply that adaptation to climate change is the only sensible strategy.

In practice, actual political activity is far more complex than this account suggests, in that official positions taken by demo-cratic governments more often than not show confidence in more traditional accounts of science which then overlay and compete with more subversive notions of science as represented in Gaian theory. In this case, a competing narrative emerges in tension with Gaian narratives that is more Promethean and far more optimistic about humanity's ability to manage its own affairs using technological knowledge, including, according to this understanding, the problems associated with climate change. Mitigation and adaptation are viewed as both desirable and possible, such that collective human action is sufficient to coun-ter any dangers or threats to human survival. The trajectory for this official political position in this case is humanistic rather than fatalistic, but the optimism about human inventiveness over and against the natural realm generates an ideal that has more utopian overtones. At its limits it may, indeed, ironically encourage a revolutionary politics such that human beings are inevitably caught up with social, political and cultural change in such a way that weakens any sense of individual agency. This, ironically again, amounts to a disassociation of the human as a political being from an understanding of its embeddedness in the natural world, a way of perceiving political life as that constructed both by and for human agents. Of course, perceiv-ing the human in political terms as disassociated from nature has been a dominant strand in the history of the politics of nature. Peter Scott argues convincingly against such a view in favour of a postnatural politics such that humanity's embeddedness in the natural world becomes not just an adjunct to human affairs, but a new approach to the political realm. This approach weaves in a deeper understanding of human beings as both part of nature, where the meaning of nature is complex and takes account of unsettled boundaries such as that between the natural and artificial.[8]

By contrast drama includes lyric in its brief and mediates between narrative and lyric. Lyric accounts of human history express themselves through a 'volatile, highly individual, immediate and emotionally coloured mode of response and expression' (Quash, 2005: 42). It is important to note that drama does not eclipse all narrative; rather, by giving attention to the lyrical it ensures that it does not slip into epic mode. Ancient literary criticism argued about the extent to which drama as a genre contained narrative, or whether drama imported narrative accounts, as it were, from the outside. Philodesmus, for example, argued against the position of Aristotle, who, in *Poetics*, distinguished epic clearly from tragedy, calling the former narrative or *apangelia* Halliwell (1986: 128–9). Yet, the figure of the messenger (*angelia*) in Greek tragedy allows drama to express the narrative voice in a way that closely resembles an epic account. Hence the mix is present in the drama, but narrative is mediated through the messenger. But what precisely is the difference between epic narratives and drama? Drama is most commonly represented as that which displays human actions and temporal events in specific contexts. Drama reflects the indeterminacy typical of human life, including the unforeseeable interactions of circumstances, and the ambiguities of existence (Balthasar, 1988: 17). Drama also has the characteristic of 'event' through the dynamic staging of particulars in a particular way. It also has an irreducibly *social* dimension, including the audience as much as those taking part in the play. In addition, drama includes the idea of anticipation, but this is not the same as resignation, rather, it is ongoing consuming involvement in the work of interpretation (Quash, 2005: 35–7). Drama certainly has the capacity to take up narrative elements, as is in evidence in classical Greek tragedy, but the difference from epic is striking, so that 'Greek tragedy confronts the spectator directly with a multitude of voices, each with an equal claim, in principle, to truth and authority. The absence of a narrator renders all speech on stage equally authoritative or suspect, equally bound by its status as a rhetorical creation' (Barrett, 2002: xvi). These encounters of different voices produce both opacity and ambiguity in language, and to some extent reproduced what occurred in the ancient political arena of Athens.[9]

Beyond Humanity's End: Interpreting Apocalypse as Drama

In facing the likely end of humanity and the earth it is easy for climate discussions to slip into apocalyptic language. While apocalyptic rhetoric may be used in contemporary climate change discourse, a more detailed analysis of the meaning and significance of apocalyptic has been the provision of theology since the birth of the Church, and a debated topic of religious studies in post Enlightenment studies. Stephen O'Leary has presented a case for the rhetorical interpretation of apocalyptic literature in narrative form. His interest seems to be primarily in tracking the rhetorical form of apocalyptic traditions in religion, especially as those found in the biblical book of Revelation. This last book of the New Testament records a mystical apocalyptic vision allegedly given to the Gospel writer John. It is a dramatic account of the last scenes of history, recording the Christian belief in the second coming of Christ, symbolized as a Lamb that was slain. It is important, however, to note that apocalyptic for the book of Revelation is not identical to many highly popular renditions of its content. In John's account the majority survive, rather than a small minority that is more common against a Jewish background of prophecy. At the heart of the message of Revelation there is hope in Christ's resurrection, as symbolized by the martyrs, even though there is grim realism about the power and presence of evil, as symbolized by the atrocities represented through the Roman Empire. This is an account that is heavily wrapped in symbolic form, but the overall message is one of devastation followed by the promise of a new creation, a new heaven and a new earth. The new creation is not one that is removed from the earth, but arises from its transformation. Rhetoric is, O'Leary suggests, persuasive discourse, in that it is 'a discipline located at the intersection of aesthetics, politics and ethics, it is a method of inquiry whose object is to discover how audiences are moved or persuaded through the interplay of style, form, content and context in texts both spoken and written' (O'Leary, 1994: 4). His interest is also historical, namely, *how* the apocalyptic form might have changed over the centuries of, most specifically, Christian witness. His attention to history seems to be constructed in such a way as to generate a particular narrative about apocalyptic rhetoric. It is therefore hardly surprising that, when coming to the more specific apocalyptic traditions, he leans towards an interpretation that stresses the narrative, so that the cosmic drama portrayed is simply the dramatic *form* of the narrative that can take the shape of either comedy or tragedy. O'Leary portrays the book of Revelation in terms of mythic secret knowledge of the coming of the end, within what he terms 'the dramatic narrative', an attempt to resolve the crisis precipitated on the occasion of the vicious persecution of the righteous (ibid.: 63). While O'Leary recognizes that some biblical scholars view the book of Revelation as 'an opportunity for a performative enactment of its cosmic drama', he is critical of Collins' description of the effect of the text on the audience in terms of tragic catharsis, for there are comic aspects as well, since the ending is a movement upward, rather than an unhappy tragic ending (ibid.: 66–7). He seems satisfied with the characterization of Revelation as a 'double plot', where the wicked are subject to a tragic fate, while the end anticipated for the righteous is heavenly comic triumph. However, for O'Leary the comic and tragic need to be read as 'frames of acceptance' within a particular eschatological narrative. But this particular reading of Apocalypse has serious consequences, for it *subsumes* the dramatic within the narrative in a way that serves to damp down the dramatic characteristics that are more properly understood as core to apocalyptic literature in general and the biblical book of Revelation in particular.

In weaving through the labyrinth of apocalyptic claims, Duncan Forrester casts a salutary warning on those who turn to apocalyptic rhetoric in an indiscriminate way, for '[r]eligious symbols may inflame rather than illumine, and religious rhetoric excite rather than clarify', but at the same time apocalyptic religion is not necessarily as pathological, divisive, dangerous or irrational as it might appear from its presentation of absolute good and evil in Manichean terms (Forrester, 2005: 53–7). Christian apocalyptic is characterized by a confident hope not only that things *can* be different, but *will* be different. The book of Revelation was written in a specific context of a minority who considered themselves powerless before an oppressive power. Yet in order to understand the power of apocalyptic in terms of its impact on the audience, it seems to me that the imaginative power of the book of Revelation is related to its use of language. Unlike conventional language that is straightforward in its ability to reveal due to its transparency, and hence 'disappears' when being spoken, 'poetic language asserts itself as translucent. At least we are led to believe it is translucent, in actuality it is opaque, but the promise of translucence, the assurance that something is beyond language, must be kept' (Plate, 1999: 4). In this the 'obscure' imagery gives an inkling of undiscoverable mystery, and this sense of obscurity leads to a fascination and gripping attention. This poetic, lyric element in drama shows its pedigree as that related to the mystical tradition that O'Leary largely ignores. Hence, according to Christopher Rowland, 'there was probably an essential continuity between the religious outlook of the apocalypticists and that of the earliest exponents of *merkabah* mysticism among the rabbis. Both seem to bear witness to the possibility that the study of Scripture could, in certain instances, lead to a direct apprehension of the divine world' (Rowland, 1982: 444).

The form in which apocalyptic is conceived is also significant, in that, given the lyric element, the possibility of *post-apocalyptic* comes dimly into view. The question now becomes, what remains, if anything, after the end? James Berger has delved into the cultural meaning of 'post-apocalypse', in that he argues that 'the narrative logic of apocalyptic writing insists that post-apocalypse precede the apocalypse. This is also the logic of prophecy. The events envisaged have already occurred, has as good as occurred. Once the prophecy is uttered, all the rest is post-apocalyptic' (Berger, 1999: 6). Yet this language of post-apocalypse seems somewhat forced, in that all apocalyptic literature has elements that are both 'realised' and 'not yet' understood in eschatological terms. It also seems to focus on envisaging apocalyptic as a sequence of events, and the disruption to that sequence; in other words, it remains in character wedded to an epic narrative, rather than drama. Skrimshire suggests as much in his comment that apocalypse does not simply end in postmodern deconstruction of the future, rather, it seems to have 'a life of its own' (Skrimshire, 2008), but this life, this appeal as to what might be 'beyond' tipping points can, I believe, be resolved far more successfully by shifting the genre of its characterization from narrative to drama.

APOCALYPSE AS DRAMA: SOCIAL AND ETHICAL IMPLICATIONS

The characterization of apocalypse as drama offers, I suggest, a much greater sense of the importance of particularity and individual response compared with more fatalistic narrative approaches. Apocalypse understood as a way of bringing the truth about the situation invites a sense of what is, to what must be done. It differs from narrative in that for narrative it is possible to remain detached and distant from the events being described. Drama is much more engaging in that at minimum it invites the audience to get involved by imagining that they are one of the players in the drama. Where identification is complete, a drama allows the audience to be caught up as participants in the drama itself, so that a deep sense of individual agency is evoked. This attention to the individual that drama brings, opens out a greater sense of the human agent's responsibility. Hence it is less likely to resort to the kind of political resignation and associated ethical reactions that follow in the wake of narrative accounts. It is also less likely to foster the alternative political stance of galvanized action that is dependent on an idealized vision of humanity. While narrative accounts can, theoretically, include other creatures, as demonstrated by the characterization of the history of the earth as a cosmic creation story,[10] such more inclusive accounts, like the epic narratives that focus narrowly on human history, tend to diminish the place of the individual creature(s). Dramatic rhetoric may, of course, fall prey to considering non-human creation as merely 'the stage' on which human activity takes place. But it need not be so narrowly conceived, and certainly it is entirely possible to include other creatures as active agents in the drama, rather than merely the 'stage'.[11] The book of

Revelation makes just this point, in giving a role to beasts as much as to human beings.

What might be the shape of ethics arising out of this more dramatic rendering of apocalyptic traditions, specifically, that connected with climate change discourse? As a starting point I suggest that the fascination with climate issues by those on the receiving end relates as much to a sense that we are all part of this cosmic climate drama in which our role as players really counts. We may, therefore, be rather less likely to try and appease our sense of guilt of our own impact on climate change through the use of all manner of environmental indulgences. This is because we have a much greater sense of our agency as having a positive impact, rather than simply accepting that we are inevitably guilty and that we somehow have to try and recompense for that guilt. The idea of climate rendered as dramatic also matches common experience, that the climate crisis has a different meaning to different people. In this it resists any overarching, epic account. Indeed, a focus on the dramatic would lend itself to a more active sense of responsibility. It would imply that the inevitable march of history in epic narrative is not all there is to be said, for we are participants as much as observers. If we allow ourselves to be caught up in the drama, the fear of what might be beyond death itself becomes re-enacted in the play.

Hans Urs von Balthasar sought to confront this fear beyond death by his dramatic theology of Holy Saturday, where Christ underwent a 'second death' by entering Hell; arguably one of the most original aspects of his theological oeuvre (Quash, 2006: 106–23). In much the same way, Christian rhetoric in the book of Revelation about post-apocalyptic fears of a barren waste-land is one where the light of Christ is seen to penetrate and offer hope. In Balthasar's account, drama pervades the whole Gospel, and its starting point is the passion of Christ. After his death, Christ entered not just into Sheol, or the place of the dead, but in a mythical way Christ may be envisaged as entering Hell, and as one who confronted the chaos that is beyond the devastation of creation, epitomized as absolute evil in the world (Balthasar, 1993: 172–3). Can we understand such a dramatic account of Christ's shadowy existence beyond death as in some sense pre-figuring that of climate change, where there is a sense of not just a death, but a fear of what might happen beyond that death? Does it thereby help to confront the awfulness of the situation before us, living in and through the experience, but in a way that does not lead to despair? Rather than resignation, such a reading of Christ's descent into Hell resonates with that fear, for it includes it as part of the dramatic encounter between Christ and the earth.[12]

Regardless of how far we find such a characterization convincing either as Christian believers or not, the purpose of including it here is to demonstrate how the rhetoric of drama does have the capacity to express the inexpressible that seems to be surfacing in climate discourse. It therefore offers not so much a fateful resignation, as a way of portraying what seems to be the case without coming to any firm conclusions about its meaning. We are dealing here as much with *post-history* as pre-history, for the first and last books of the Bible reach out beyond human knowing and what we might imagine to be realistically the case in that they are based on visions. Such readings lend themselves to dramatic rather than narrative portrayal, so that poetic imagination reaches out for more than can be characterized through a simple mapping onto present history. In other words, future hope is not so much for a return to paradise, but a hope for the transformation of this world beyond apocalyptic ruptures that threaten its integrity. Christian theological traditions insist on a retention of the comic end, one that arguably has the potential to invite a deeper involvement in political activity and responsible decision making.

The political implications of such a move towards the dramatic are, I believe, highly significant. In the place of resignation fostered by narrative accounts there is a greater stress on the importance of individual human agency. Yet because such agency is one that is caught up in a drama, it does not collapse into individualistic liberalism, but invites what might be called a version of postnatural politics. This is where the human and non-human creatures are embedded and woven together in a drama. Collective and communitarian action is one, therefore, that is inclusive rather than exclusive of the non-human realm. Here one might envisage climate as being much more than simply a stage on which human activity is played out, since it is responsive to the multiple activities of all the different agents in the play. Yet I would press against the idea that the earth as a whole has agency in such a drama. Rather, other players are all those creatures living in relationship with human beings. While humanity will be aware of its role in such a drama, much will be hidden from view; since the way the drama unfolds will not be known from its beginning, middle or end.

CONCLUSIONS

The argument of this chapter is fairly straightforward but not, I believe, widely appreciated. I suggest that in thinking through the ethics and politics of climate change we need to be more aware of how that change is portrayed in narrative or dramatic form. A common narrative dominant in the Western world is one that assumes a Promethean view of the human, where the assumption of human progress includes the ability to deal with difficult problems such as those associated with climate change. If such a view is interpreted as a collective ideal, it may lead to revolutionary political action as a way of expressing the power of human dominance of the natural world. There is an inevitability latent here, but it is one that assumes human activity is inevitably good. An alternative narrative approach is one that attempts to dethrone the central place of the human and work against the anthropocentrism that is assumed to be at the heart of the problem, reflecting an arrogance about human agency. Here the dominant narrative, expressed in, for example, Lovelock's Gaia hypothesis, is one that stresses the incapacity of human beings to manage the earth. Further, humanity is more likely to be a liability, or even a negative influence on the planet. Stronger versions of this hypothesis take up the idea of the earth itself having agency, such that it will take revenge on humanity that seems to be bent on its destruction. In political terms this means either no action at all, or adaptation to climate change. Both accounts are narrativistic in that both lead to a sense of resignation about what may or may not be the case. I suggest, therefore, that both are disempowering in terms of galvanizing social and political engagement with this issue. A different approach is one that draws more fully on the rhetoric of drama, rather than narrative. It is here that we find close connection with apocalyptic religious literature. Such apocalyptic accounts were intended to empower individual and collective action in the present realm, rather than be escapes into altern-ative imaginary worlds. Drawing on the work of theologian Hans Urs von Balthasar, I have pressed the case for a recovery of the dramatic, and in theological terms this takes its cue from the dramatic accounts of Christ's life and passion. Further, in the context of climate change that seems to present the spectre of the end, Christ's descent into Hell offers a way of pre-figuring in dramatic imagery what might be after humanity's end. In as much as it is a theological account it makes most sense within the household of Christian faith, but it also has wider ethical implications in helping humanity to engage with and consider what might be beyond humanity's end.

NOTES

1 This chapter is based on a presentation delivered at the third Future Ethics Workshop entitled *A World Without Us? Imagining The End of the Human* held on 16 January 2009 and organized through the Lincoln Theological Institute at Manchester University. I would like to thank Stefan Skrimshire and Peter Scott for their generosity in inviting me to take part in this event, as well as the helpful feedback during the meeting that gave me the opportunity to develop the chapter for this book.

2 See, for example, Intergovernmental Panel on Climate Change, IPCC, Working Group 111 to the Fourth Assessment Report, edited by B. Metz, O. Davidson, P. Bosch, R. Dave, L. Meyer *Climate Change 2007: Mitigation of Climate Change* (Cambridge: Cambridge University Press, 2007); IPCC Working Group 11 to the Fourth Assessment Report, edited by M Oarry, O. Canziani, J. Palutikof, P. van der Linden, C. Hanson *Climate Change 2007: Impacts, Adaptation and Vulnerability* (Cambridge: Cambridge University Press, 2007).

3 Stefan Skrimshire, 'What Are We Waiting For? Apocalyptic Narrative and the Theology of Extinction', paper presented to 'Religion in Dangerous Environmental – and Climate Change', Trondheim, Norway, 9–11 October 2008.

4 For a discussion of these various forms of narrative see Stroup, 1984. All five potential uses of narrative could be rhetorical in as much as it deliberately seeks to convey a meaning that will have practical outcomes. Other writers who have given particular atten-tion to narrative include Frei, 1993 and Lindbeck, 1984. It is possible to name two broad ways of doing narrative theology, one takes its cue from scripture or the experience of the church; the other is founded on a general theory of religious experience. For further discussion Loughlin, 1996: 35–66.

5 I develop a more detailed appraisal of the science and ethics of Gaia theory in Deane-Drummond, 2004. However, I did not discuss an understanding of Gaia as a form of narrative.

6 A good example of this approach to narrative is found in the work of Paul Ricoeur. I consider the Kantian undertones to his work detected by authors such as Kevin Vanhoozer to be highly significant in that it imposes a particular shape and direction on the narrative and so seems to nudge closer to epic by doing more than simply supply form to otherwise heterogeneous material. Vanhoozer believes, for example, that Ricoeur is Kantian when Ricoeur claims that 'narratology constitutes the rational reconstruction of the rules underlying poetical activity' (Ricoeur, 1991: 24). On the other hand, given Ricoeur's deliberate comparison between metaphor and narrative, it seems less likely that he slipped into epic forms of narrative. See Vanhoozer, 1990: 89.

7 Lovelock is inconsistent with the implications of strong versions of his theory in this respect. He argues for far greater use of nuclear power as a technological response to burning of fossil fuels that seems to come from a positive model of humanity, but then doubts if humanity will be able to respond adequately to meet the challenge that climate change represents. See Lovelock, 2006.

8 For Peter Scott postnatural does not mean so much *leaving behind* the natural as being aware of and conscious of how deeply we are embedded in natural processes while at the same time aware of the breakdown of boundaries between the artificial as human construct and the natural and between the human and non-human animal. The postnatural can, it seems, be applied to the condition in which we find ourselves, to humanity as such, and to the political realm. But just as nature itself is a term full of complex meanings, so too postnatural can absorb and engage with the different dimensions of what nature means. Scott's position is not utopian in the sense of denying individual agency, but such agency sits uneasily alongside a communitarian approach to the politics of nature, such that he supports an 'abstract notion of the free, eco-productive individual, living cooperatively in a determinate ecological condition' not a 'general notion of community'. While this avoids the kind of determinism emerging from narrative accounts that I have critiqued here, since it puts stress on individual freedom, it is still an abstract and therefore idealized notion of the human so that the shape of human agency in relation to determinate ecological relationships veers rather more towards a particular narrative of the human in particular and therefore seemingly stable natural relationships. See Scott, 2009.

9 The figure of the messenger allowed for implicit claims to a more secure form of knowledge, such that his report presented itself as an unproblematic and non-rhetorical account of events offstage. The figure also allowed for some narration of events which could not easily be presented in a play, such as miracles. See Irene, 1991: 117.

10 I am thinking here of Brian Swimme, Thomas Berry and other influential writers in this vein, including James Lovelock. See, for example, Swimme and Berry, 1992; Lovelock, 1987; 2006.

11 I develop this aspect in more detail in Deane-Drummond, 2009.

12 There is, however, some ambivalence in making this move in that Balthasar envisages Hell in somewhat abstract terms, rather than his more earthbound understanding of Sheol, or the place of the dead. As such, authors like Quash believe that this has Gnostic overtones that function to separate Christ from the earth in all its contingency. Yet if we view such an act as just part of a drama, one that weaves together both lyric and narrative elements, then this dramatic reading of history allows us to perceive what may be difficult to perceive otherwise, for what is beyond death inevitably calls on an imaginative response, as we have no tools to think of it in any other way.

BIBLIOGRAPHY

Barrett, James (2002), *Staged Narrative: Poetics and the Messenger in Greek Tragedy.* Los Angeles, CA: University of California Press.

Berger, James (1999), *After the End; Representations of Post-Apocalypse.* Minneapolis, MN: University of Minnesota Press.

Boykoff, Maxwell and Jules, M. Boykoff (2007), 'Climate Change and Journalistic Norms: A Case Study of US Mass Media Coverage'. *Geoform* 38 (6), 1190–204.

Brent, Plate, S. (1999), 'Introduction: Words, Images, Aesthetics, Ethics and the End of the World', in S. Brent Plate, ed., *The Apocalyptic Imagination: Aesthetics and Ethics at the End of the World.* Glasgow: Trinity St Mungo Press.

de Jong, Irene, J. F. (1991), *Narrative in Drama: The Art of Euripidean Messenger and Speech.* Leiden: E. J. Brill.

Deane-Drummond, C. (2004), *The Ethics of Nature.* Oxford: Blackwells.

—(2009) *Christ and Evolution: Wonder and Wisdom.* Fortress/SCM Press.

Forrester, Duncan (2005), *Apocalypse Now? Reflections on Faith in a Time of Terror.* Aldershot: Ashgate.

Frei, Hans (1993), *Theology and Narrative: Selected Essays*, eds George Hunsinger and William, C. Placher. New York/Oxford: Oxford University Press.

Halliwell, Stephen (1986), *Aristotle's Poetics.* Chapel Hill, NC: University of North Carolina Press.

Intergovernmental Panel on Climate Change (2007), IPCC, Working Group 111 to the Fourth Assessment Report, edited by B. Metz, O. Davidson, P. Bosch, R. Dave, L. Meyer *Climate Change 2007: Mitigation of Climate Change.* Cambridge: Cambridge University Press.

IPCC (2007), Working Group 11 to the Fourth Assessment Report, edited by M. Oarry, O. Canziani, J. Palutikof, P. van der Linden,

C. Hanson *Climate Change 2007: Impacts, Adaptation and Vulnerability.* Cambridge: Cambridge University Press.

Lindbeck, George (1984), *The Nature of Doctrine, Religion and Theology in a Postliberal Age.* London: SPCK.

Loughlin, Gerard (1996), *Telling God's Story: Bible, Church and Narrative Theology.* Cambridge: Cambridge University Press.

Lovelock, James (1987), *Gaia: A New Look at Life on Earth.* 2nd edn. Oxford: Oxford University Press.

—(2006), *The Revenge of Gaia.* London: Penguin.

O'Leary Stephen (1994), *Arguing the Apocalypse.* Oxford: Oxford University Press.

Primavesi, Anne (2000), *Sacred Gaia: Holistic Theology and Earth System Science.* London: Routledge.

Quash, Ben (2005), *Theology and the Drama of History.* Cambridge: Cambridge University Press.

—(2006), 'Hans urs von Balthasar', in *The Modern Theologians,* ed. D. Ford and R. Muers. Oxford: Blackwell, pp. 106–23.

Ricoeur, Paul (1991), 'Life in Quest of Narrative', in *On Paul Ricoeur: Narrative and Interpretation,* ed. David Wood. London and New York: Routledge.

Rowland, Christopher (1982), *The Open Heaven: A Study of Apocalyptic in Judaism and Early Christianity.* London: SPCK.

Scott, Peter (2009), 'Right out of time? Politics and nature in a postnatural condition' presented on 17 May 2009 for conference entitled *Religion, Ecology and the Public Sphere,* EFSRE 11, Abo/ Turku, Finland.

Skrimshire, Stefan (2008), 'What are we waiting for? Apocalyptic narrative and the theology of extinction', paper presented to 'Religion in Dangerous Environmental – and Climate Change', Trondheim, Norway, 9–11 October.

Stroup, George, W. (1984), *The Promise of Narrative Theology.* London: SCM Press.

Swimme, Brian and Thomas, Berry (1992), *The Universe Story.* San Francisco: HarperCollins.

Vanhoozer, Kevin, J. (1990), *Biblical Narrative in the Philosophy of Paul Ricoeur.* Cambridge: Cambridge University Press.

von Balthasar, Hans Urs (1988), *TheoDrama Vol 1, Prolegomena.* Trans. Graham Harrison. San Francisco, CA: Ignatius Press.

—(1990), *Theodrama, Volume 11, Dramatis Personae: Man in God.* Trans. Graham Harrison. San Francisco: Ignatius Press *TD2*, p. 56.

—(1993), *Mysterium Pascale.* Trans. Aidan Nichols. Edinburgh: T & T Clark.

CHAPTER TWELVE

ARE WE THERE YET?

COMING TO THE END OF THE LINE – A POSTNATURAL ENQUIRY

PETER MANLEY SCOTT

What, will the line stretch out to the crack of doom?
Macbeth (IV: 1)

APOCALYPTIC SHOCK?

In that it presents human beings one more time with 'the transience of the earth and its species' (Anderson, 2008: 9), climate change is not new. This transience – that species become extinct and that the life of the earth will eventually end – is widely known and will surprise no-one. Although this transience forms an old story, nonetheless our politics – the politics of the North and West – is inscribed by the refusal of this story. Modern governments are not in the electoral business of managing the end of the human. Rather, they seek to reassure that all will be well and that human living can continue much as before. As the UK government's then chief scientific adviser, David King, put it, government policy on energy in the United Kingdom will not be premised on moving the British electorate out of its 'comfort zone' (King, 2007). No society likes to consider its demise; no administration seeking re-election will wish to foreground that demise and will rather stress technological innovation – to preserve resources and develop fresh sources of energy – and careful management – to conserve non-renewable resources.

Of course, climate change activists refuse this comfort. They present the wider electorate and governments with the shock of the claim that unless we change this society and our lifestyles, the future of the human will be shorter (possibly much shorter) and more miserable (possibly much more miserable) than most of us would like. (A history of the interaction in the United States between environmental issues and apocalypse is nicely presented by Buell, 2004.) Yet, of course, they offer this shock in order to help the rest of us to see that the human has a long-term future. (Buell notes that this older strategy of apocalyptic shock has given way to – although without replacing – what he calls *slow* apocalypse: the sense of living in a crisis rather than being confronted by a crisis.)

How shall we approach this association of anthropogenic climate change on the one hand with the sense of an apocalyptic ending on the other? There is much evidence of this association in the activist, scholarly and media discussion of climate change; the chapters in this volume are additional, and important, witnesses. Moreover, it is clear that there is little agreement – even across the essays presented here – on the correct understanding of the association. How then is the relation best understood?

In what follows, I seek to answer this question in two stages. In the first, analytical, stage, I give an account of many meanings of 'end' and 'apocalyptic' to show the variety of ways in which they interact, and explain why the association is rhetorically powerful and theoretically fruitful.[1] I argue that apocalyptic poses a set of fundamental questions and suggest how these fundamental questions may be worked out in the context of a changing climate. In a second, interpretative, stage, I try to 'expand' apocalyptic discourse a little as it occurs in the context of climate change. That is, I experiment with the claim that apocalyptic as it occurs in the context of climate change makes reference to nature and to humanity in the debate over the future of the human. I work to show that this discourse has limitations as well as strengths.

At the conclusion, I return to the matter of the activist deployment of apocalyptic 'shock' to shake people out of their complacency. Applying such a shock may be beneficial if you are trying to show how a system works: let us 'shock the monkey' in order to show the interactions between humanity and nature. Apocalyptic provides the energy for a grand experiment to demonstrate the proper functioning of Earth's system. Yet such a display is only convincing if the system is in good repair and only lacks energy. Thus, shocking the system rests upon a claim to a balance of nature and thereby requires a conservative reference back to how things once were. It is not clear to me that political energy is best directed in this way.[2] Moreover, I shall argue from a theological perspective that there are non-political aspects to apocalyptic: the threat appears to be external, its reality is authorized by experts and any sustainable future is unlikely. Thus my conclusion is that without the substantial development of apocalyptic in terms of political theory, reference to apocalyptic is de-politicizing and thereafter demoralizing. Moreover, it makes sense to shock the *populus* only if the vision of a long-term future of the human is proffered as the alternative to apocalyptic interruption. On the basis of a re-working of apocalyptic, I seek to show that theology has no investment in such a long-term future of the human and that the theological roots of activism must therefore lie elsewhere.

END; APOCALYPTIC

Let me begin by returning to the question I posed earlier: how is the relation between climate change and apocalyptic to be understood? Part of the answer is informed by the ambiguity of the term, 'end'. In imagining the end of the human, what precisely is this ending? Are we discussing the final 'destination' of the human – which of course raises the question of teleology? That is, as regards teleology: is the historical/earthly destination of the human (1) accidental, or is it (2) part of a general tendency towards, say, complexity, or is it (3) the outworking in a much stronger sense of the essence of the human? All three senses are teleological but with rather different strengths. Or, alternatively, in referring to the end are we discussing the demise of the human? And demise in what sense? – in the sense of the eventual extinction of the human species or the more immediate partial extinction of the human species as a result of changing global conditions resulting from climate change (often linked with imaginative portrayals as to how the human remnant will live in reduced circumstances – see McCarthy's 2006 novel *The Road* or the 2007 film *The Day after Tomorrow*)?

A third option involves combining aspects of the first two options to assert that the 'essence' of the human is not embodied and that, as in trans-humanism, there is the possibility of a new existence for the 'human' beyond the conditions of extinction – that the future of the 'human' is non-material and there is a way beyond the demise of the human with its embodied conditions (Peters, 2006). Mind is separable from meat in a culture of hyperexuberance (Buell, 2004: 261). A fourth, religious, option now presents itself: in the foregoing, the destination of the human – whether embodied or not – is always this-worldly; we are speaking of the destination of the species and not always about the destiny of individuals. Yet, the destination of the human can be imagined as other-worldly: a movement from time into eternity, the *eschatological* fulfilment of the human; here the end is also a new beginning and may also have a cosmic dimension (Scott, 2000; Kerr, 2008: 13–14).

A hermeneutical question now emerges: is it possible to think of a temporal ending without also thinking of the end as culmination? Are we able to think of *terminus* without *telos?* In an influential essay for western philosophical traditions, Immanuel Kant argued that it is not possible to separate the two (Kant, 1794/1998: 195–205): an end is always a completion or a fulfilment, he argued. For, Kant continued, we cannot propose a fulfilment of the human and yet also maintain the continuation of time. If we do that, what can the historical content of this fulfilled time be? It will be an abstract time, lacking content, which means in turn we cannot grasp what it might mean to be human in it. Yet, we cannot imagine what it means for time simply to end and for fulfilment to take place in a different reality because that would mean that we, as historical beings, do not enter an historical fulfilment, but some other kind. Our present history is thereby rendered alien to our fulfilment, with deleterious consequences for our moral life. Kant is therefore arguing that to speak of the end of the human as terminus and fulfilment is *rational*. It seems wiser, then, to maintain *terminus* and *telos* together. Of course, through imagining a different end, we may decide to adopt an irrational stance but that would mean not that we are being illogical but that we have just rendered ourselves alien, as if our nature is unrelated to other worldly natures. The recent developments in genetic science in the context of an evolutionary understanding of the emergence of species seems to me to strengthen Kant's point because it is now harder to imagine ourselves as resident aliens on this earth.

If we add to this presentation the matter of the ending in theological apocalyptic, the discussion becomes even more complex. According to Kerr, an apocalyptic end in Christian tradition must be understood as transcendent, in the sense of granting priority to God's action. Moreover, such an ending is also an interruption (Kerr, 2008: 12–13) and is always 'political' – we are concerned here with the rule of God (Hauerwas, 1994: 109). Moreover, there is some scepticism in theology as to whether ecological crisis and apocalyptic are truly speaking of the same sort of end. In that we may be destroying the 'natural' conditions of human life, ecological problems may herald the end of humanity but this human end – although serious for us – is different from both the end of this earth and the end of this cosmos (Pannenberg, 1998: 590). We are confronted with the destruction of the earth and such a confrontation may be presented in apocalyptic terms but these are 'secularizations of biblical apocalyptic, and now have in common with it only the catastrophe, no longer the hope' (Moltmann, 1996: 226–7). Nonetheless, there is some overlap between these theological interpretations of apocalypse and the convergence between climate change and apocalyptic.

For example, a sense of apocalyptic ending can be interpreted both actively and passively. *Actively*, this sense of an ending presses the question: how shall we act to avoid this apocalyptic ending or interruption? Conversion, change and renewed human action may be encouraged thereby. A sense of time running out, of coming to the end of the line, is often evident. On this view, the timing of the apocalyptic end may not be fixed or imminent: that is, suitable human action may be commended to ensure the continued postponement of the end. Or, human action in the present can be understood not as the effort to avoid apocalyptic rupture but instead as action to provoke it. This is the apocalyptic version of 'Bring it on'. This active construal is why reference to apocalyptic raises the matter of human agency.

Passively, an apocalyptic ending can be presented as a script written from elsewhere – perhaps by a god whose wrath cannot be expiated – and so is not avoidable. Fatalism, based on a sense of history's ineluctable destination, is one outcome here. The god of this apocalypse may be understood as rescuing those who are identified as faithful in the script; the notion of 'rapture' is a good example of such rescuing. Or the script written from else-where can be understood as 'written' by Nature or Gaia: now the human is understood as alienated from – and a threat to – Nature or Gaia. Nature is here the stronger force and will perhaps seek its revenge on the human (Lovelock, 2007, 2009).

Together with these active and passive interpretations, a third, more ambivalent, interpretation is possible. That is, it is possible to understand apocalyptic in a sense of permanent crisis; in this sense, we are living at the 'end of the end', in a condition in which we are always accompanied by crisis of one sort or another which is best understood as a crisis in our thinking about crisis (Skrimshire, 2009a).

The answer to the question posed in the context of climate change, Are we there yet?, can thereby take a number of forms because any answer depends on decisions taken about the range of variables presented above. These variables include: what is the meaning of 'end' – is it this-worldly or other-worldly? Moreover, is this end a reference to a terminus – the end of the line for the human? Or is this end a reference to the human's culmination or fulfilment? Or both? In sum, apocalyptic presents us with the theme, variously understood: the *future of the human*. In addition, does reference to the apocalyptic recommend human action to avoid catastrophe or resignation in the face of inevit-able disaster? Apocalyptic thereby also presents us with the theme, variously understood: the *basis of human action.*

Third, we are presented with the question as to what is the source, so to speak, of apocalyptic: who/what is the agent on the move in apocalyptic? Apocalyptic thereby also presents us with the theme, variously understood: *what forces – natural or divine – are being disclosed or unveiled in apocalyptic?* Lastly, we encounter a troubling question: how does the human participate in apocalyptic? If apocalypse is an event the script of which is already written, *in what sense do human beings participate in apocalypse?*

APOCALYPTIC AND CLIMATE CHANGE

We can now appreciate how appropriate the association between climate change and apocalyptic is. The association is far from arbitrary. What is commended by apocalyptic is the moral significance of human action, the association of the human with its context and intimations of the end.

That is, first, apocalyptic thinking protects the claim that human action is appropriately judged by moral categories in that human action contributes to an open future. The human is genuinely free, and without such freedom responsibility is rendered unintelligible. Even when apocalypse is understood to be closing down the human future, that is itself based on a moral judgement. The apocalyptic supports the view that a human response to climate change is possible, even when there is considerable pessimism as to whether human beings will act in time. Such pessimism indeed turns upon the claim that human beings will fail to respond adequately. Nonetheless, such failure is premised upon an implicit acknowledgement that human beings could respond differently and thus that the future is open.

Second, a variant of apocalyptic thinking insists that the future of the human is not to be considered without the non-human; there can be no consideration of a new heaven without consideration of a new earth also. Indeed, apocalypse is sometimes associated with a return to Eden or paradise with the pastoral associations of a return to a garden. In that climate change raises the question of the nature of the ecological conditions for the long-term sustainability of the human species, a further connection between climate change and apocalyptic is clear: the human is placed in a wider – indeed, sometimes cosmic – context (see Kerr, 2008: 13; on the historical development, see Pannenberg, 1998: 527–32).

Third, apocalypse protects the significance of thinking about the end. The epistemological status of such thinking about the end is not at all obvious (Skrimshire, 2009b). For example, in that the end will be unknowable by the human – that we cannot know our own death is analogous – it could be argued that to consider the end of the human is irrational. It is not an event that can be known by the human and, as such, what sort of event can it be? Certainly, it is not an event that can be related to the human by knowledge. However, apocalypse keeps alive the idea that there are intimations of the end – whether the reference is to an original creation (the garden of Eden), the vision of a peaceable state (as in the vision in Isaiah that the lion will lie down with the lamb) or the new creation evidenced in the resurrection of Jesus Christ – that are knowable by the human. And, as knowable by the human, these may help the human in thinking about the end. In that climate change seems also to be pressing the matter of the end or disappearance of the human, the association with apocalyptic is intelligible.

Moreover, as a matter of logic, we may also appreciate that through this association certain options in understanding climate change are excluded. Among these are: cyclical notions of history, the unreality of human action and the indifference of the natural context to the human. These are, as we have already seen, all challenged by strands of apocalyptic thought. For apocalyptic thought, the direction of time cannot be seen as either cyclical or reversible; history develops, is the place of moral action and heads towards an unrepeatable fulfilment. Moreover, this future is often to be understood as open to participation and thereby an invitation to act responsibly. Even where the apocalyptic script is understood to be written from elsewhere, such an intervention from elsewhere is often a judgement on the immoral actions of human beings. Apocalyptic is not a shadow of history but rather its ending; apocalyptic does not provide an alternative history but rather brings history historically to a culmination. Moreover, at least in some versions, apocalyptic is understood to happen on a cosmic scale; the scope of the event thereby encompasses more than the human.

At this point, I want to stress the importance of appreciating the full force of apocalyptic discourse as we encounter it in the context of climate change. Put differently, it is easy to dilute the strength of that force by considering such a combination of apocalyptic and climate change as a practical matter. For example, a fictional climate camp activist might argue as follows:

> By my actions, I am trying to avoid the apocalypse of a rise in global temperature of more than 2°C and thereby avoid or mitigate the consequences. These consequences will of course be felt first and most strongly by poorer countries and communities who are also those who have contributed least to carbon emissions over the last 20 years or so. Moreover, the moral urgency of avoiding this apocalypse outweighs your decision to fly from Manchester to Glasgow and this gives me the moral justification to interrupt the operations of this

airport to draw attention to your flight's contribution to CO_2 emissions and the warming of the planet.

While this is clearly a deployment of apocalyptic discourse with important practical implications or consequences, I claim here that apocalyptic discourse is fundamentally and primarily a discourse on *judging*. It is an effort to judge what the true basis of action is. As such, of course it enjoys practical implications. Yet the fundamental point is prior to practice. Apocalyptic discourse risks an interpretation of what is and is to come, and thereby enquires into the true basis of action. That is, it offers an epistemology based on a judgement of what is to come; it seeks to provide knowledge based on conditions that are not yet fully in force; these conditions are actual but not fully realized; there is some evidence for these conditions but the evidence is not definitive. The epistemology at issue here is thereby an eschatological epistemology: a 'theory' of thinking about the end from the perspective of the end (imaginatively or 'literary-ly' construed). This process of realization is underway already.

And this means – indeed, it follows – that apocalyptic discourse is always a religious discourse: it requires that this world is passing away and yet is also commandeered by a different reality. Whatever force it has is derived from the claim that the present – including the conditions of knowledge in the present – are in process to a different, yet still recognizable, reality. Even secular uses of apocalyptic discourse trade upon this tension, although the tension between what is and is yet to come is usually transposed to an intra-worldly sphere and its power reduced thereby. For example, the 2008 film *The Age of Stupid* refers to this different reality in a sophisticated way: by having the action of the film presented by a narrator who speaks from the future (the year 2055), we are presented both by a different reality (the narrator is viewing film footage about climate change from the year 2008) that encourages the viewer to act as if the present could be commandeered by a different futural reality, that of human mitigation of climate change. Both projections – the disaster scenario and the scenario of mitigation – are 'conservative': these futures are predictable. Moreover, the two realities are without hope for it cannot be determined from *within* the two projections of a future which is to be preferred. In this domestication of apocalyptic by the secular, the viewer is in effect denied by the fantastical construction of the film the ethical resources required to respond to the moral issue presented by the film.

I have already argued that by the apocalyptic four questions are posed: What is the destiny of the human? What is the human contribution to that destiny? Which agent is the source and guarantor of that destiny? How does the human participate in that destiny? Let us reconsider these to get a fuller sense of what it means to designate these as acts of judging. These four questions refer the reader to the future; they seek to identify that which cannot be fully identified because it is yet to come. Therefore one has to judge, to discriminate, and to identify traces of the yet-to-come that is already present. Apocalyptic is a means for doing this.

Here it is important to affirm that apocalypse is a mythic discourse that cannot easily be translated into other terms or straightforwardly de-mythologized. It is easy to sideline the mythical aspects and try to translate such discourse into a different idiom. Or to restrict its impact by using it only to make people fearful and thereby to understand such discourse only instrumentally. Instead, at its most fundamental apocalyptic poses the question of the destiny of the human, of appropriate action by that human, and who the agent of that destiny is. It is important to try to work with the full force of the discourse if its power is not to be truncated (Bonhoeffer, 1971).

ACTION

Given that apocalyptic raises the matter of the basis of human action, how does apocalyptic relate to climate change? We may approach the matter of the apocalyptic politics of climate change by noting the demand for political action. There is a range of political actions: from activism on the one hand to parliamentarianism and international treaties on the other. Few proposals in the context of climate change suggest that we may go on as before and most work from the assumption that free human action into an open future is possible. (Even right-wing discourse, if the United States is any guide, stresses action: for example, an emphasis on unleashing the power of the free market [see Buell, 2004: 25–7].) Of course, it is debated how fundamental the change is required to be: a deep ecologist might argue that we need to develop forms of bioregionalism whereas a technocrat may argue that what is required is the unleashing of the human spirit for technological innovation (Giddens, 2009). Yet given the convergence of apocalyptic and climate change, what is the basis of this action?

We can begin to appreciate what is attractive about this convergence. If the action is truly human it must in some way be making a contribution to the destiny of the human. And climate change raises the matter of global human action – of the action that the human might take to secure its future as a species. Thus some account of the end or *telos* of the human as a species is being presupposed here: that the human is in some fundamental sense 'at home' on this planet. Additionally, as we have seen in my brief comment on Kant, this 'at home-ness' may be read back from the claim that human fulfilment is also and always an historical fulfilment. Moreover, whatever account of the human is being presupposed, with it must come some account of the relationship between the human and the non-human. Climate change poses the question about the quality of the interaction between humanity and nature, and in some of its formulations so does apocalyptic. It is of course possible to answer these questions by recommending that the *telos* of the human is achieved through its own work or that the *telos* cannot be represented. And it might also be argued the relationship between the human and the non-human is a negative one; only the human makes a contribution to its own destiny. Yet, in most of its formulations, apocalyptic instead promotes an end of the human in a wider cosmos – a new heaven and a new earth – and by reference to an external event or agent such that the *telos* of the human is not only secured through its own work.

Here we begin to encounter limitations in apocalyptic thought. To enquire after the basis of human action in the context of anthropogenic climate change is problematic because it must perforce take place in a postnatural condition. (Buell, 2004: 233, associates posthuman and postnatural; I contrast these terms [Scott, 2010].) By postnatural condition, I mean that although it is legitimate to maintain a distinction between the natural and the artificial, there is a sense in which the human is mutually entangled in nature in new and ever deeper ways (Ingold, 2009). Geo-engineering projects – for example, the sequestration of carbon through conversion by biomass or through underground storage – are large-scale, industrial projects in the (attempted) human domination of space (spaces for planting trees or the 'empty' spaces of underground wells). Moreover, we may appreciate this phenomenon of entanglement even in global warming: a rising global temperature is to be traced to increasing levels of carbon introduced into the atmosphere by humans so there is a sense in which even the weather now is postnatural. Our climate is a hybrid phenomenon: a joint production by the human's industrial works and this earth's global support processes. This means that action can no longer only be about emancipation from; it makes little sense to seek to emancipate ourselves from our natural conditions; freeing ourselves from the climate makes as much sense as trying to free ourselves from oxygen. We are placed beings, situated in time and space, not least by climate.[3] Action must thereby be directed to emancipation into [attachments] (Latour, 2007). Part of the pedagogy of action will therefore be about education into an acknowledgement of constraints, the practice of finitude 'which does not leave us chafed by our own skin' (Stanley Cavell, cited Kerr, 1997: viii). Action must therefore both identify constraints and emancipation into these constraints.

At this point, difficult political problems arise with which, I think, apocalyptic does not adequately engage. That there is a fit between apocalyptic and climate change is not in doubt; the reasonableness of that convergence was amply demonstrated above. However, this is not the same as saying that all issues are adequately handled. For example, if we are to speak of the *telos* of the human in a postnatural condition, will we not need to decide in what way the human finds its fulfilment 'in' nature? Apocalyptic rhetoric on climate change stresses human responsibility but if *hubris* is to be avoided, we need to be careful not to indicate that the fulfilment of the human takes place without nature. Yet thinking about this common fulfilment is difficult. I doubt whether it is helpful to appeal to some natural condition of hierarchy, as in the work of Leo Strauss, which functions as a kind of perduring beginning (Strauss 1953/1965). Yet there must be some way of indicating the mutual entanglement of the human and the natural. Moreover, drawing on apocalyptic discourse, there is a temptation to appeal to an 'end' that functions in a similar way to a kind of natural order: by insisting on some apocalyptic interruption of nature by nature – as in the revenge of Gaia – a sort of imposing constraint is pressed upon us. Both natural hierarchy and interruptive end are non-negotiable. We are thereby plunged into the problem of ecological authoritarianism, of which the recent appeal to the merits of nuclear power as a 'clean' technology is a good example. If at any cost, the 'end' of plentiful energy must be avoided, nuclear power – whose disasters are 'smaller' than any imagined apocalyptic 'end' – suddenly appears attractive. Moreover, with nuclear power comes the issue of the security of nuclear materials and thereby the justification of security measures to keep such material 'safe'. Authoritarianism has here two functions: as the justification of nuclear power and the justification to ensure the safety of the materials. Both matters reinforce the security state: this state will save us from the 'end' – turn on the nuclear power! – and will secure our safety – maximize the surveillance! – from dangerous nuclear materials. We may free ourselves from such authoritarianism by noting that there is neither natural order for us to ground our actions in nor any force of nature imposing an ending on us. Yet the victory may be a Pyrrhic one. For what is true in ecological authoritarianism are the matter of constraints and the effort of trying to acknowledge these. There is a need for the articulation of a kind of post-natural ordering: a compact, a co-operation of the human and the non-human.

The articulation of such a compact will, I think, require more than apocalyptic theory offers. I have already said that apocalyptic theory poses the question as to the destiny of the human and the basis of human action. Moreover, the matter of the scope of human action is also raised: to what extent is it the human alone that contributes to the securing of its destiny? It is not clear to me that apocalyptic theory answers these political questions successfully. It is likely, first, that a political theory will require an exploration of how the human represents the non-human. There are steps in this direction in the work of Bruno Latour (Latour, 1993) yet it remains undeveloped and is in need of correction (Scott, 2010). Moreover, if a species ethic is to be developed in which the *telos* of the species is to be understood as co-implicated with the *telos* of non-human nature, we shall need a theory of needs – that is, an historical attempt to differentiate between true and false needs that is resourced by an account of the nature of the human in which the non-human is also implicated. That is, a theory of human needs is now required to be also an ecological theory of human needs. As such, this ecological theory will have to give some account of the 'needs' of non-humans. Finally, to complete our political theory for the context of a changing climate, we need a concept of right that presents us with the free, eco-productive individual, living co-operatively in a determinate ecological condition.

These emphases on negotiation, needs and free action in a postnatural condition offer ways of affirming ecological dependencies but avoiding ecological authoritarianism. As such, we move beyond the implications of apocalyptic theory and begin the process of re-working the theory so that climate change and apocalyptic inform one another rather than merely being convergent. Why should apocalyptic theory be weak here? I think that we can see the outline of the basic problem. It is an old issue, moreover. The problem is the relation between human freedom and the systems of nature. In other words, if apocalyptic theory poses the question: Which agent is the source and guarantor of human destiny? – the answer is either Nature or Humanity. And we can see this ambivalence in responses to climate change: we must conform to the cyclical processes of the stabilization of the planet or alternatively humanity's technological inventiveness may yet rescue us. There are many epicycles here but basically either nature or humanity is the source and guarantor of human destiny. Yet, as I have already argued, apocalyptic discourse is always a religious discourse: it works from the promise that the world is passing away but not only into nothingness. It operates from the premise of divine agency and the primacy of God's love in creating. In the secular use of apocalyptic discourse, such reference to divinity is downplayed or marginalized. However, it cannot finally be expelled altogether without grave damage being done to the discourse itself. Once downplayed and marginalized, apocalyptic discourse may function only as a discourse of fear or terror or may tend towards prediction.

Either Nature or Humanity – what other answer is there? Of course, for theology in its articulation of apocalyptic theory, there is a further answer. I shall not here claim that reference to God as the answer to the question, Who or what is the source and guarantor of human destiny?, yields clear answers and effective political solutions. Yet reference to God does, I consider, reduce the emphasis on Humanity and Nature as answers in competition. We may thereby be enabled to see beyond abstractions of Humanity and Nature to the material processes by which human beings interact or produce natures. It may well be that our knowledge of God is always a mediated knowledge. Thereby, there can be no knowledge of God except by way of human works and, perhaps, natural events (Scott, 2003a). Yet, if God is to be known through God's own action, and a God-borne history is part of that action, and if that history includes what we commonly call nature (Adorno, 1932/1984), then it seems to me there is the opportunity to re-consider apocalyptic as the disclosure of God. Thus, reference to nature, yes – but qualified by reference to God; the human – yes, but qualified by reference to God. In other words, the use of apocalyptic could be expanded by reference to its original foundation in God. What would that achieve?

NATURE IN APOCALYPTIC

One matter it would force us to pay attention to would be nature itself. The theme of nature has not been strongly featured in our discussion so far. There are good reasons for this, of which I shall mention two here. First, apocalyptic discourse is often used by those who find themselves to be marginalized or dispossessed; apocalyptic is thereby a profoundly political discourse and has been used to advance the interests of the human. Second, dispossessed groups tend to be suspicious of reference to nature in that oppressed groups have sometimes had animal status pressed upon them as a way of justifying their oppression. If you are deemed to be in some way beyond the human pale, to claim that duties are owed to you by other humans makes little sense.

However, if we fail to pay attention to nature in apocalyptic then inappropriate understandings of nature may be smuggled in. To avoid this problem, I want to begin by stressing the diversity of nature's interactions with humanity. I have elsewhere (Scott, 2003a) written of nature as the in-between of human projects. Moreover, I think we can understand nature in three ways: *pro nobis, in nobis* and *extra nos*. That is, the full complexity of our interactions with nature requires us to see nature as oriented on us or as being for us, as 'in' us in the sense that we by our bodies are placed with and interact with nature, and that nature exceeds or surpasses us (Scott, 2003a). It seems to me that this is not so different from the suggestion that humans live from, in and with nature: that nature supports us, that we inhabit nature and that nature pre-existed us and may survive the death of the human species (O'Neill et al. 2008: 1–4).

At this point, we may now appreciate that there are further limitations to apocalyptic. The problem seems to be the way in which nature is present in apocalyptic theory. Once we refuse the view that nature is writing a script that seeks to write the human out of the cosmic plot, we are confronted with the issue as to how nature is present. In short, apocalyptic thought does not provide a theory of human obligation to nature or the representation of nature to the human. This requires some explanation so let me try to provide one. Earlier, I suggested that there is a convergence between apocalyptic and climate change. Why is there this convergence? And I have suggested that the reason lies in the fact that apocalyptic is the edgiest of doctrines and in that it calls into question the present order, is often articulated by those with least stake in the present order. (The best textual example is Engels, 1850/2000.)

Yet we should not fall into the trap of thinking that apocalyptic is a political *theory*. Even if my argument that apocalypse is always religious is not found to be convincing, it remains the case that apocalypse has the quality of a doctrine rather than a theory: it contains a transcendent impulse. Of course, a political theory may be found in it but that requires some supplemental work. I find the major deficiency in apocalypse as a political theory for a changing climate is that is struggles to find a way of exploring the relationship between humanity and nature. Moreover, what is required here is a *political* theory of the relationship between humanity and nature.

Difficult issues confront us at this point. It seems to me that there are two likely candidates that might serve as such a political theory. These are a theory of human obligation and a theory of representation. That is, during political processes some reckoning of nature could be given by a process of obligation on the part of the human towards nature. This is one way of honouring the fact that humans live from nature, that nature is *pro nobis*. The second way would be to argue that in political processes of deliberation and decision, the human represents nature in some fashion. Neither of these positions is easily developed but would, I think, offer some repair to the political deficit in apocalyptic.

COMING TO THE END OF THE LINE?

At the beginning of this chapter, I posed the question of apocalyptic 'shock': is this enabling or disabling? We may note that the shock is premised upon a claim to the longevity of the human; this is arguably evidence of an advanced anthropocentrism. In the film, *The Age of Stupid* (2008), the narrator (played by actor Pete Postlethwaite) ponders whether humans failed to act to avoid global warming because we humans did not feel we were worth the effort. In a way, such apocalyptic reinforces the question of *human* worth through its appeal to human longevity – the line of humanity really does stretch to the crack of doom, does it? This anthropocentrism may offer a profound humanism but in what sense is it an acknowledgement of our 'naturalness'?

In this anthropocentrism we are presented with the convergence of apocalyptic and climate change one more time. Yet, I have argued that there are problems with this convergence: first, human action needs to be interpreted in a postnatural direction by stressing the ecological situatedness of such action and yet all the while avoiding authoritarian resolutions; second, the way in which nature is present in apocalyptic thought needs careful consideration in order to offer a political theory of the presence of nature in human action.

In the light of these considerations, the meaning of apocalyptic shock is altered. Apocalyptic shock should commend us to acknowledge nature's care of us – even through a changing climate and warming world. Human beings are not placed in some script of which nature is the author nor are human beings the sole author of a script that narrates the existence of the human stretching out to the crack of doom. Although these are possible apocalyptic 'messages' of climate change, I have throughout this chapter been arguing in favour of a different apocalyptic and a different message. My theological reading proposes the end of an anthropocentrism, the end of nature as in opposition to humanity, and an invitation to our postnatural end. Apocalyptic ecologizes – this has been my argument – and thereby identifies sources of hope. From this theological message a fresh answerability for the human species towards ecological dependencies is founded and the possibility of a hopeful anti-climate change praxis emerges. Who threatens these dependencies, and by what power? Responding strenuously to this is activism's task. We are not there yet.

NOTES

1 I use the nominal adjective, apocalyptic, to indicate that such discourse is wider than the literary genre of apocalypse and to acknowledge that this discourse has moved beyond its religious birthplace.

2 In making this point, I am agreeing with Buell in his argument that some reference to the 'reality' of nature is important; the field should not be left to the social constructionists (Buell, 2004: 366, fn. 79). However, I think that a defence can be made for notions such as a pristine nature or an ordering of nature. I am less convinced by the appeal to a 'balance of nature', as it implies either an atemporal nature or one that can be accessed only by looking back, so to speak.

3 There is a useful discussion of the cultural representation of climate in Hulme, 2009: 1–34.

REFERENCES

Adorno, T. (1932/1984), 'Idea of Natural History'. *Telos* (60), 111–24.

Anderson, P. (2008), *Spectrum: From Left to Right in the World of Ideas*. London: Verso.

Bonhoeffer, D. (1971), *Letters and Papers from Prison*. London: SCM Press.

—(1978), *Christology*. London: Fount.

Buell, F. (2004), *From Apocalypse to Way of Life: Environmental Crisis in the American Century*. London and New York: Routledge.

Engels, F. (1850/2000), *The Peasant War in Germany*. New York: International Publishers.

Giddens, A. (2009), *The Politics of Climate Change*. Cambridge: Polity.

Hauerwas, S. (1994), *Dispatches from the Front*. Durham, NC: Duke University Press.

Hulme, M. (2009), *Why We Disagree about Climate Change*. Cambridge: Cambridge University Press.

Ingold, T. (2009), 'The Wedge and the Knot', in *Nature, Space and the Sacred: Transdisciplinary Perspectives* (S. Bergmann, P. M. Scott et al., eds). Aldershot: Ashgate, pp. 147–61.

Kant, I. (1794/1998), *Religion within the Boundaries of Mere Reason, and other Writings*. Cambridge: Cambridge University Press.

Kerr, F. (1997), *Immortal Longings: Versions of Transcending Humanity*. London: SPCK.

Kerr, N. R. (2008), *Christ, History and Apocalyptic: The Politics of Christian Mission*. London: SCM Press.

King, D. (2007), Lecture on climate change, The University of Manchester. 9 November.

Latour, B. (1993), *We Have Never Been Modern*. London: Harvester/ Wheatsheaf.

—(2007), 'Is there a Cosmopolitically Correct Design?', Fifth Manchester Lecture on Environment and Development, delivered at the University of Manchester, 5 October.

Lovelock, J. (2007), *The Revenge of Gaia*. London: Penguin.

—(2009), *The Vanishing Face of Gaia*. London: Allen Lane.

Maslin, M. (2004), *Global Warming*. Oxford: Oxford University Press.

Moltmann, J. (1996), *The Coming of God: Christian Eschatology*. London: SCM Press.

O'Neill, J., Holland, A., and Light, A. (2008), *Environmental Values*. London and New York: Routledge.

Pannenberg, W. (1998), *Systematic Theology*. Vol. III. Edinburgh: T&T Clark.

Peters, T. (2006), 'Perfect Humans or Trans-humans?', in *Future Perfect*. (C. Deane-Drummond and P. M. Scott eds). London and New York: Continuum, pp. 15–32.

Scott, P. (2000), 'The Future of Creation', in *The Future as God's Gift* (D. Fergusson and M. Sarot, eds). Edinburgh: T&T Clark, pp. 89–114.

—(2003a), *A Political Theology of Nature*. Cambridge: Cambridge University Press.

—(2003b), 'Creation', in *The Blackwell Companion to Political Theology* (P. Scott and W. Cavanaugh, eds). Oxford: Blackwell, pp. 333–47.

Scott, P. M. (2010), *Anti-human Theology: Nature, Technology and the Postnatural*. London: SCM Press.

Skrimshire, S. (2009a), 'The end of the future: Hegel, progress and apocalypse', unpublished paper.

—(2009b), 'Revenge of an ageing earth: Kant and the future of the human', unpublished paper.

Strauss, L. (1953/1965), *Natural Right and History*. Chicago: University of Chicago Press.

INDEX